CW00469188

*In the service of love and brotherhood, like all great projects,
I dedicate this work. To you my friends, I can't thank you
enough. We keep going.*

*To you my dear readers, past, present and future. For reaching
out, for your encouragement, my eternal gratitude. This is for
all of you.*

*"And consequently! Consequently! Consequently! Do you
understand me, my brothers? Do you understand this new law
of ebb and flow? Our time will come!"*

Friedrich Nietzsche

CONTENTS

INTRODUCTION

Early last year was a moment of gratitude, gratitude towards all those readers, followers and subscribers who found me online and bought my book. Gratitude is one of the nobler emotions, and it spurred me to write, but moreover it encouraged me to think. Heidegger in one of his interviews referred to 'the Thinking not being adequate', which was very much the position I was in. I had plunged into writing without any grand ideological mission, and the thinking slowly took shape over time. I've had time to reflect on what is important and urgent about the Stone Age Herbalist project. Nietzsche distinguishes between two types of nihilism - passive and active. Passive nihilism is the endpoint of renunciation, of turning one's face away from the world and embracing the spirit of meaninglessness. Active nihilism is instead a process, more akin to a wildfire or a cleansing tonic. The nihilistic attitude is a cleaning out, a shaking off of all previously held beliefs and ideas, to make way for new ones. It is like a gardener pulling up all the weeds, leaving healthy soil for new growth.

Without sounding too conceited this is the guiding philosophy of my writing project, to use truth as a sickle, to cut away all the obfuscating foliage which covers the reality of the world. Do I think I have succeeded? No, but I have made my attempts and put them out there for public scrutiny. I believe that modernity has pulled a veil of pretty lies down over our heads, a soft and woolly veil that whispers the reassuring and familiar maxims, "everybody everywhere is the same", "the better angels of our nature have won the day", "the evils of the human condition can be excised", "we are all brothers". I don't revel in cruelty myself, I don't glorify all the awful tendencies of Man, but I do believe that Life and nature are beyond good and evil, and the first way to tear away this veil is to write honestly, and accurately, about how the world really is. If you are religious you might disagree, and that's fine, but we can probably agree that Truth is a fundamental good, one worth protecting and preserving.

You might ask, why would this 'active nihilism' be important? Why now? My answer would be that I can't rouse instincts that were never there to begin with. My readers contact me on a regular basis, and I've begun to distinguish the different aspects of my work that appeal to different people. For some they enjoy learning, the itch to discover new and interesting things is the impulse which led them to seek me out in the first place. For others they have a personal fascination with particular topics, like prehistory. Some are on their own projects, and sometimes it dovetails with my own. Finally a few admit that they find my explorations of dark and uncomfortable subjects to be distressing, even upsetting, but they feel the drive to confront the world anyway. This affirmation of the world, with all its horrors, is the end goal of active nihilism. Life is beautiful and joyful, and encompasses all of its children and fruit. So if you have those instincts then perhaps you'll feel the need to read on. If you've ever felt that modernity is too flat, too grey, too tame, then maybe read on. Whatever you get from this collection of essays I hope it changes you in some way, and spurs you towards your own reconciliation with life, an aesthetic creation - but I've said too much! Read on!

◆ ◆ ◆

Disclaimer - these essays were for the most part written for Substack and other online platforms. Many articles originally contained images, maps and diagrams, which cannot be transferred to a book without permission. I have made minor alterations where necessary to ensure the text flows, but if you wish to read them with images then please visit my Substack page at https://stoneageherbalist.substack.com/.

PART ONE – MODERN ANTHROPOLOGY

THE TALE OF RICHARD HOSKINS: A LIFE MOST CURSED

*A modern story of a criminologist
caught up in witchcraft
and child sacrifice*

I t's hard to imagine what a modern curse would look like today, how that would affect your life, but the story of criminologist and religious scholar Richard Hoskins comes as close as we might possibly get. His tale is one of almost unbelievable sorrow, witchcraft, murder and adventure, the kind of life one associates with an era gone-by. Hoskins' biography touches on some of the most bizarre events in recent British history, from investigating Yoruba human sacrifice in London to VIP Satanic sex-rings. He has lost three of his children in tragic and disturbing circumstances and has undergone hormone therapy and the removal of his testicles through NHS gender affirmative care, an act he regrets. A haunted figure, a man half in touch with the supernatural and demonic. Let us explore this, a life most cursed.

Part One - Twins In The Congo

Hoskins was born in Beaconsfield, Buckinghamshire in 1964. His schooling led him to Sandhurst Military Academy where he gained a Special Short Service Commission in the 3rd Battalion of the Royal Anglian Regiment. Not much is known about his early life, but his story really begins when he married a medic, a woman called Sue, and went with her to the Congo in 1986. She was working for the church, providing basic medical care and vaccinations to the most rural communities and Hoskins was excited to be travelling and working alongside her, a great new adventure for a newlywed couple. Kinshasa was not what he expected - warned that Sue would be kidnapped at the local market and sold into slavery in Dubai and rattled by the flagrant aggression and corruption of the local regime thugs, he was pleasantly surprised when he landed in Bolobo, a small town on the Congo River in the western-most region of the country.

The local Bantu tribe, the Bateki, welcomed them both with open arms, teaching them to speak Lingala, how to pilot a dugout canoe and hunt with handmade muskets. Hoskins fully immersed himself in the culture and his work, installing a solar powered vaccine fridge and carving trails through the bush for their battered Land Rover. He learnt about the Congolese belief in *kindoki*, a form of low-level witchcraft which afflicted people from time to time and the *nganga* healers, who would restore ailments both physical and spiritual with herbal remedies and animal sacrifices. In 1987 Sue fell pregnant and both were troubled by the late scan which revealed twins, one positioned for a dangerous breech birth. Twins in the Congo, as in other parts of Africa, are both revered and feared, believed to be more in touch with the spiritual world. The eldest twin is always known as Mbo and the youngest as Mpia. Distressingly one twin was born dead, amid a frightening and primal labour, far away from the benefits of a hospital. The second twin, premature and sickly, miraculously survived the night. They named her Abigail.

They briefly returned to Britain in 1988, where Abigail was declared fit and healthy, but on returning to their work in Bolobo Hoskins learnt that the villagers were worried about their daughter. He was approached alone by a man called Tata Mpia, himself a surviving twin and given a warning:

> 'But . . .what's this to do with my Abigail? You said she was being called? What . . . what do you mean by that?'
> 'Ah.' Tata Mpia nodded his head slowly. 'She is a twin. She is a Mpia – a younger twin – like me.' I felt the heat of Abigail's fever on my own forehead. 'Twins have a special power, Mr Richard. They call to each other and you must listen to their call. Mbo is calling your Mpia to come and join her in the shadowlands. I am sure of it.' 'Her twin sister? Calling her? But she's—' I stopped myself. 'No, Mr Richard,' Tata Mpia said gently. 'Mbo is not dead. That is the thing I am trying to say to you. She is one of the living dead. And she is calling out to her twin sister, calling her to the world of the living dead.

His worst fears were to come true. Both Hoskins and his wife began to feel that something was wrong, they heard distressed voices calling out sometimes, Abigail seemed full of life but also haunted by something. As Hoskins recalls, in one of his most chilling anecdotes in an already unpleasant book:

> 'Abigail?' I stepped towards her. 'What are you up to?'
> She turned her head, and the expression on her small face – normally as bright as a new flower – made me

stop dead and lifted the hairs on the back of my neck.
There was something in her eyes I had never seen before.
Something that made her look old beyond her years.
Without a sound, she turned away from me to stare
out of the window again. I realized then what held her
attention so completely. This was the only point in the
house from which it was possible to see the graveyard.

Tata Mpia urged Hoskins to find a *nganga* and have him perform a sacrifice, to placate the soul of his dead child, but Hoskins refused. He recounts watching a similar ritual and felt that he could not go down that path, no matter how tempting. Abigail died in her sleep shortly afterwards, peacefully and with no explanation. Hoskins was overcome with grief. Burying his second child next to the first with shaking hands he felt a hand on his shoulder, the village elder - 'Mr Richard,' he said, 'now you are truly an African.'

The pair came back to the UK shortly afterwards, battling with their demons. Hoskins was privately tortured by the thought that he could have spared Abigail by ordering a sacrifice; he never told Sue about Tata Mpia's suggestion. They attempted to salvage their lives and had another child, a boy called David in January of 1990. Despite this nascent familial bliss, they were drawn back to the Congo, where they continued working until the country became too dangerous for them to stay. In the autumn of 1991, an explosion of violence rocked the country, as rebel soldiers demanded their wages and went on a looting spree through Kinshasa. Sue and David fled to South Africa and were evacuated to Britain. Hoskins attempted to keep their medical centre running, but was forced to flee across the Congo River in a canoe, under a hail of bullets. Finding themselves back home again and with Sue expecting another child, they seemed to live in two worlds. Becoming ever more drawn into his faith, Hoskins successfully applied to Oxford to read Theology, but spent a month in 1992 helping the UN coordinate supply lines from Kinshasa to Bolobo. The UN offered him a job, working on the Congo-Rwanda border, as the country rapidly spiralled into warfare and mass murder. Wisely, he refused, and came back home to continue his studies. Their next daughter Elspeth was over a year old, and Hoskins was happy and relieved to dedicate himself to his studies. He achieved a doctorate from King's College London, but at this point he and Sue were practically strangers to one another. The intense grief, the travels and turmoil of their lives, combined with differing views on their religious convictions had resulted in them both retreating into their inner worlds. They divorced and separated when Hoskins was offered a lectureship in African religions at Bath Spa University in 1999. Despite having experienced enough grief and hardship to last a lifetime, Hoskins had no idea what the future had in store for him.

Part Two - The Boy In The River

It was an IT consultant on his way home from work who noticed him first. A strange dummy-like figure covered in a red-orange cloth. After realising what it was and phoning for the police he stood watching, as a team fished the torso of a young boy out of the Thames. He was missing his head, his arms and his legs and had been clothed only in a pair of girl's shorts, bright orange in colour. The police were baffled. The pathologist identified him as a 7–8-year-old African male. His limbs and head had been expertly removed and his neck bore a strange surgical wound from back to front where he had been held upside-down and drained of his blood. Hoskins was a senior lecturer at this point, one of the few experts in Britain on African religious practices. He had started a new relationship with a student called Faith and the pair had moved in together after a research trip to his old stomping ground in the Congo. Scotland Yard was convinced the boy's death was connected in some way to an African religious practice, they tossed out words like voodoo, *juju* and *muti*, a South African practice which, in its darkest forms, involved using the internal organs of a person for their medical and spiritual power. In the absence of any identification the police had named the boy Adam.

To do full justice to Hoskin's involvement in the Adam case would be to rewrite his book, *The Boy in the River,* which details his specialist expertise and research into West African sacrificial practices. Adam was eventually identified as a Nigerian, based on the new technique of assessing bone and teeth isotopes, a first in British criminal history. His stomach revealed that he had been fed a vile potion, made up of charcoal, plants and animal bones. Significantly the forensic team discovered the potion contained the Calabar bean, a toxic legume which was traditionally used as a witchcraft ordeal in Nigeria and surrounding countries. If one vomited after ingestion they were guilty, if they died, they were innocent. In very small amounts the bean acted to paralyse and numb the victim. A gruesome picture was eventually painted of the boy's fate. With his orange shorts and final deposition into the river, Hoskins could infer that the ritual was linked to the Yoruba people. The shorts themselves were only sold in Germany and Austria, providing a clue as to his movements before his death. It would seem that Adam had been somehow smuggled into the country, starved and then force-fed the paralysing concoction, before having his throat slit and his blood drained. His limbs and head were removed and kept, and his torso dressed and put into the Thames. Who committed this atrocity and why are unknown to this day. Despite the police travelling to South Africa and personally requesting Nelson Mandela's help in broadcasting the crime, no developments or leads emerged.

For Hoskins this case was to resurface painful old memories, connecting the death of a child, Africa and sacrifice. His mental fragility became evident as he was bombarded with threats from angry Yorubans, furious he had mentioned their religion on the news in connection with the murder. He even had a teacher from Yorkshire phone him, shrieking that he was undermining 'racial harmony'. His life with Faith became strained as he worked long hours, absorbed in memories and pain. One day she eventually confided that a souvenir African death mask they had bought on holiday together was causing her immense distress:

Just then Faith pushed the door ajar and peeped in. She looked uneasy. 'You're going to think I'm nuts. It's that damned mask. There's something weird about it.' I'd never liked the Chokwe death mask. I'd been uncomfortable when Faith had seen it on a trader's table in the Brazzaville market. It would have been shaped around a dead girl's face so that whoever wore it thereafter might draw up the spirit of the deceased. It was strangely beautiful, but the first night we'd had it in the room with us we'd both had chilling nightmares. We'd hung it on the wall of our home in Bath, and occasionally, when I'd been working late, the thing had given me the creeps. 'I put it up on my study wall when I unpacked,'she said. 'And I've been getting blinding headaches ever since.' She hadn't told me before because she couldn't see how her headaches could possibly have anything to do with the mask. But as soon as she took it out of the room, the headaches stopped. As an experiment, she'd passed the thing on to her mother, for whom it had no connotations. But her mother had started to have awful nightmares in which the mask featured, and now she wouldn't have it in the house. 'And she smells,' Faith went on, 'of wood smoke.

She always did a bit. But sometimes it's really strong. Almost choking.' I didn't like the way Faith had called the mask 'she', as if it had a personality of its own. That wasn't something I wanted to consider.

Progress was slow on the Adam case, eventually a Yoruba woman called Joyce Osagiede was arrested in Glasgow. She was wanted in Germany for immigration crimes and her evidence led to a joint Italian, Irish and British police operation which busted an international child trafficking ring based out of Benin City in Nigeria, where Adam was from.

Part Three - Child Witches In London

By 2003 Hoskins was a man much in demand. Police forces across the UK began to call him for advice regarding any crime with a religious or occultic bent. He worked on the savage murder of Jodi Jones in Scotland, before being handed the case file for a Congolese child witchcraft case in London - Child B. The story of Child B is a disturbing glimpse into modern multicultural Britain: An Angolan war orphan, smuggled into the UK by her aunt and brutally tortured by her and her friends who believed she was possessed by *kindoki*. This wasn't Hoskin's tame jungle *kindoki*, this was a new and mutated form which had arisen in the darkness of the Congolese Civil Wars. Rather than *kindoki* being a diffuse but mostly mild form of bad spiritual energy, the new revamped version had blended with a sadistic form of Christianity, where children in particular were held to be possessed agents of the Devil. For 8-year-old Child B this meant her guardians had beaten her, tortured her with knives and rubbed chili pepper extract into her eyes, as well as refuse her all food and drink for days. For Hoskins this was to become his new reality, and he became obsessed with finding out exactly what was happening in London. His blood ran cold when a limp-wristed council lawyer phoned him and sheepishly asked if he would sanction a child being sent back to the Congo to undergo an exorcism. Incensed, he demanded the council pay for him to go to the exact church the child was destined for in Kinshasa.

To his amazement, they agreed. In February of 2004 he flew out on an erstwhile fact-finding mission, discovering to his horror that the Congo he knew had been twisted into something unrecognisable. Tens of thousands of street children, some lying dead in the road, crowded the city. Churches were holding many of them in metal pens and sheds, having been abandoned by parents or taken in as orphans. They were starved, mistreated and forced to undergo violent and frightening 'deliverance' rituals, to cast out the demons. Hoskins returned again in 2005, this time with a camera crew, attempting to locate a small boy called Londres, who had disappeared from Britain. Despite nearly being torn apart by a mob during a street funeral, the team found the boy, but they could do little to help. With casework mounting in the UK, Hoskins was called to be an expert witness in the Child B case. His testimony that *kindoki* was a sincere belief, but one which had been warped over the past few decades, was instrumental in putting the accused behind bars.

In his fixation on child witches, his relationship with Faith began to crumble. Sensing it was near the end, he threw caution to the wind and abandoned his work, utterly despondent at the state of UK law enforcement and the reality of child suffering in the Congo. He sold their London flat and moved with Faith to Devon, near her parent's farm, where they had a son in 2007 - Silas. Four happy years ensued, a scene of rural bliss, until a police officer managed to track him down in 2011. Another child had been murdered in London, they suspected it was a *kindoki* case. Unbeknownst to Hoskins, he was about to walk into possibly the worst case of child abuse in British criminal history - the torture and murder of 15-

year-old Kristy Bamu. The Bamu children, Congolese in origin, had been invited by their eldest sister to come to London for Christmas. They arrived into a nightmare. Their sister's boyfriend, Eric Bikubi, immediately accused the children of being witches. A three-day horror scene unfolded as Bikubi beat and starved the children until they confessed, but Kristy Bamu refused. After he wet the bed from sheer terror and panic, Bikubi turned his attention to the teenage boy. Forcing his siblings to help, he rained down on Kristy a frenzy of violence - knocking his teeth out with a hammer, shoving a metal bar down his throat, smashing ceramic tiles across his head, mutilating his ears with pliers. At the trial the court handlers had to use two trolleys to cart in the number of makeshift weapons used on the boy. Finally, Bikubi ordered the children into the bath where he granted Kristy's last plea - "let me die". He made his brothers and sisters sit on his chest until he drowned, whereupon he sprinkled them all with the water in an act of purification. At the trial the barrister noted the sibling's disgust at their eldest sister's refusal to intervene:

> 'And then, when Kristy staggered across the room, blood pouring'– Altman paused, betraying his own distress for the first time – 'all you could say to your own fifteen-year-old brother, who was dying in front of you, was, "Don't sit on the sofa, or you might spoil it . . ."'

Yet again Hoskins had been dragged into another case of Congolese witchcraft and the death of a child, he had been chained to the country and seemed fated to be gripped by its pain. In August of 2011 he returned, yet again, to Kinshasa, this time with another TV company to document the deteriorating situation of its children. After battling with a cold-hearted pastor to give a small toddler a glass of water, in defiance of the fast ordered by the church, he vowed never to return. He would again take the stand as an expert on

Congolese religion in the Bamu trial, outraged that Bikubi was attempting to plead insanity as a defence. At this point in his story his autobiography ends, with a despairing reflection on the state of affairs:

> *I didn't believe that Europe was just seeing a momentary overspill of misguided religious fundamentalism. Something much worse was beginning to flourish beneath the farcical ignorance and superficiality of the pan-European multicultural agenda. Children were being trafficked and used for benefit fraud, sold into sex slavery and subjected to physical and mental abuse. Porous national borders, splintered churches, broken family ties and a fundamental lack of understanding and communication amongst the relevant authorities had fostered a litany of depravity. Victoria Climbié, Child B and now Kristy Bamu were unlikely to be the only victims.*

Part Four - Sex And Gender

So far, we've been following Hoskins' life through his own published words, in his book. But his life after Kristy Bamu was anything but easy. What he didn't mention in his book was the fate of his children from his first marriage. It appears that his son, David, was not a well man, and at age 19 had climbed an electricity pylon and touched the 33,000-volt cable. After 42 days in hospital Sue made the decision, alone it seems, to switch off his life support. Sometime after 2011 he and Faith also parted ways, leaving him fully alone with his thoughts. Hoskins, clearly a traumatised and broken individual, fell into the Youtube transgender rabbit hole and became convinced that taking oestrogen might help him feel better. He purchased some from a dark web vendor based in Vanuatu. The side effects drove him to seek medical help and he was 'fast-tracked', in his own words, through the NHS gender clinic in 2015 and began to call himself Rachel. In 2016 he travelled to Bangkok and then to Malaysia, combining his own personal torments with his desire to track down and uncover child trafficking networks. He returned to Bangkok that December and paid £15,000 to a private surgeon to remove both his testicles. This clearly did not have the intended effect he hoped for, and despite being scheduled for a vaginoplasty in March 2017, he instead checked into the Nightingale clinic in London. There, he was finally diagnosed with severe post-traumatic distress, stemming from the death of his twins, his son and the police work he had been undertaking for nearly 20 years. Through intensive trauma counselling he began the process of detransitioning, taking male hormones and returning to his name - Richard. Writing in the Mail on Sunday:

> For a decade, I ran and ran. I tried to escape my life, my very identity. I changed my gender to leave Richard and his life behind. Inspired by youthful images of smiling women, I grabbed the chance for a different life. I know I'm unusual and that few others have experienced the multiple traumas to have befallen me

While not bitter, he wrote that he was incorrectly diagnosed by the NHS gender services and was never questioned as to why he wanted to change his sex. This is both revealing of how the transgender medical industry operates and of how complex trauma can lead to bodily dysmorphia. Tragically he will have to live the rest of his life on hormone therapy, an avoidable mistake.

As if this tale was not baffling enough, while he was in the process of transitioning towards his short time as 'Rachel', Hoskins was asked to consult on the confusing case of Operation Conifer by the Wiltshire Police in 2015. Operation Conifer was a national investigation into accusations made against former Prime Minister Edward Heath that he abused young children. This included a string of different allegations, and the final report documents inquiries into sex workers, use of maritime vessels, bodyguards and intelligence officers, amongst others. Hoskins was asked to work on a particularly lurid investigation based on the testimony of 'Lucy X', who gave a description of a satanic ritual during which Heath and other figures of authority abused a young boy on an altar, killed him and feasted on his body. The police were concerned that her testimony was rational, structured and 'evidence-based', and that it should be taken seriously. Hoskins ultimately dismissed the report, citing the controversial use of hypnosis and 'memory-retrieval' techniques by psychotherapists working with Lucy X. He chose to leak his findings to the press, believing that the police would ultimately bury or ignore his work. Whether or not one trusts Hoskins' judgement at this time in his life, it is telling that he was allowed to work on such high-profile cases, given that he was obviously suffering from extreme mental distress. The total acceptance of transgender ideology within the senior ranks of the police services meant he was relied upon for his expertise at a time when he clearly needed help.

Hoskins continues to write for various publications, including the *Mail on Sunday*, and has clarified his position on transgenderism and the NHS, taking a moderately 'gender-critical' stance. It's hard not to see his life as ultimately tragic, a man broken by the Congo and haunted by the spiritual world of its inhabitants. Death, the suffering of children, witchcraft, ritual sacrifice - these themes have attached themselves to him ever since he refused to perform the rites to save his child. Despite this, he has struggled and persevered to help bring an end to the scourge of modern witchcraft accusations and deaths, particularly in Britain, and has relentlessly pointed out the failings of a world with open borders, where children can be trafficked and tortured with impunity. No doubt he will find himself on the front lines of this battle again as cases of witchcraft continue to grow in England. He has never shaken whatever attached itself to him all those years in the jungles of central Africa, but maybe this is how some curses work, a man must suffer to see what he is made of, and what he might do with his life.

WAS LOLA DAVIET'S MURDER MOTIVATED BY WITCHCRAFT?

*Zouhri Children, Tasfih &
culture-bound psychosis*

O ver the past few weeks I've been inundated with messages asking me if the murder of Lola Daviet was motivated by some kind of witchcraft or belief in magic. The wound is still fresh for my French friends and I don't want to be distasteful in coldly analysing Lola's death, but many people want answers and an explanation. What I want to do is lay out the facts as best we know them and see if there could be any substance to the claim that her death was motivated by a belief in witchcraft.

As far as a timeline for her death has been made public this is what we know:

The Case

12 year old Lola Daviet was last seen entering an apartment building in Paris at 15:17 on October 14th, 2022, following a

woman. At 16:48 a woman, Dahbia Benkired (24 years old), then left the apartment carrying two suitcases and a trunk. Lola's body was discovered by a homeless man inside the trunk, which had been left outside the building. At 16:30 Lola's father had reported her missing, having failed to come home from school. Many of these details are confusing, between different news reports, but this seems to be a general timeline of events.

Benkired was arrested after police discovered duct tape and box cutters in or around the apartment. The description of Lola's body is that she was naked, bound at the hands, feet and mouth, and her throat cut and mutilated. Initial news reports described post-it notes on her feet with the numbers "1" and "0", but this was later changed to red pen. The official cause of death has been listed as asphyxiation.

The fragments of Benkired's interview with the police make for disturbing reading. It seems that she lured or ordered Lola upstairs, before making her take a shower. She grabbed her by the hair and forced her between her thighs, to perform cunnilingus, during which Benkired says she had an orgasm. Somewhere in this horror she taped Lola's mouth and nose shut, which is most likely the cause of death. She then drank a coffee, listened to music, and then attempted to decapitate or mutilate Lola's body, almost removing her head using scissors or a knife. After which Benkired claims to have drunk some of Lola's blood and preserved some in a bottle. The police have not confirmed if this bottle has been found.

Her interview is made more confusing by some incoherent and strange statements, including that it was all a dream, not reality, that she was fighting a ghost or a mysterious attacker, that she could never hurt a child, and that pictures of Lola's body made her feel nothing:

"It doesn't make me hot or cold. I too was raped and saw my parents die in front of me"

Benkired's sister apparently informed the police that she had been waking during the night a few days prior to Lola's murder, saying nonsensical things. The police conducted a psychological assessment of Benkired and decided she was mentally stable enough to be held under normal custodial procedures. Benkired claims the murder was motivated by a personal dispute with Lola's mother, who refused to issue her with a building pass to her sister's apartment. Her lawyer has denied the killing was racially motivated.

Benkired arrived in France in 2016 and was known to the police only as a victim of domestic abuse in 2018. At the time of Lola's death she was in the country illegally, and had been ordered to leave France in August, but she was not detained since she had no criminal record. Picking this case apart to look for motivations connected to religion, faith or witchcraft is, on the face of it, not easy. Clearly elements of the murder do not make sense, in particular the sexual aspects, the labelling of her feet with numbers and the consumption of blood (assuming we believe everything that she said during her interview). If Lola had simply been killed, without any of these disturbing additions, it would appear like a revenge killing for a personal dispute. But the incoherence, strange story and weird additional and gratuitous nature of Lola's death, make one suspicious that other motives were at play.

In other witchcraft related murders I've looked at there are some consistent patterns:

The victim is the source of some malevolence, either by being a witch or possessed or something else.

The victim's body, age, sex or some other attribute makes them the object of a ritual, eg their internal organs can be turned into medicine or the way they are killed fulfils some religious requirement.

Lola's murder does not fit either of these, since she was used as the object of personal sexual gratification, and then haphazardly disposed of with little to no ritualistic aim. Benkired seems to have acted alone, apart from a confusing report that an older man was arrested for helping her transport the body.

But then, why drink her blood, force her to perform sex acts and why write numbers on her feet?

Zouhri Children

In 2016, a 9 year old boy was discovered bleeding to death in Sidi Abed, Tissemsilt Province in northern Algeria. It transpired that the boy had been kidnapped and assaulted for the purposes of extracting his blood, but why? A mediaeval belief, common to Morocco and to a lesser extent, Algeria, is the existence of a special kind of child - a Zouhri - the offspring of a union between a woman and djinn spirit. These children are marked by distinct eye or hair colours, certain lines on the palm and tongue or head. Since unrecovered buried treasure in the desert belongs to the spirit world, the belief amongst some North Africans is that a blood sacrifice of a Zouhri child will lead them to great wealth. The details of this practice seem murky at best, but certainly reports in the press suggest that a number of children in Algeria and Morocco have disappeared and have been labelled as Zouhri children.

Beyond this, the practice appears to be tangentially linked to modern organ-trafficking networks, a subset of the general human and contraband smuggling and trafficking between Africa and Europe. Whether this link is real or merely an overreach I can't say, but certainly organ-trafficking is a common-place problem across the Maghreb and Middle East, with poor children sometimes killed for their organs. Interpol's Overview of Serious and Organized Crime in North Africa report from 2018 lists Algeria amongst the offending nations - in 2008 the country had to use military police to break up an organ-trafficking ring run by a university professor. Although the Anglophone world has not linked the Zouhri phenomenon to Lola's death, social media and even civil officials have made the connection across France and the rest of Europe. According to some circulating pieces, the French magistrate George Fenech made this statement:

> *"This reminds me of the story of the Zouhri children, blondes with blue eyes, considered to be the custodians of powers in Algeria (...). They are kidnapped, sacrificed and their blood is drunk (...). On this poor girl there was the number 1 on the sole of her left foot and the number 0, it is exactly the satanic rite of the Zouhri of North Africa"*

Personally this seems overwrought, there is very little detailed information on the Zouhri phenomenon and the connection to organ-trafficking seems tenuous at best. But it can't be denied that certain aspects of the case superficially line up with Lola's murder. Given that several news pieces reported witnesses hearing Benkired talking about organ-trafficking when she left the building, and that a man was arrested for allegedly transporting Lola's body in his car, the temptation is to jump from blood drinking Zouhri child to organ harvesting conspiracy. But running against this narrative is the sordid sexual assault, botched mutilation and chaotic disposal of Lola's body. If we entertain the Zouhri hypothesis seriously then we have to imagine Benkired was a well connected profit-seeker, who saw an opportunity to use a mediaeval ritual and a young body to her advantage. Her behaviour seems to testify to the opposite - a homeless, unstable, unemployed single woman who unnecessarily violated a child for her satisfaction.

So what else could explain her bizarre behaviour?

Tasfih, Virginity & Psychosis

One phenomenon we can look at is the North African magico-religious practice of 'tasfih'.
Tasfih is a virginity ceremony conducted mainly in North Africa, particularly Tunisia and Algeria, although not a lot of data exists for how widespread the practice is. Before the age of 13 a girl must be ceremonially 'locked', to protect her purity. This is done by her mother and an older woman making incisions into the girl's thighs and then making her eat wheat grains or raisins soaked in her own blood. The trauma of this experience is enough to make women suffer all manner of sexual dysfunction throughout their lives, and the psychiatric literature is full of case studies relating to tasfih. Women interviewed by the Independent gave some revealing testimonies:

> Fatima told Independent Arabia about her feelings when recounting how "the taste of blood mixed with the sweetness of raisins still remains in my mouth to this day". "I never believed in these superstitions, but in my first romantic relationship I had mixed feelings as I was haunted by the memories of cuts and bleeding. In successive relationships, I wasn't even able to reach the euphoria during sexual intimacy."

Now this might be entirely unrelated, but it is telling that the themes of a young girl, tasting blood, thighs and sexual gratification all appear during Lola's torments and murder. Second to this we can look at the Francophone psychological concept of 'Bouffée délirante'. Bouffée délirante is described as an acute psychotic disorder, characterised by:

> an acute, brief nonorganic psychosis that typically presents with a sudden onset of fully formed, thematically variable delusions and hallucinations against a background of some degree of clouding of consciousness, unstable and fluctuating affect, and spontaneous recovery with some probability of relapse.

Alongside this we can add some other descriptors from Pichot:

> Sudden onset: 'a bolt from the blue'.

> Manifold delusions without recognizable structure and cohesiveness with/without hallucinations. Clouding of consciousness associated with emotional instability. Rapid return to premorbid level of functioning. Age: usually between 20 and 40 years of age. Onset: acute without prior mental illness (with the exception of previous episodes of bouffée délirante). Past history: no chronic mental disturbance after resolution of the BD episode. Typical symptoms: delusions and/ or hallucinations of any type. Depersonalization/ derealization and/or confusion

The literature on bouffée délirante describes North Africans as vulnerable to the condition, particularly after they have migrated to France, where a new environment and the culture shock can provoke an acute form of psychosis. If Benkired had overstayed her visa, was ordered to leave but did not, was homeless and unemployed and suffered a series of sexually related traumas, from tasfih to rape, and watched her parents die in front of her - then she would be likely to suffer some form of mental breakdown. Of course, this is not an excuse nor a justification, purely a speculative approach to explaining her actions. Had she been removed from France by the authorities, then Lola's murder would not have happened.

I have no evidence of course that Benkired underwent tasfih as a child, nor any evidence more than was presented for any psychological breakdown. But her hallucinatory stories, lack of affect, derealisation and inconsistency do match some of the descriptions for an acute psychotic episode. Culture and psychological pathology are highly interlinked, and so how her hallucinations or feelings of persecution manifested would depend on her background. With the belief in magic, witchcraft and sorcery still prevalent in parts of Algeria, this may have contributed to how she viewed Lola and her family. If the Zouhri children story was familiar to Benkired, then she may have attempted to act it out in some way, or believed in its power in some way. It also seems the case that some form of sexual jealousy, fantasy or need for gratification played a part here, potentially bound up with Islamic Algeria's emphasis on virginity and/or sexual abuse she suffered in the past. But this is again speculation.

My instinct, based on the little information we have, is that Lola's savage murder wasn't the result of some organised ritual, or any overt belief in witchcraft or magic, but rather a horrible complex of mental pathology bound up with sexual fantasy. The murder seemed relatively disorganised, unplanned and unstructured, the disposal of her body without premeditation. I don't have a good explanation for the numbers, but given that psychosis is hardly rational, we never have a good explanation. As the facts come into public view we may get a completely different story of motive and means, but for now I don't think this is a witchcraft case in the same vein as those I've previously described, nor of the Maghrebi Zouhri murders. This was a shocking and depressingly preventable murder, of a young girl with her whole life ahead of her. Those to blame are obviously the murderer herself and the French authorities for failing to remove her, even when her visa had been noted as expired. It's a damning indictment of many Western countries that illegal, homeless and unemployed people can slip through the cracks for many years. I hope the Daviet family can eventually find some peace in this world, may it start with justice.

GHANA'S CONCENTRATION CAMPS FOR WITCHES

Academics, NGOs and the struggle to explain why Ghana has had witch camps for over a century

From the years 2005 to 2011, over 3,000 people were put to death in Tanzania for the crime of witchcraft. Before that, around 50,000 to 60,000 more were killed between 1960 and 2000 for the same reasons. The majority of these victims were elderly women, who fit the Tanzanian witch stereotype.

However, accusations have been made on all grounds, such as if a woman has red-tinted eyes. Others were accused of simply living in poverty. Or if the village had a poor harvest. Or blamed for uncontrollable diseases such as HIV. No matter the justification, these women were shown no mercy in their deaths: beaten, chased, stoned and in more dramatic cases, burned or buried alive. In most instances, the murderers did not face punishment as law enforcement is stretched thin over the region.

This quote, taken from an LA Times piece about the modern witch hunts in Tanzania, highlights the scale of social violence across many African countries related to witchcraft. Tanzania is not alone of course in carrying this burden - in 2009 the Gambian president Yahya Jammeh had 1,000 people kidnapped on suspicion of witchcraft, and forced them to drink hallucinogenic potions in order to confess; witch-lynchings in Kenya are common enough that officials have turned to sanctioned exorcisms to prevent murder, and sporadic outbreaks of unknown diseases can cause communities to turn on one another, as happened in the Congo in 2001, where around 400 people were killed in a spasm of witchcraft-related violence.

Many of these incidents are the result of intra and inter community tensions, where the authorities attempt to mediate and pacify to prevent rising violence. But sometimes the state itself can look to purge a country of witches, often resorting to magical methods itself to track them down and interrogate suspects:

> Through provincial and district conferences, documented in print and radio media, state actors drew on local understanding of witchcraft to construct a standardized witch other' (Ciekawy 1 998) - a deadly figure capable of inflicting magical harm on peasants or state agents in the name of 'feudal lords'. Unlike antisuperstition campaigns launched elsewhere (e.g., in The People's Republic of China), the rhetoric of the Beninese campaigns never construed witch others as the delusions of ignorant peasants (cf. Feuchtwang and Wang 2001); the deadly practices of witch others were regarded as actual challenges to state sovereignty. As such, the goal of liberating the masses did not hinge on ideological reeducation and infrastructural change alone; it depended on a battle between the progressive

forces of the state and an army of evil witches, sorcerers, and vodun priests (see d' Almeida 1976).

- Kahn, J., 2011. Policing 'Evil': state-sponsored witch-hunting in the People's Republic of Bénin

Benin is a fascinating example here, a country which underwent a Marxist-Leninist coup between 1972 and 1991, led by the militant revolutionary Mathieu Kérékou. Benin's modernisation project placed witchcraft front and centre, but as the above quote reveals, the regime took witches seriously on their own terms. In doing so Kérékou and his forces courted and made use of other spiritual and religious figures. This led to the bizarre position that an avowedly atheistic revolution deployed a private army of Fa diviners, Sakpata and Xebyoso priests and *azeglio vodun* anti-witchcraft voodoo cults against non-sanctioned witches.

In 1979, the Beninese government continued to simultaneously uphold and blur the distinction between legitimate state authority and illegitimate witchcraft by awarding three seats to 4 animists in the Assemblee Nationale Revolutionnaire under the condition that each cult- group has to consider itself as a revolutionary cell and that no sorcerers will be accepted in the priesthoods ranks' (Sulikowski 1993, 386). Throughout the 1980s, President Kerekou called on the vodun priest Daagbo Xuno Xuna to conduct state-sponsored rain-inducing ceremonies in service to the nation. By 1989, on the eve of his fall from power (see Heilbrunn 1993, 286), it was widely believed that Kerekou depended on Malian diviners as mystical protectors and political advisors (Sulikowski 1993, 387). In addition, rumors circulated that several of Kerekou's top ministers, including former Minister of the Interior and reported architect of the antiwitchcraft campaign, Martin Azonhiho, were now fully initiated witches (Sulikowski 1993, 387)

Amongst the many strange policies of the Benin project was an attempt to corral and confine suspected witches to special camps or prisons, usually called azexwe - a house of witchcraft. These were largely informal and poorly provisioned places, where the suspects were left to fend for themselves. Strikingly the overwhelming majority of the inmates were older and childless women, a theme we'll return to with the case of Ghana. Of course the logic of the internment was somewhat undermined by the widespread belief that witches could transform themselves into animals and fly around at night, unimpeded by walls or doors, a contradiction which led to guards and officials seeking magical protection against their detainees.

Witchcraft In Ghana

Ghana is considered to be a modest success story, relative to many of its neighbours. Looking at measurements of democratic institutions, healthcare, poverty and economic growth, Ghana has performed well since its independence in 1957. However, belief in witchcraft is highly prevalent across the country, manifesting in a number of ways. One such is the well documented phenomenon of the 'spirit child', called chichuru or kinkiriko. These are believed to be malevolent spirits who inhabit the body of a newborn child, often manifesting in disabilities or deformities. Infanticide in these cases is very common, but difficult to study. One analysis recorded that 15% of all infant deaths under 3 months old was due to chichuru infanticide, typically using a concoction of lethal herbs and/or exposure to the elements. Such is the strength of belief in chichuru that health professionals will fail to report suspected infanticide cases, even in hospitals:

The day after the birth, I went to the hospital to see how mother and infant were progressing. On the ward, the midwives explained that Jampana was fine. However, her daughter had died during the night. The midwives explained further that Jampana's mother, Lamisi, had been with the child during the night. Lamisi reported to the night duty midwife that she had been feeding the infant a herbal preparation when the infant started choking. She had pinched the infant's nostrils to force her to swallow in order to start breathing again, but she had subsequently died. Lamisi wrapped up the dead infant and laid her in a cot, before calling for help. When the midwife examined the infant, she was dead.

In spite of support from a medical officer, Jampana insisted that the incident not be followed up with the staff on duty. Most of the nursing staff were local and were very reluctant to challenge traditional beliefs and practices, some of which they themselves held. Instead it was reported to family and friends that the child was stillborn.

In 1930 the British colonial government outlawed judicial witch-finding, following the previous abolition of the death penalty for sentenced witches. In place of executions came a focus on confession and voluntary examination, particularly by oracles. But even these were far from ideal:

The controversy began in 1926 when J. E. Gresham Williams, a British employee of the Akim Limited mining company, witnessed Nkona priests trying to rid a young mother of witchcraft. Williams reported that he saw the Nkona priest, Kwasi Adjai: "Dance up to the woman and drag her hair with both hands shaking her head from side to side, pulling her cloth down, stripping her naked to waist in the pouring rain. Placing his muddy foot on her head, he would order her to confess...." Williams, a World War I combat veteran, was painfully sensitive to violence. Over the course of four rainy days, he became increasingly convinced that what he was observing was the "most gruesome torturing of a defenseless native woman." The woman, Akosua Darebuo, was a new mother and a widow. Darebuo had been living in a nearby town earning her living as petty trader and caring for her baby when her husband, Kwaku Asante, came down with smallpox in the epidemic of 1926. A priest determined through the Nkona oracle that Darebuo was causing her husband's illness through witchcraft

- Gray, N., 2001. Witches, oracles, and colonial law: evolving anti-witchcraft practices in Ghana, 1927-1932

The shift towards social gossip, rumour, exorcism, therapeutic interventions and confession is a legacy of colonial rule, although lethal violence does still occur from time to time. A meningitis outbreak in 1997 killed nearly 550 people across northern Ghana and led to vigilante attacks on older women. Several were lynched and others beaten and stoned to death. Outraged NGOs and journalists began investigating the conditions for women, particularly in northern Ghana, and discovered a shocking reality. Not only were women being killed as witches in higher numbers than expected, but many thousands of women were fleeing to makeshift camps - witch's camps. Pieces appeared in the international cosmopolitan press, decrying the conditions, particularly at the largest such camp - Gambaga - in the north east region of the country.

Between the 60's and the 90's there was a feeling amongst scholars that African witchcraft would simply 'go away', under the combined pressures of modernisation and globalisation. But this didn't happen. Researchers such as Jean and John Comaroff and Peter Geschiere began pointing out that witchcraft and the fears surrounding it intensified and morphed as different African nations began to develop, both politically and economically. Fears of zombies, evil factories, possessed politicians, ambulances roaming at night stealing blood, Satanic murders, ritualistic killings for company profit, the international trade in body parts, digital curses and hexes, penis-snatching, killer mobile phones and more proliferated under what scholars called 'occult economies'. Success and failure in this new world took on the extra dimension of witchcraft, and whoever might be jealous enough to hold you back could be using magical powers against you.

This 'African witchcraft in modernity' paradigm hasn't really added any value to the scholarship in my opinion. The ghost in the machine for the first wave of researchers was 'neoliberalism', which at this point is like the term 'ritual' in archaeology, it serves to fill in the blanks when things don't make sense. Papers trying to explain modern witchcraft as a reaction to the anonymising forces of urbanisation and modernity clash with other studies showing that witchcraft accusations start at home, between intimate family members. Often a young person feeling thwarted in life turns on his mother or grandmother, accusing them secretly of malicious intent and action. Defining Ghanaian witchcraft has been a preoccupation of anthropologists since British rule. The general term bayie is translated as witchcraft, but it is a slippery term, shifting between a person, a spirit, a physical substance and its transformations. Bayie can mean the voracious appetite for human flesh, or the bewitching spells placed on another person. Sometimes witchcraft can be good and helpful, and the position of authority and wisdom that elders possess can oscillate between benevolent and evil.

Bayie, hideous but hidden, became the most trenchant symptom of the contradictory feelings which close relatives may have for one another. Imputations were secretly levelled at people one could not openly criticise, let alone accuse. I agreed with Kennedy (1967: 273): 'Witchcraft is primarily a manifestation of strongly held negative emotions. Any student describing it inevitably finds himself involved with materials which have been the province of psychoanalysis-hatred, fear, anger, jealousy and frustration.' But a psychological interpretation of bayie also falls short of the 'facts'. Several of those who accused someone of bayie denied any ill feeling towards that person. They stressed that the 'witch' was not guilty of his/her deeds since he/she was not even conscious of them. Accusing often went hand in hand with excusing. Bayie remained elusive, typically a concept not to be caught by one-dimensional reasoning, let alone a dictionary

The most remarkable public appearance of bayie, however, is on public transport: lorries, mini-buses and taxis. Again, it was Field (1960: 134-45) who drew attention to the meaning of the popular inscriptions which drivers painted on their cars. In them, she wrote, they express their worries about the future, their anxiety that misfortune may strike. Their security lies in the hands of other people, and it is witches in particular who pose a threat. Some inscriptions beseech God for protection, others are aggressive and refer directly to the potential evildoer: Obi mpc obi yiye,

'Someone does not like someone's success', Sura nea obcn wo, 'Fear the one who is close to you', Abusua d:J funu, 'The abusua loves a corpse', and tan firi fie, 'Hatred come from the house'

- Van der Geest, S., 2002. From wisdom to witchcraft: Ambivalence towards old age in rural Ghana

It seems obvious that swapping out the words 'success' and 'prestige' for 'neoliberalism' hasn't added anything productive to the conversation. The frustration for modern NGOs and liberal-minded development workers and academics is that witchcraft defies simple explanations, and attempts to intervene can simply make things worse. Poverty relief programs or targeted charity towards accused and banished witches breeds the very resentment which fuels further accusations. NGOs working in the witch camps are seen as benefiting from the arrangement:

The popular image of total banishment and isolation turns out to be more complex in practice. Young children sent to care for the accused also benefit from funds given by the GoHome project to pay for school fees. The local hospital no longer charges for visits. The banished are then ironically resented for charity received. As one informant cynically commented, "The NGOs are happy they (the women) are there" because they are so popular as a source of donor funds

- Crampton, A., 2013. No peace in the house: witchcraft accusations as an" old woman's problem" in Ghana

The Witch Camps Of Northern Ghana

As of today Ghana has around six functioning witch camps, although others have opened and closed. Three of them - Gushegu, Nabuli and Kpatinga - are located in the Gushegu district. The infamous Gambaga witch camp is in the East Mamprusi district, and the Gnani and Kukuo camps are located in Yendi and Nanumba South districts. The exact number of residents is unclear, several thousand is a rough estimate. This is in part because these camps are not like a standard prison compound, they are more like an open market/village, demarcated but porous. People come and go and many NGOs and charities are semi-permanently settled. There is no doubt that the majority of the inhabitants are older women, with some younger women and children amongst them. Many anthropological assessments have now been written about the camps, drawing the traditional candidates looking for studies on female autonomy, mutual solidarity and gender subversion. Food is scarcer, life is harder than at home and women typically arrive with little to no possessions. Many combine agricultural work with cottage industries and firewood collection to make a living. Some camps are ruled over by local chieftains, who exchange the women's labour for protection.

Why are they there? Ultimately the most common reason is that life is better at the camps than at home. Petty accusations, harassment, violence, gossip and local power politics often sees widows targeted for their home and property, at least, that is the view of the aid workers and journalists. The claim that Ghana's northern ethnic groups are more patriarchal, as compared to the apparently relaxed matrilineal Akan peoples of the south, has become a staple of articles and experts trying to explain the camp phenomena:

Ghanaian sociologist and criminologist Mensah Adinkrah observes that Ghana is very diverse in terms of ethnic composition. In this regard, a woman's political and social status and recognition depends on the ethnic group to which she belongs. He argues that people in northern Ghana who are mostly Mole-Dagbani, have patriarchal structures that tend to undermine the social status and power of women as against the matrilineal Akan-speaking ethnic groups in southern Ghana who are more powerful than their counterparts from the north

- Mutaru, S., 2018. An anthropological study of "witch camps" and human rights in northern Ghana

This idea that the Akan are somehow more immune to violence against women is easily countered by looking at Akan notions of witchcraft, which seem just as dangerous and misogynistic as any northern tribe.

In Akan society, as in many others (Niehaus, 1993), accusations of practicing witchcraft are based on mere suspicion, rumor, or gossip (Bannerman-Richter, 1982). Often, after a witchcraft accusation is leveled, the suspected witch is threatened, drugged, beaten, forced to submit to humiliating ordeals, or is coerced into confessing to imaginary witch activities (Assani, 1996; Parish, 2000; Simmons, 2000). Many accused witches vehemently deny allegations of witchcraft (Drucker-Brown, 1993). Those who "confess" or agree with their accusers often do so simply to avert physical assaults and retributions that may follow denials (Gray, 2000; Niehaus, 1993; Simmons, 2000; Ware, 2001). In some instances, accused witches are banished from their families and communities with threats of violent, retributive reprisal should they return.

- Adinkrah, M., 2004. Witchcraft accusations and female homicide victimization in contemporary Ghana

Neither neoliberal modernity nor simple anti-female sentiment easily explains Ghana's camps, which are virtually unique in Africa. We must instead look for another motivation or reason as to why they exist. A good place to start is their age. While a number have formed in the last few decades, many go back over a century, before national independence. So whatever this is, it predates the modernity argument.

Ghana's history is long and complex, too long for this article. But of crucial importance to the history of witchcraft are the tensions between the different northern kingdoms and ethnic groups. Sometime in the 15th century, the Dagomba people moved into northern Ghana and established the Kingdom of Dagbon, displacing the prior Konkomba peoples of the area. The results of this were catastrophic for the Konkomba, who were not only captured and sold as slaves across the Sahara initially, but were then doubly subjugated as the Ashanti conquered Dagbon and demanded slaves were sent south towards the Atlantic coast. This continued from 1744 until 1874, when the British won the Third Anglo-Ashanti War and abolished the slave trade.

The Voltaic peoples, which include the Konkomba, are known for their spiritual attachment to the earth. Not only is the earth a deity, the prime mover of fertility and life, it can also be defiled and polluted by impure activities, which includes the spilling of blood. This is one reason why pre-colonial witch executions often involved strangulation or poisoning, to avoid bloodshed. Amongst the religious structures of the Konkomba is the office of 'earth-priest' - ten'daana - whose duties include protecting and conducting rituals at particular 'earth shrines'. The Dagomba invasion destroyed many of these shrines and resulted in an assimilation of the priestly class into Dagbon society. For the most part these shrines and their priests were allowed to continue operating, but the ten'daana lost their political power to their new overlords. As Ghana became a closer union under the Ashanti, British and then as a new nation-state, there was considerable diffusion of Akan, Voltaic and Dogomba religious belief between the different regions and kingdoms, as well as the presence of Islam and denominations of Christianity.

Over time there was a movement to stop executing witches, as previously discussed, and banishment became more commonplace. Both earth-shrines and chiefly residences became sanctuaries for women and men fleeing persecution. Inhabitants of the camps even today refer to themselves as bagbenye, a 'witch-slave', harkening back to when a witch and her children would throw themselves on a chieftain's mercy.

As far as ethnohistory is concerned, we only have limited sources to draw conclusions from. In 1918 Arthur W. Cardinall, a colonial official cum anthropologist reported about the shrine at Gnani:

> *Witchcraft is very much feared. There are at Gnani and near Wapuli special villages where the fetish of the place has the power to prevent "child- or man-eating" people – invariably women, in these instances – from continuing to do so. The Gnani village is very large and is divided into three sections, Konkomba, Dagomba and Nanumba. The women seem quite happy and are looked after by their men-folk, who visit them and make farms for them and keep their huts in repair. The fetish is a stone under a big tree. Trees seem generally to have evil spirits, and many baobabs are cut down to drive them away (Cardinall 1918: 61).15*

In another source from 1969 Cardinall writes: In Dagomba, Mamprussi and Nanumba and to some extent in Gonja, separate villages are set apart for the use of witches. In Gonja confessed or "convicted" witches become the slaves of the sub-divisional chief (Cardinall, cited in Parker 2006: 353).

- Riedel, F., 2018. The sanctuaries for witch-hunt victims in Northern Ghana.

Complicating the connections between witch camps and shrines is the fallout from the 1994-5 war between the Konkomba and Dogomba-Nanumba-Gonja. Sometimes called the 'Guinea Fowl War', this conflict seems to have been forgotten, not even appearing on Wikipedia's History of Ghana page. Several thousand people died and tens of thousands fled their homes as over 400 villages were destroyed. The root cause was the perceived inequality between the Konkomba and their historical overlords, who still demanded tributes, food and labour from the Konkomba. Many witch camps, in particular Kpatinga, became sanctuaries for women and children fleeing violence, adding another complicated layer to the gender-witch-mistrust mixture.

The camps today seem to be under the aegis of different chiefs and priests, along with NGOs, churches, missionaries and government agencies. The ten'daana still practise different annual rituals, including sacrificing a chicken and giving the women herbal potions to cleanse them of any magical ailments. Attempts to send women home have produced mixed results, with some projects claiming great successes and others watching impotently as the women are chased back to the camps. At least one report cites the underlying ethnic composition as the prime factor in whether reintegration is possible - that where the chief and priest are the same person, as in western Dagbon, there are no Konkombas, and trust is more easily established. But where the chief and priest are different people, and the priest is a Konkomba, such as the Ngani camp, then women who are sent home will most likely be killed.

The Future of the Camps

Mirroring the mood in scholarship regarding witchcraft in Africa more generally, the future of the witch camps seems stuck and unsure. On the one hand the camps are an embarrassment for the urban elite of Ghana and the NGOs who hold the country up as an example of African success, on the other hand closing the camps down seems both impossible and dangerous - vulnerable women and children will lose their protection and livelihoods. No amount of government legislation can force a village to accept an accused witch back in their midst, nobody can abolish the belief in witchcraft overnight, or likely ever.

In 2014 a camp at Bonyasi was shut down by the government, who quickly made it a priority to close all the camps as soon as possible. Whilst lauded by the UN and international media, the complex reality soon hit home. Almost immediately women from the Bonyasi camp relocated to the Gnani camp. The Anti-Witchcraft Allegation Campaign Coalition wrote to the Minister for Gender, Children and Social Protection, making the case that the camps were a pragmatic necessity, and that re-education and poverty initiatives were essential. Similarly, a 2020 opinion piece on GhanaWeb made the case that, until all the underlying belief, economic and social systems which produced witch camps were undermined, the camps should remain open to protect people from harm. Note though that the focus was again on patriarchy and poverty, with no mention of ethnicity or land ownership, two crucial factors in explaining why the camps exist in the first place. Ultimately the interventions to tackle witchcraft accusations and violence will almost always fall short, as a 2020 paper by Johanneke Kroesbergen-Kamps notes:

> *Combating witchcraft violence is not high on the agenda of many African governments (Secker 2012). Even if laws are in place, they may not be enforced, and mob justice even involves traditional and community leaders (Eboiyehi 2017: 260). Community groups and civil organizations are called upon to support the fight against witchcraft violence (Federici 2010; Secker 2012). However, this solution proves to be complicated as well, since civil society in many African countries consists mainly of foreign institutions. On a local level, where the witchcraft accusations are made, communities place their trust in traditional and religious leaders, who share the community's fear of witchcraft, rather than in the more skeptical foreign institutions (Kleibl and Munck 2017). The human rights discourse that civil organizations use has also come under close scrutiny in different African countries, where the feeling is that human rights constitute an imposition of specifically Western values (Secker 2012: 33). Finally, accusations of witchcraft often take place in a context of conflict and contest within families. Social action and programs aimed at teaching people about their rights do not solve the problems within families that lie behind witchcraft accusations (Crampton 2013). Studies that take the human rights approach are not unproblematic. Even in the quantitative scholarship discussed at the beginning of this section, witchcraft is always labeled as a superstition. Despite repeated urges to understand local*

ways of viewing the world better, there seem to be few attempts to see witchcraft as anything else than an evil, backward illusion

This position is a square peg in a round hole. Western NGOs do not want to be accused of being patronising, colonial or condescending, but neither do they want to give witchcraft any legitimacy. This is probably why Christian denominations which accept witchcraft as real and can offer some protection against it flourish in Africa, particularly the Pentecostal Churches. Approaches which demand a redress in gender relations often seem to miss the mark as well. As missionary Jon Kirby notes in his 2015 essay Toward a Christian Response to Witchcraft in Northern Ghana:

Unlike in the West, in Africa there is nothing more sobering than the threat of witchcraft. The media portray accused women as victims, but few Africans believe this—often not even the accused. As Fr. Joseph points out, in the African mind they are outcasts, and helping an accused witch is itself antisocial witchery. How, then, might one approach a Christian ministry when even the most basic care risks being so grossly misinterpreted?

A new anti-witchcraft bill has been proposed in the Ghanaian Parliament, and the language surrounding the debate sounds very familiar to anyone versed in the concept of 'The Blob'. If rural villagers accusing one another of transforming into cats or invading their dreams is the reality of witchcraft, the NGO-stakeholder approach looks like another reality entirely:

The discussion forms part of the on-going "Engaging Media and Minorities to Act for Peace building (EMMAP)" project, a two-year intervention that is running from March 2022 to February 2024. As part of the project, 10 Journalists from Ghana, Sierra Leone and Liberia participating in the online course were selected to undertake the five-day face-to-face training and field visit to some selected Ghanaian communities that host minority groups.

The purpose of the EMMAP programme, which is funded by the European Union (EU), is to raise public awareness of the inter-connections between conflict, migration, and minority exclusion to help build and consolidate sustainable peace in Ghana, Senegal, and Sierra Leone. The EMMAP is being coordinated by Uganda-based Minority Rights Group International (MRGA) and implemented by the Ghana-based Media Platform on Environment and Climate Change (MPEC) and Media Reform Coordination Group (MRCG) of Sierra Leone, NGOs. Prof Alhassan reminded the media that, "journalists have the power to frame and therefore let's use that power to re-frame and shape our narratives."

Speaking on the topic, "Conflict, Migration and Minority Rights: Media Perspective on Community Livelihood", Prof Alhassan insisted he was strongly against advocacy against the disbandment of the Gambaga and other witch camps in the country

In the end, the last words should probably go to the women who actually live in these camps. In a piece published on April 4th 2023, the residents of Gambaga camp had this to say to journalists:

"We're safe, happy and comfortable at Gambaga Camp"

SPIRIT SPOUSES & CORPSE BRIDES: MARRYING THE DEAD - PART ONE

Posthumous marriage, necrogamy
& ghost brides in rural China

In 2013 a family in Shaanxi Province, China, attempted to sell their 19 year old handicapped daughter to another family, where she was going to be killed and then married to their dead son. In 2002 a Yoruba woman was taken to her church by her husband, she had begun waking after midnight, screaming and rolling around on the floor like a baby. She had lost weight and was terrified her family would all soon die from HIV. Her pastor diagnosed her as suffering from ogun oru - dreamtime spiritual warfare - brought about by her malevolent 'spirit husband'. In 2005 a young woman called Julia began having terrible dreams, in which a demonic woman started having sex with her, trying to use her as a conduit to sleep with her boyfriend. Julia learnt through her Pentecostal church that this 'spouse' was an evil spirit sent to torment her by her extended family, as a punishment for her failure to honour her ancestors. What is happening here?

One of my writing goals is to show a contemporary audience that the conceit of modern humanism or pseudo-cosmopolitanism is false. It is easy to imagine as a Westerner today that everyone around the world is basically the same, except for food and language, mostly interchangeable. I want to tear away this illusion and have people realise that pre-modern ideas of witchcraft, sorcery, magic and superstition are key features of the modern human landscape around the world. If the idea of marrying a demonic spirit in your dreams or purchasing the corpse of a young woman to wed to your dead son sounds alien and unreal, then prepare to be shocked.

Necrogamy: The Ghost Brides Of China

Marriage between two or more living people is already a hellish institution to define universally, and the concept of 'ghost marriages' throws the whole thing into disarray. In general when we talk of a ghost marriage we mean that one or more participants to the ceremony, the spouses themselves, are deceased. This seems to come in two flavours - one purely legalistic and the other with spiritual and religious consequences. Being able to marry a dead person has many customary and lawful advantages: the legitimation of children, the preservation of inheritances within a family line or to access the social benefits of matrimony. Many western nations have allowed ghost marriages in exceptional circumstances, such as Nazi Germany during WW2. France permits dozens of ghost marriages every year, since it is permitted under Article 171 of the Civil Code. Some recent examples include the widow Magali Jaskiewicz, whose fiancé had been killed by a car two days after seeking permission to wed from the town hall, and the spouse of Xavier Jugelé - the police officer killed by a jihadi on Paris' Champs Elysees in 2017. Other notable countries and cultures which permit legalistic ghost marriages include the Nuer and Atwot Nilotic peoples of South Sudan. Here the constant feuding and raiding between pastoralists has led to a practice whereby the brother of a dead man acts as a living substitute, allowing a woman to marry the deceased. Any children are considered to be of the dead man's lineage, and wealthy women often choose to marry a ghost groom in order to protect their wealth and hand it off to their children.

The second type of ghost marriage has much deeper implications. In both China and Japan the institution of ghost marriages resonates in the spiritual world. In China and Taiwan it is known as yinhun (阴婚) or minghun (冥婚), translating as 'dark marriage' (yin from the well known yin-yang) or using the term for underworld. To understand the origins we need to delve into the mists of time, reaching back to the Shang dynasty (1,600 - 1,050 BC). One of the classic features of this period was a shamanistic focus on divination and human sacrifice; many victims have been recovered from royal tombs. With the accession of the Zhou dynasties and the blossoming of Confucian, Daoist and Legalist thought, human sacrifice became to be regarded as something evil, something contrary to proper human nature. In its place came an early version of yinhun, where the deceased could be married in the spiritual realm. In the Confucian text, The Rites of Zhou, ghost marriages were prohibited, indicating that the practice was already widespread. The later Han dynasty era warlord-poet Cao Cao married his 13 year old dead son, the child prodigy Cao Chong, to a dead young woman Miss Zhen, underscoring how popular ghost marriages continued to be.

Why would anyone feel the need to marry dead children to one another? To understand this we must first appreciate the uniquely Chinese preoccupation with filial piety, ancestor worship and debt-care. To fall back on an illuminating quote

I've used before:

> *Among the various forms of virtuous conduct, xiao comes first (baixing xiao weixian !"),"* declares a well known Chinese proverb. In the Shuoyuan , Confucius is quoted as saying, "Among human practices, none is greater than xiao." Xiao is commonly rendered as "filial piety... Some scholars contend that the character xiao appears in the oracle bones; most agree that it occurs in Western Zhou (1045–771 BCE) sources, frequently as a verb in texts about the performance of sacrifices... probably at the very earliest stages in their history, the Chinese gave filial piety an extremely exalted position – treated it as something one might almost call an absolute, a metaphysical entity*

> *Holzman's study describes "the peculiar passion [for filial piety] that took hold of the country at the beginning of the Later Han dynasty (25–220 CE)," and explains how "the excesses to which filial piety was carried at that time illustrate an aspect of Chinese psychology that, once understood, will help us appreciate much that usually remains incomprehensible in Chinese history." According to Holzman, the centrality of the homage children rendered to their parents and ancestor worship in Chinese culture, which create a strong tie binding succeeding generations one to another, explain both its enduring character and the difficulty of adapting it to the modern world*

Xiao likely first emerged as a moral principle to feed one's ancestors, and by extension one's parents. The degree to which

Han children were expected to undergo self-sacrifice for their parents is extreme to a Western ear, including: killing one's own child in order to better care for your parents, feeding parts of oneself to a sick parent, not enjoying foods or comforts that your parents could not afford during their lives, sacrificing one's ambitions or job to take care of one's parents and so on.

Filial sons, thus, do distasteful, even appalling, things to restore or ensure their parent's health, such as sucking pus out of wounds, tasting vomit, or sampling feces. Their willingness to do so was admirable precisely because they enthusiastically performed these acts that were normally considered repulsive.

> *A wife typically has to choose between being loyal to either her father or husband, or between her brother and husband. She usually commits suicide to avoid disloyalty to either one. In other cases, a mother has to choose between saving her own child or a relative's child. Almost invariably, she saves the child that is not her own, whether it is her brother's child, master's child, or stepchild. Many tales suggest that filial sons even risked their lives to obtain their parent's desired food. For example, due to his mother's fondness for the water from a river's main current, Wei Tong always rowed out into the treacherous waters to get it for her. In short, these accounts stress that reverent care is so important that any sacrifice is justifiable.*

- Filial Piety in Chinese Thought and History
(2004). Alan Chan & Sor-hoon Tan

One important aspect of filial behaviour is to take one's place in the patriline and produce children, specifically sons, to preserve the family and bind the ancestors together with the living. To not have children is to show a lack of pious character. To quote a common proverb: "of the three kinds of unfilial behaviour, dying childless counts as the most morally reprehensible" (不孝有三, 无后为大). Marriage is an institution of adulthood, and the vehicle of legitimation. It also has its own customs, such as the eldest son marrying first, creating an imperative to marry a dead child in order to allow the younger sons to marry and produce heirs. In contrast to the sons, the daughters of a family were not considered to be part of that line, and not the responsibility of the family, since she would marry into another. If she died before that could happen, she would be left with no-one to remember her.

> *She had no right to be enshrined as an ancestor on her natal family's altar. If she died unmarried, nobody would offer her anything to appease her neglected and dissatisfied spirit. Indeed, some Chinese believed that placing the spirit-tablet of an unmarried daughter on the ancestral altar would only provoke the wrath of the other ancestors, and invite disastrous consequences*

-Corpse Brides: Yinhun and the Macabre Agency of Cadavers in Contemporary Chinese Ghost Marriages (2018). Chris K. K. Tan, Xin Wang & Shasha Chen

The spirit of an unmarried daughter, like other ancestral spirits and ghosts, could become restless and aggressive. Seeking to re-order their situation they might harass or punish the living. Creating familial harmony therefore would necessitate soothing her spirit, or the spirit of a son, by placing them in wedlock with a suitable spouse.

So how does it work? Some of the best studies come from diaspora communities in Singapore, Hong-Kong, Taiwan and Macau, but there has been a steady revival in ghost marriages since the 1970's. Typically the process begins by a family seeking out a spiritual matchmaker, usually the family of a dead son. The matchmaker then searches for a deceased bride of a similar age, an unmarried young woman. The groom's family then asks the dead man for permission, before contacting the bride's family to discuss a dowry. The ritual itself often involves effigies of the couple, along with paper money, bamboo furniture, sometimes even modern kitchen appliances and wedding gifts. After a feast, the families might then burn all of these things and the effigies together, and rebury the corpse of the bride with the husband. Naturally this involves someone digging up a body and transporting it to the groom's house or a temple.

Needless to say ghost marriages are illegal in modern China, the enforcement mechanism being the 8th and 9th articles of the Body Exit and Disposal of Dead Bodies Regulation, which states that the buying and selling of corpses is prohibited. While we have looked at the theoretical and abstract background of ghost marriages, which seem perhaps like a macabre but harmless ritual, the reality of the practice is very different.

> *In April 2016, three men from Gansu Province murdered two mentally disabled women in order to sell their bodies as ghost brides (Global Times, 2016). In a case in late 2016, a woman with speech, hearing and intellectual disabilities narrowly escaped being buried alive. Fed powerful sedatives meant to kill her, she nevertheless regained consciousness during the burial, and alerted the frightened family who had bought her by loudly thumping on her coffin walls. These victims were perhaps specifically chosen because of their intellectual disability. Not only could they offer less resistance to the violence inflicted on them, but their disability also diminished their personhood in the Chinese moral worldview (Guo, 2008), thus making it easier to morally justify their murders. The police have since charged six suspects with abduction, human*

trafficking and attempted murder (Gao, Niu, & Cui, 2016)

-The Macabre Affective Labour of Cadavers in Chinese Ghost Marriages (2020). Chris K. K. Tan

Ghost marriages are not 'big business' in the manner of organised crime. But they are profitable enough that rural regions, particularly in central China, now abound with small-scale criminal networks who supply corpses for families on demand. One novel feature is the extension into hospitals and morgues, where a family might learn through an intermediary that a woman is dying of cancer or was just in a car crash, and begin contacting matchmakers and traders to acquire her nearly-cold body.

> *Wang Yong, an employee at a Shanxi hospital, is quoted in Chinese media as saying that once the news of a young girl dying spreads, tens of families who had lost their sons would rush to the hospital for an "auction war". 30 years ago, it reportedly cost around 5,000 yuan ($1,035) to buy a female corpse and host a ghost marriage wedding, a "matchmaker" who had been in the business since the 1990s told Chinese media. Professor Yao told the ABC that there have been at least 12 prominent murder cases related to ghost marriages, and more cases of kidnapping and grave robberies.*

-ABC News 2018

Prosecutions seem rare, and where they do occur it often lifts the lid on a network or organised operation. For example, in 2006, a family in Nanzhuang Village spent RMB14,000 on a corpse bride for their son. What they didn't know was that the provider, a local farmer, was serially killing young woman to supply families in the area. In one incident he strangled a mentally disabled woman in the woods. In this case he attempted to sell the family a dried, older corpse. They refused and he killed another woman to supply them with a 'wet', fresh body.

According to T. Wing Lo, in Ghost Brides and Crime Networks in Rural China , only 84 cases have been prosecuted in 15 years across the whole of China. From these we learn that around 65% involved stealing a corpse from a grave, morgue or elsewhere; around 10% of cases involved murder or violence; two cases involved kidnapping and four cases involved bribery. These 84 prosecutions altogether comprised the trade of 250 corpses, and four living people. As Lo points out, this is surely the tip of the iceberg, and perhaps many thousands of bodies every year change hands and become wedded through secretive rituals and traditions.

Next time we turn to the marriage and sex lives of spirits themselves, and customs and cultures where engaging in spirit spousal activity is something of the norm. I leave you with this ghost marriage prayer, taken from an observed ritual by Professor Ping Yao.

> "So and so, I hereby inform you: You died at young age and thus did not realise the great principle of marriage. You sleep alone in the dark world and lack the intimacy of man and woman. Just as living people long for companionship, the dead fear loneliness as well. Unexpectedly, so and so's family had a daughter who just passed away like an autumn leaf. We sent a betrothal for you so your souls might meet. We selected this auspicious day for the rite of your union. We also set out an offering next to your shrine tablet, furnished with all kinds of food. Please send your spirit down to the banquet and eat the meal."

SPIRIT SPOUSES & CORPSE BRIDES: MARRYING THE DEAD - PART TWO

Yoruban spirit husbands, Afro-Brazilian demon spouses and Siberian shamanism

Marrying the dead, whether by legal fiction or physically exhuming a corpse to stand at a ceremony, is just one half of the spirit spouse phenomenon. We now turn to the more ephemeral and unsettling realities, where people engage in relationships and sexual activity with a spirit, or a ghost, or a demon. For European readers familiar with elements of late mediaeval or early modern Christianity, there are parallels here with the incubi and succubi. Similar creatures or malevolent beings are staples of folklore all over the world, generally manifesting as a shapeshifter or violent and ugly spirit who sexually assaults and rapes both men and women: the tikoloshe of Zimbabwe; the Swahilian Popobawa; the Chilean Trauco and so on. For this article we'll explore a few lesser known examples where such relationships are consensual, to some degree, rather than involving a named being. We start with the Yoruban spirit husbands, then look at Afro-Brazilian demon spouses, and end with Siberian shamanic beliefs in spirit spouses.

Yoruban Spirit-Husbands

"During sleep the spirit seems to desert the body, and as in dreams we visit other localities and even other worlds, living as it were, a separate and different life, the two phenomena are not unnaturally regarded as complements of one another..."

This quote from Sir John Lubbock, the esteemed archaeologist and anthropologist, helps explain the basic dualism found among almost all peoples - that there is a world of the living and awake, and another, which connects to the dead and the invisible. What Lubbock does not explain though, is how someone could engage in romance and even sexual activity with a spouse who was never alive to begin with. This is the position some women in Nigeria find themselves in, being married to a living, breathing husband during the day, and then having a separate marriage to a spirit spouse while asleep.

The Yoruba of West Africa are one the largest ethnic groups on the continent. Their home, Yorubaland, stretches across Togo, Benin and Nigeria. The Yoruba, like many of their neighbours, possess a complex animistic and polytheistic religion, one which shares features with the Vodun (Voodoo) tradition. Their belief in the Orisha deity pantheon, the ability for spirits to enter the world through childbirth and the importance of the ancestors has had a profound effect on global religion - in particular through the syncretism of Yoruba cosmology in the

Americas leading to the development of Umbanda, Santería, Candomblé and many other belief systems. The permeability of the spirit world for the Yoruba often leads to all kinds of trouble - many spirits, demons and mischievous entities can enter the life of a person, such as an abiku child, who wishes to constantly be reborn and so dies during infancy as a human baby, only to reincarnate again and again, bringing misery to the mother.

"Abiku" and "ogbanje." have also been linked and/or culturally explained with affliction from water spirits popularly called "Mammy Water" or "water goddess" or "Queen of the Coast" or "Eze nwanyi" (in Igbo land) or "Yemoja" or "olokun" (in Yoruba land). It is believed that these water spirits are very powerful, troublesome, unfriendly and wicked. They are said to live under streams, rivers, seas and oceans. Water spirits are further believed to appear on few occasions as handsome men but usually as beautiful ladies to the extent that beautiful ladies in real life are usually nicknamed "mammy water" to show how they resemble the female water spirits. The cultural link between "ogbanje." and "abiku" is the belief that during transition, the water goddess who is pretty and very tempting will try to bring one away from his/her original life contract to fulfill her own. Those who get enticed by the water goddess will be under the influence of her group and herself

-Culture–bound syndromes and the neglect of cultural factors in psychopathologies among Africans (2011) OF Aina, O Morakinyo

Alongside these spirits is the universal phenomenon of witchcraft, typically performed by females amongst the

Yoruba, sometimes translated as aje. Nocturnal attacks by witches can result in a form of dream-time warfare known as ogun-oru, where an individual might be tormented in the early hours of the morning by magical forces.

An interesting combination of both these aspects of Yoruba culture is the phenomenon of the 'spirit husband' or occasionally 'marine husband' (oko orun). This arises from the belief that a man and woman can be married in the spirit world, and that sometimes a man will allow the woman to enter the physical world. He will continue to visit her, to have sex with her, even to impregnate her. But he might also torment her, become jealous of her earthly husband or make her barren.

> *Another experience that confirms the reality and manifestation of the spirit husband is the sexual encounter that transpires between it and its victim. The encounter is usually so real that the woman not only enjoys it but also experiences ejaculation. When she wakes up, she sees virginal discharge which confirms the fact that her experience is not an illusion. In consequence of the frequent sex in sleep, another manifestation is that the woman might see herself pregnant in her dream; while at the same time she begins to notice physical changes in her body anatomy which confirms the reality of her dream. Such changes include fullness of the breast, nausea and in some cases, temporary seizure of her menses, breastfeeding in dream etc... Yoruba women who have spirit husbands believe that there are certain benefits and privileges that they enjoy from spirit husbands such as lavishing them with gifts of varying kinds and magnitude. When they physically lack or are in need of anything, the spirit husband appears to them in dream with the promise to*

fulfil their needs

Women who have spirit husbands also claim to enjoy maximum protection from them. The spirit husbands guard them jealously and attack their perceived enemies even if it needs soliciting the supports of other members of their spiritual cult. They all rise in support of the spirit husband and in defense of their member (the woman) by attacking the adversary and causing disruptions in his or her affairs.

-The Yoruba Concept Of Spirit Husband And The Islamic Belief In Intermarriage Between Jinn and Man: A Comparative Discourse (2015) Shaykh Luqman Jimoh

The advantages of this system for some women are obvious - being happily married to a good spirit husband might prevent her from being married off to someone she doesn't like, or she can enjoy a personal and private satisfaction that others can't interfere with. However, many women do not want the attention of these husbands, and go to great lengths to be rid of them. A quick internet search reveals hundreds of Facebook, YouTube, LinkedIn and other social media pages offering relief from the oko orun. Worse still are the potential physical side effects of spirit spousal conflict, which can turn into an exhausting protracted form of nocturnal combat:

Mrs MO, a 38-year-old housewife and mother of three children, two girls and a boy, was apparently well until six months before presentation when she developed an irrational fear of having contracted a venereal disease following a generalized body rash with pruritus in her last child. She slept only very briefly at night and relatives noted that characteristically between midnight and 5 a.m., she would be awake and exhibit very strange behaviors. She would shout at top of her voice to the extent of disturbing the neighborhood. She sometimes cried like a baby and rolled on the floor, making statements of regret for her life and saying that her family was doomed to be wiped out by HIV/AIDS. She disorganized items around her home. Usually, she would not remember these actions at daybreak, and she might burst out crying when told by relatives of her strange behaviors during the night. During the day, she had occasional panic attacks with brief episodes of breathlessness and weeping. Over time, she became socially withdrawn, unable to carry out her housekeeping tasks, and was very sad most days. She had poor appetite with slight weight loss. Her husband and a pastor interpreted this behavior as evidence of being bewitched and also under the influence of a curse. Prayer and deliverance sessions were organized to cast out the spirit of witchcraft and sever the patients' connection to a spirit husband who might have been tormenting her with the ogun oru. However, there was no response to the spiritual treatment, hence the patient was taken to a babalawo (native healer) for further intervention for the problem. Several items were procured for deliverance activities including: pieces of white candle, a piece of red cloth, spiritual perfume, a whole coconut, and a white egg laid. She was made to rub her whole body with the raw egg, the candle and coconut in turn saying, 'my illness should go back to my enemy, and I don't want this sickness.' Thereafter, she threw the piece of red cloth, the intact egg and candle into the bush (where the major trash dump of her village is located). Under cover of darkness, she broke the coconut in pieces at a T-junction of a road. Next, she was made to bathe with water fetched in a black pot from a stream, using a new sponge and soap. After *this bath, she was made to break the pot into pieces and throw away the soap and sponge to be carried away by the flowing stream. Finally, she was given a native concoction to drink.*

-Ogun Oru: A Traditional Explanation for Nocturnal Neuropsychiatric Disturbances among the Yoruba of Southwest Nigeria (2007) O. F. Aina & O. O. Famuyiwa

Despite Christian and Islamic inroads into Yoruban culture, belief in spirit husbands continues, and both preacher and imam struggle to cast out these devils and jinns from their faithful. Nigeria might be a relatively prosperous and modern country by African standards, but the spirit world still breaks through and torments its denizens, by both night and day.

Afro-Brazilian Demon Spouses

"Since childhood, Mariza had known that she was married to a spirit. Her mother had tried to free her by going to curandeiros and prophets at African Independent Churches, but without success. Mariza married but she had no children and then got divorced. Initially, she refused the marriage proposal of her current husband, as she knew the spirit would act, but she finally relented. Her husband got a job in Maputo where Mariza's spirit spouse began to operate fervently: she often fell over in the middle of the street and when her husband received his salary at the end of the month, she became so ill that they had to spend all the money on doctors and healers. Finally, after much praying, the spirit left her:

"One night I saw the Devil in my dream, he looked very ugly, and said that he would go away because he was tired of God. God had burned him too often."

When Mariza began to organize her civil marriage, the Devil/spirit spouse returned to tell her that she would not marry. Right up until the day of her wedding it was uncertain whether she and her husband would get married or not. But Mariza knew that this was part of a spiritual battle: she was being tested"

The previous example of Yoruban spirit-husbands leads us nicely onto the topic of how Christianity in contemporary Africa deals with the phenomenon of spirit-spouses. If the transfer of indigenous African religions into the Americas led to the blossoming of syncretism, then so did the transfer back again of new types of Christianity. Pentecostalism in Brazil is just such an example. This denomination has gained significant ground in a traditional heartland of Roman Catholicism - emphasising spiritual warfare and appealing to the youth - it takes seriously the existence of demons, devils and evil, especially emanating from Afro-Brazilian folk religions. Not only is it spreading in Brazil, but this form of Pentecostalism has made its way into other Portuguese-speaking parts of the world, such as Mozambique.

Many of the different Bantu-speaking groups in Mozambique, such as the Ndau, Tsonga and so on, share a belief that angry spirits can intrude into the physical world to bring harm. Two types are often listed - the muhliwa and the matlharhi. The muhliwa is the spirit of someone who was killed in a magical rite, to make use of their spirit for nefarious purposes (the muhliwa is 'one who is eaten by a muloyi', a sorcerer). A matlharhi is someone killed in battle, someone who seeks revenge. Interestingly many of these spirits persist from times of great conflict, such when the Nguni, under the command of King Shoshangana, launched a war to subjugate the Tsonga and other tribes during the 1830's. How the living deal with these 'vengeance spirits', who are a subset of all the spirits which move in and around their world, is complex, and can involve eating the murdered man to prevent his spirit from causing trouble, or appeasing his spirit by bringing him a flesh-and-blood woman to marry.

In 1992, Adelaide was very sick. She had pain in her head and her body. Her life was not going well and all her children were sick. She went to a diviner, who performed the kulhaluva and gave voice to a spirit:

Spirit: You don't know me?

Adelaide: No, I don't.

Spirit: When you are in bed alone, don't you have the feeling that you are with a man?

Adelaide: Yes, I do.

Spirit: I am this man. Your mother and father know me. I am your husband.

-Gender, self, multiple identities, violence and
magical interpretations in lovolo practices in
Southern Mozambique (2005) Brigette Bagnol

This quote is taken from a long piece, explaining that Adelaide's mother had visited a healer when she was pregnant with her. She was on the verge of miscarrying, but with the help of a diviner, a spirit told her that she would not miscarry. The spirit wanted to make his presence known, and to claim the child in her womb as his future bride. Further investigation revealed that the spirit was attached to the family, and had been killed by a long distant male ancestor. The spirit had methodically attacked every generation of the family, but was ready to name himself and be compensated. The story gets very complex, but this should give an impression of the phenomenon.

So how does a woman end up marrying a spirit? In Mozambique there are two main ways - first is to be sold to a spirit for profit, and second is to be gifted to a spirit as part of the traditional libolo/livolo bride price ceremony. Either way can result in a young woman being spiritually bound to an angry, vengeful being, one who may take great offence if she were to marry a real man. In this convoluted way the youngest member of the family carries the punishment for their ancestor's crimes, and is tied, intergenerationally to actions performed maybe centuries earlier.

This is one reason why Pentecostalism is becoming more popular amongst younger Mozambicans, they see in the religion a way to throw off this yoke, and the church takes such 'demonic' interferences very seriously:

In this spiritual war, Pentecostal women often expressed their distrust and fear of those people who were closest to them, such as kin, partners and neighbours who were 'eating' from their wealth. A deep sense of (spiritual) insecurity involving danger and doubt plagues them and many others I met, which is part of the instability and redefinition of social networks based on kinship in Maputo. Acts of witchcraft can mostly be expected from those within intimate networks who share or want to share one's reproductive wealth in both monetary and sexual terms, such as in the case of the spirit spouse linked to a person killed or stolen through witchcraft. Convert Julia (aged 40), for example, tried to explain the burden she and various others felt:

My kin visit a curandeiro to get protection. The healer will drive the evil spirits away. But these evil spirits have to go somewhere, if they leave one person they have to go to another and they go through blood relations. The evil comes into me or into my sister. I am so tired of this vicious circle and want to leave Mozambique. I want to live elsewhere where you are less liable to be affected.

The possibility of distancing oneself from this vicious circle by going 'elsewhere' is found by joining the Brazilian Pentecostal domain where through different prayer modes, converts learn to close off their bodies to demanding kin and spirits. These Pentecostal arms of prayers and 'burning' have real breaking effects. For example, as an effect of their embodied disconnection converts choose a confrontational position towards elders. The Pentecostal women I met who succeeded to arrange a marriage, refused to participate in certain lobolo procedures, such as the presentation of gifts to the ancestor spirits. The relations with their elderly kin *became tense as contesting the power of ancestral spirits can provoke misfortune for the whole extended family. In several of these cases converts stopped visiting their kin or did not speak to them for some time.*

Far more than in Western countries, Pentecostalism in Mozambique must feel like a real liberation, a freedom from the burden of endless cycles of witchcraft and spiritual conflict. Armed with the shield of religious faith, these women are able to refuse participation in the perpetuation of their own misery. Their spirit-spouses can be banished and their personal power and happiness increased.

The current high number of spiritual spouses that forcefully penetrate and 'eat' female bodies demonstrates the crisis in gender roles, as witnessed by difficulties in relations between kin, between partners and between people and spirits in the reproductive order in Mozambican society. Upwardly mobile women are frequenting Pentecostal churches to get rid of this spirit of war and witchcraft, and of kin who force them to be married to such a spirit. Pentecostal women are learning to close off their bodies to spiritual intruders and demanding kin by becoming filled with the Holy Spirit.

-Converting the Spirit Spouse: The Violent Transformation of the Pentecostal Female Body in Maputo, Mozambique (2011) Linda van de Kamp

Siberian Shamanism & Spirit-Spouses

Shamanism is a slippery and ill-defined concept, and books

continue to be written contesting the meaning of the term. For our purposes we'll stick to that 'northerly' tradition which emanates from Siberia, which has made its presence felt from the American Arctic to the Tibetan mountain strongholds. Siberian shamanism generally refers to a tradition of specialist healers, who use 'altered states of consciousness' to travel in spirit form through this world and other worlds, communicating with the dead, with animals, and attempting to help people through manipulating the forces between these worlds. Siberia and the high Arctic in general is a place which tests the nerves: long periods of darkness, endless cold, isolation, vast spaces, and physical dangers seem to prompt several 'culture-syndromes', including piblokto or 'Arctic hysteria'. Descriptions of other Siberian peoples, like the Chukchi, often refer to an acute sensitivity or neurosis amongst people, and a frightening ability to 'snap' at the slightest trifle:

> *Each unexpected contact, for example, on the sides or on the other sensitive parts, sudden shouts and whistling, or other frightful and quick manifestations bring these people beside themselves and almost into a kind of fury. Others, much like the berserkers of Norse mythology, would fall into uncontrollable rages, get hold of knives, axes or other lethal instruments, and go after the people who had disturbed their tranquillity... If they cannot give vent to their rage, they beat about themselves, scream, shake violently, and are completely like madmen.*

-Shamanism and the Eighteenth Century
(1992) Gloria Flaherty

Possession by spirits and engaging with them sexually seems commonplace, perhaps helping to explain the strange changes in mood and personality experienced by people living in such a harsh environment.

> *The first one I remember was when I was eleven, twelve or thirteen years old. When my cousin was going through that. There was a lot of people involved in that exorcism, I think you would call it but I only know from the stories they gave. I knew her. She was very outgoing, very outgoing; in a way, she was promiscuous. And she had a stepmother who started to notice something strange about her. But, then she was always telling her she's strange. She's the stepmother, she's not the actual mother. So she felt that there was something wrong with this girl and it was, in a way, now that I look at it, true you know. What actually happened was true. I only know one incident that - not what actually happened. Well, I only know one story that she had many babies not from her own, not from another man, but from a spirit. She was with, she had relations with... that's one story I know. Her children, they were make believe like. . . for her it was so true, for her they were alive but other people could not see them... uirsalik, it's someone who has a spirit for a husband*

-Spirit work: Nunavimmiut experiences of affliction and healing (1997) C M. Fletcher and L J. Kirmayer

Probably the most extreme example of this is the shamanic spirit-spouse, a male or female being who 'marries' a shaman and assists them in their work. A point we need to recognise here is that Siberian shamanism is renowned for its complexities of transvestism and belief that shamans can be inhabited or even become the opposite sex. All of which makes the spirit-spouse situation that much more strange. In contrast to the Yoruban and Mozambican experiences of spirit-spouses, the Siberian shaman engages in such relationships as part of their initiatory place as an outsider to the general community. Shamanism is a religious practice of isolation, of the individual and their internal experiences of the spirit world. Many feel the 'calling' to shamanhood at a young age, and are marked out as different. But what the shaman does share with the African experience is the involuntary and sometimes forceful nature of the encounter:

> In his interesting treatment of the growth of religion, Western La Barre remarked that "the shamanistic dream-vision... often proposes sexuality with a succubus animal, a spirit marriage, or some other 'forced' choice, which if disobeyed will drive the initiate mad". A refusal may even terminate in death.

- The Nature of Shamanism: Substance and Function of a Religious Metaphor (1993) M Ripinsky-Naxon

The principal aim of these spirits is to guide the novice shaman through the difficult process of becoming a healer and the suffering which must be borne by a fully-fledged practitioner. Suffering is a key part of the journey, involving extended periods of isolation, starvation, travelling into lower worlds where the initiate might be sliced with knives, or even dismembered and eaten by angry spirits. A shaman's power with animals comes from their mastery and acceptance of animal spirits, which may penetrate them, possess them, enter their body without forewarning. To be a shaman is to have one's physical and spiritual body at the mercy of other beings, and a spirit-spouse might be exactly the help they need. In Leo Sternberg's 1905 work Die Religion der Giljaken he describes how a Goldi Siberian shaman began to be visited by a young woman, a spirit, who told him she would help him become a powerful healer. His refusal would lead to his death. The man became her husband, and he slept with her. She would transform into different animals, a tiger, a wolf, and help him travel between worlds. Eventually she left him with his own animal spirits, her job done. In a similar fashion, Darkhad Mongolian shaman-initiates would engage in relationships with tutelary spirits:

> *"There is a fierce area (lit. Earth and water) in the Darkhad territory of Mongolia called Algag which has male and female chthonic spirits (lus). From early times the female shamans became companions of male chthonic spirits, the male shamans became companions of the female chthonic spirits and became powerful and good shamans initiated by earthly lus-spirits." The above narrative motif and Pürew's data refer to the importance of non-hereditary shamanic initiation, through interaction with a "spirit-spouse". In the case of shaman Mend – obviously the gender of the initiator spirit is female (emegčin lus). Even if the narrative motifs do not mention the presumably sexual relationship between the spirit and the shaman candidate, other case studies illuminate the real nature of such an encounter with a spirit of the opposite gender. The male spirit-spouse narrative is described in more detail by Sanžeev in the case of Nādmat (cf. Khalkha Nadmid) udgan "shamaness", whose spirit spouse visited her climbing down from a cedar tree and having sexual intercourse with her every day since she was ten years old while she was pasturing the flocks. Nadmid became a shamaness when she was twelve years old and had a family in the spirits' world (a husband and three children). Sanžeev did not specify what kind of spirit was the initiator, but he emphasised that the spirit helped her during rituals and was talking in the Tuwa language through the mouth of the shamaness17*

(Sanžeev 1930, p. 58).

-Delden Mend – The Darkhad Shaman and
Outlaw (2016) Ágnes Birtalan

Acceptance of these spirits' help seems to produce real benefits, and they become more like partners or guides than aggressors, there being no need to banish them or engage in conflict to be free of them.

Spirit-Spouses & Culture Syndromes

These two essays have covered a lot of strange ground - Chinese ghost brides, jealous Yoruban spirit-husbands, vengeful Mozambican spirit-spouses and helpful shamanic spouse-guides. To a modern reader each of them sounds incomprehensible, and there is no one explanation which can cover them all. One topic to return to though is the concept of a culture-syndrome. These are bounded physical and psychological conditions which only manifest within particular cultures, most likely as an interplay between faith, placebo, expectation and childhood experiences. If you believe strongly enough in witchcraft, you may experience symptoms. Each cultural manifestation may have its own scientific rationale (losing babies to disease may prompt a belief in spirit children, or fairies etc), but together they form a cohesive sociobiological package. This is why the Mozambican case is so interesting, since here we see the use of a different 'magical' or 'spiritual' system to defeat the default and accepted status quo.

Despite filling two articles with multiple descriptions of the spirit-spouse phenomena, I have only scratched the surface on a global scale. Every time I researched further there were more and more examples from all around the world. Perhaps the human ability to visit somewhere else in a dream, and be visited by other beings is indeed at the root of it?

A MUMMIFIED MODERN MURDER - THE CASE OF THE PERSIAN PRINCESS

How an archaeological wonder became a macabre murder investigation

I'm currently interested in the whole topic of archaeological fraud and forgery. In particular the motivations and characters of the people who find themselves creating entire legacies of fake objects, often they seem compelled to keep going, creating ever more outlandish scenarios, presumably in their aspiration for fame and glory. Some impulses though are much more basic, simple financial gain, and this one can lead to some dark places, as I discovered when I first read of the case known as the 'Persian Princess'. Others have written about it, but I thought I'd outline the case myself for my readers, and add some more archaeological context to a story already worthy of a novel or a film.

October, 2000, Pakistan

Our story begins with a VHS videotape. Sometime in October, 2000, police in Pakistan were made aware of a tape circulating around individuals known to be involved in various black market activities. The tape was a sort of advert, showing that someone in the country possessed an ancient mummy, and it was for sale. After a tip-off, the police found a Karachi man called Ali Akbar, who denied possessing the mummy or its sarcophagus. The asking price for the mummified remains was a cool $11 million, a significant sum, even for a valuable archaeological artefact. Akbar led the police into Balochistan province, an area split between Iran, Afghanistan and Pakistan, and riven with ethnic conflict. In Quetta, the police located the mummy in the house of a local leader, Wali Mohammed Reeki, who claimed it had been given to him by an Iranian man called Sharif Shah Bakhi. Sources seem to vary on what happened next, but it appears that the Pakistani authorities managed to find Bakhi, question him and corroborate the story that he discovered the mummy after an earthquake in a small Iranian border town. After that Bakhi was never heard from again. Akbar and Reeki were both charged under the country's Antiquity Act and the mummy was taken to the National Museum in Karachi.

A Big Announcement

A mummy in Pakistan is big news, and one of the nation's most prestigious sons knew it. Ahmed Hasan Dani (1920-2009) was a giant in his field, responsible for essentially creating archaeology as a discipline in Pakistan. He apparently spoke dozens of languages, wrote as many books, and was showered with awards and honours from all over the world, including the coveted French Légion d'honneur in 1998, the German Order of the Merit in 1996 and an Aristotle Silver Medal from UNESCO in 1997. He would have known what was at stake when he first approached the sarcophagus, with its cuneiform stone carvings, gilded wooden coffin and Zoroastrian iconography.

On October 26th, in front of TV cameras and journalists, Dani announced the museum's preliminary findings: the mummy and its coffin and sarcophagus dated back to 600 BC, Persia, and appeared to be a princess, potentially from an important family. She had been preserved in the Egyptian style and laid atop a mat coated in honey and wax. She could have been an Egyptian princess, married into the royal family, or potentially a daughter of Cyrus the Great himself. Either way, here was an extraordinary find, the first remains of a Persian royal, and mummified in a way not known to the region.

A Diplomatic Meltdown

Almost immediately Dani's conference provoked outrage, first and foremost amongst the Iranians, who felt that they should now take over the care and investigation of the mummy, since she had been identified as Persian royalty. The Iranian Cultural Heritage body lodged a complaint with UNESCO, prompting a war of words between Pakistan and Iran, the former highlighting that the mummy was recovered on Pakistani territory. To complicate matters, the Awan tribe of Balochistan filed a petition with the High Court, insisting that the mummy must belong to them instead. Finally, a month later, the Taliban of all people chimed in, saying they had interrogated a group of cross-border smugglers, who revealed that the mummy had surfaced originally in Afghanistan. This was quite a bold move for a regime which was renowned for destroying its pre-Islamic inheritance, but they threw their hat into the ring - a showdown between Pakistan, Iran, Afghanistan and Balochistan was underway.

Dani tried to sidestep the problem by negating everyone's claims, saying that the princess was most likely Egyptian, and therefore did not belong to Iran. The Iranians played their own cards, announcing that an Italian archaeologist by the name of Lorenzo Costantini had validated the Iranian claim to the mummy, by authenticating the inscriptions on her coffin. Costantini, bewildered and angry, hit back on Iranian television, retorting that he had been shown a photograph sent by the Iranians, which possibly said the word 'Xerxes' or 'Cyrus', sources seem to vary. The name 'Rhodugune' is listed in many articles about the princess, but Constantini himself is quoted as saying:

> *"I never gave an interview to any Iranian journalist...I shortly talked on the telephone with an Iranian woman of the IRNA office at Rome. During the talk, I told her that the name of Xerxes was mentioned in the [coffins'] inscriptions...she asked, 'Who's he?' This small comment reveals the degree of knowledge of the person I was speaking to"*

One has to imagine the rumours swirling around the press offices at the time led to much confusion about names of ancient Persian kings, but certainly later accounts differ from Dani's original announcement. The battle over ownership and authentication was to continue for some time. Before Christmas 2000, the mummy underwent a CT scan at Aga Khan University Hospital in Karachi, revealing her to be a young woman with a broken spine.

The Dealer And The Archaeologist

Before any of this happened, back in March 2000, a letter with four Polaroid pictures landed on the desk of Oscar White Muscarella at the Metropolitan Museum of Art in New York. He opened it, finding images of what seemed to be a mummy with a gold breastplate, along with a translation of the cuneiform - "I am the daughter of the great King Xerxes. Mazereka protect me. I am Rhodugune, I am". The letter had been sent by one Amanollah Riggi of New Jersey, acting as a middleman for a seller in Pakistan. They were offering Muscarella and the museum the opportunity to buy this priceless artefact.

Muscarella seems an odd choice for this venture. This was a man who was not only an expert in ancient Persia, Anatolia and the Near East, but had a reputation for being the 'conscience of the discipline'. He had devoted much of his life to stopping and undermining archaeological looting, forgeries and illegal purchases. He quite literally wrote the book on the subject, "The Lie Became Great. The Forgery of Ancient Near Eastern Cultures", which accused many museums, and even his own institution of purchasing forged antiquities. Naturally he was intrigued by the photos and translation, but also suspicious. He demanded better photographs, and reached out to the academic who had supposedly translated the cuneiform on the breastplate.

Things unravelled quickly for Riggi. Muscarella discovered that the academic had written up much more than he had been shown in the letter. In fact, the linguist had determined that most of the writing had been lifted directly from the famous Behistun Inscription, which outlined King Darius I's achievements. He also highlighted numerous inconsistencies in the production, concluding that the work was most likely a forgery. The scholar had laid this out to Riggi, who in desperation sent back radiocarbon dates for the wood in the coffin. It was no more than 250 years old, a discrepancy that seemed to evade him - "it cannot be called modern" pleaded Riggi. Muscarella severed communication and went back to his work, roused only when he was invited by Archaeology magazine to give a statement on the mummy find in October, 2000. He realised the photos and the mummy now in the news were one and the same, and submitted all his evidence to Interpol. Any chance of the princess being authentic was disintegrating away.

The Iranians Arrive

The details don't seem to be available, but sometime in January Pakistan relented and allowed an Iranian archaeological delegation to come to Karachi and analyse the mummy. A joint team made up of Dani, Pakistan's National Museum curator Asma Ibrahim, and the Iranians - led by the veteran Mir Abedin Kaboli - launched a new investigation of the remains. What they found was shocking. Not only was the body covered in modern petrochemicals, the coffin carvings guided by lead pencil markings and the radiocarbon dates miles off 600 BC, but the woman herself was a modern person. She had had her heart and other organs removed, contrary to classical practice, before being stuffed with salt and bicarbonate powder. Her tendons were visible, there was fungus developing on her face, her teeth had been removed to prevent easy identification. Where traditional Egyptian mummification would have seen her organs carefully removed, cleaned and returned to her body, this woman had been crudely gutted and improperly preserved. Further radiocarbon dating placed her death tentatively around the mid 1990's.

What had originally been a story of archaeological wonder

had quickly devolved into a sordid tale. German researchers were sent samples of the body, coffin and more, confirming the joint Iranian-Pakistani conclusions. A young woman had died around 1995 of a broken neck, possibly killed deliberately, and was then subject to a mockery of a mummification procedure, and turned into a forged ensemble to be sold for $11 million to a buyer who believed her to be a Persian princess. Ibrahim released her report on April 17th 2001. The Pakistani authorities then treated the case as murder, but they had let their most valuable suspect, Sharif Shah Bakhi, disappear into thin air.

Aftermath

For all the attention paid to the mummy when it was found, nobody cared after it was announced the remains were a hoax. By all accounts the police gave up looking for the people responsible, the department in Balochistan dragging its feet for so long it took until 2008 for the mummified woman to be buried. The experts who had been so confident in their pronouncements, Dani in particular, were silent. A BBC documentary was made on the case, concluding that this had to have been the work of many skilled people - a stonemason, a joiner, a goldsmith, someone with a working knowledge of anatomy and embalming, and someone familiar enough with cuneiform and Persian history to conduct the choir. Despite the mistakes, this was a relatively sophisticated operation, and one with bravado, either killing or acquiring a body and quickly producing a mummy to be sold on the black market. Someone out there knows what happened, and maybe they've done it before and since. Someone knows who she was, and how she ended up in a sarcophagus with a golden breastplate. But we'll likely never know, just as we'll never know how many such fakes fill our museums and archives, maybe there are other bodies to be found.

PART TWO - BIOLOGY

HIDDEN COSTS: ECOLOGICAL REALISM & THE 'GREEN' REVOLUTION

*Polymetallic nodules, sand
mafias and e-waste hazards*

F rom the position of the archaeologist, technology is a
neutral term. From flint hand axes to sickles, antler
harpoons to fish traps, the earliest forms of technology
leverage efficiency and capability at the interface between the
human and the rest of the world. There is nothing unnatural
about this - crows, otters, monkeys, even crocodiles make
use of manipulated objects to exploit their dietary niche.
Where there are concerns about how modern technology
functions, they shouldn't be framed as a dichotomy between
'good' and 'bad', but rather at the specific problems created.
Too often what counts for academia today will position any
discussion of technology in a framework of 'neoliberalism'

and 'systems thinking'. Some will talk of the Anthropocene, barely suppressing their glee at the control such definitions bring. What I want to do here is outline some concrete and non-systemic threats that specific technologies pose. It is my contention that only through approaching risks to the natural world in this way will we actually retain the ability to tackle them. Beyond the nebulous outlines of international agreements and porous commitments lies the bulwark of the nation state and its capacities, let us not be shy in demanding it makes use of them.

Mining The Sea-Floor: Polymetallic Nodules

The new Green Revolution and its consequences are rolling like a tidal wave across the world. One of its most insidious children is the 'net-zero' mining industry. To be absolutely clear, the new eco-friendly techno-complex of electric cars, wind and solar generated energy and the vast new infrastructure of batteries needed to support these relies precariously on this industry's ability to extract unprecedented amounts of raw minerals. According to the World Bank's 2020 report: Minerals for Climate Action, the increase in mineral production includes a staggering 488% increase in demand for lithium, 460% for cobalt, 231% for indium and a 189% increase for vanadium. The projections for the UK to meet its target for electric cars would require the world's current output of neodymium, almost twice the world's production of cobalt and three-quarters of the global lithium production. With two of the main countries for nickel, cobalt, manganese and copper being China and the Democratic Republic of Congo, the race has started to find alternatives mining venues. European nickel mines are one option, but by far the most enticing is the prospect of under sea mining.

Back in the deepest past, earth's seawater began to slowly precipitate heavy metals. Manganese and iron oxyhydrides began to scavenge cations of cobalt, copper and nickel, freed by the actions of undersea hydrothermal vents and the imperceptible metabolism of microorganisms, they settled over millions of years into polymetallic nodules. But why is this important? These nodules lie scattered all over the sea floor, most no larger than a duck's egg, a gift from mother nature to a civilisation desperate for metals. The Clipperton Fracture Zone, a 4.5 million square kilometre expanse rich in manganese nodules, is just one prime example of the embarrassment of riches lying untapped and unused. The world has just realised that these treasure troves now need to be harvested and companies are applying for exploratory licences everywhere from Nauru to Mexico. Specialised sea craft with submarine vehicles now pioneer the extraction of nodules, suctioning, grinding, harvesting and crushing the metals before sending them up to the surface. What's the problem I hear you ask, surely we need this?

The problem is that these nodules are not sterile globules of free resources, like some computer game world. They are in fact the underpinning keystone in a complex food web which we barely glimpse through the handful of studies which have focused on them. What we do know is this: the nodules themselves are coated with living beings, one in particular, the stalked glass sponge, is considered a key structural species. The trophic webs which exist in these deep abyssal zones rely on the nodules as the only physical structural support to anchor onto, the soft sediment being incapable of supporting these species. The cascading effects of removing the nodules flows upwards to the sediment and filter feeders, the scavengers, omnivores and carnivores. Equally as devastating are the fine sediment plumes created by the harvesters and the waste dumping after extraction, these clouds smother species to death and choke up life on the precarious reefs. Added to these known factors are the unknown risks - a 2016 study into the Clipperton Fracture Zone found that half of all the collected species were new to science. More dangerous (and ironic) is the possibility that deposits of frozen methane, known as methane clathrates, could be accidentally disturbed, potentially releasing unknown quantities of natural gas into the ocean and the atmosphere.

The question before us is - do we tear up a unique and important ocean ecosystem in order to fuel the Green Revolution? The cost-benefit analysis here should look at what this Revolution actually offers and whether it is desirable? It seems unlikely that all the ocean's metals are going to remain unused, and no amount of international pressure will stop a country like China exploiting its own shoreline. But we needn't all rush onwards with the charge for an electric battery powered world, there are alternatives.

Stripping The Dunes: Sand Extraction

On a list of conversational topics bound to cure insomnia, sand has to be near the top. Yet, this basic and seemingly ubiquitous material is rapidly becoming a coveted resource. How is this possible? Sand is required for a number of fundamental industries, including construction, road building, electronics, plastics, cosmetics, detergents, solar panels and water filtration. Due to the nature of the grains, desert sand is practically worthless, being too fine to bind together. This makes rivers, lakes and any accessible ocean the major targets for sand extraction and mining. On the face of it, this sounds reasonable. However, we have two huge problems here - firstly, the amount of available sand in the world is shrinking faster than it can be replenished; secondly, the damage caused to the environment, ecology and human habitation around the mined areas.

Sand extraction accounts for 85% of all mineral production globally by weight. Roughly 32 - 50 billion tons of sand is used annually, which, according to some models, will lead to demand outstripping supply before the century is out. Virtually every country imports sand, with the leading exporters, such as China and the United States, shipping 300 million tons in 2019. These figures are notoriously unreliable however since, as we'll see later on, the illegal mining of sand is likely the largest supplier. As an example, between 2006 and 2016, Singapore imported 80 million tons of sand from Cambodia, but only 4% of that was through legal export channels. Since Singapore desperately needs sand for land reclamation and skyscraper building, the nearby countries have scoured billions of tons of sand for illegal export, so much so that Indonesia has physically lost over 20 islands, and another 80 are at risk.

Ecologically, sand mining at scale presents a number of problems: it lowers water tables, depletes wells, physically destroys habitats, alters the shape and flow of rivers, disrupts food webs, creates river bank instability, collapses bridges, changes the velocity of the river flow which can cause flooding and damage to property, leaches salt into agricultural land, dune removal can cause flooding, dust plumes can increase airborne radioactivity and damage health, and so on. The standard method for sand extraction is to dredge, at different scales and in a number of different ways. Ranging from Nigerians physically wading into the surf and carrying baskets of sand away on their heads, to Tamil truck drivers parking on tourist beaches and filling up using spades, to huge Chinese commercial ships complete with conveyor belts and barges, the nature of the work depends on the country and its legality. At the risk of repeating previous talking points, sand mining clearly has an immediate and long term impact on the ecology of the region. The physical removal of beaches, dunes, sand banks and river beds negates the ability of dependent wildlife and flora to survive, but another consequence is the spillover into violence in the human world.

Illegal sand mining seems like one of those minor headline topics, but the scale of the organisation goes far beyond what most people understand. Unauthorised sand extraction is the largest criminal enterprise in India, in particular the southern state of Tamil Nadu. In China, the Yangtze River has been a target for illegal extraction for decades, since the state banned mining in 2000. In 2019 alone police seized over 300 vessels, carrying approximately 100 million cubic feet of sand. Yet the theft continues, in part due to sophisticated GPS spoofing, which prevents authorities from accurately monitoring ship movement in real time, resulting in lethal collisions. Thane Creek, the river inlet from the Arabian Sea to Mumbai, swarms with hundreds of small wooden boats, all illegally scooping up sand from the river bed by hand. The divers used to make the plunge down to 20ft, a few years later they are at their physical limits of 40ft, soon the river bed will simply disappear. Like many similar illegal mines and dredge sites in India, they are run by mafias with the power to buy off local officials and murder journalists and protestors. On the larger geopolitical level, the tensions between Singapore and Indonesia/Malaysia have reached the point where the Indonesian navy has been deployed to arrest illegal sand miners in its territory.

E-Waste: Guiya, China & Agbogbloshie, Ghana

Along with reducing energy consumption and the replacement of fossil fuels with renewable energy is the third great eco-commandment: thou shalt recycle. Drilled into us as children and now for many an unconscious habit, the act of recycling is considered part of the virtuous package of green beliefs and an essential component in the 'circular economy'. But recent scandals have exposed the great fraud of recycling and its empty promises. In 2018, under a policy called 'National Sword', China banned 24 types of plastic entering the country. At a stroke, the entire foundation of the world's recycling system was demolished. Panic set in as countries began frantically searching for somewhere else to dump their trash. The harder questions then began to be asked, about how and why industrial nations are producing so much plastic. What was also discovered was the alternatives to China were horrifying, ranging from burning plastic in residential areas, to just dumping it in the ocean. Back in 2017 alarm bells should have been ringing when a research paper estimated that: since 2015, humans have produced roughly 6300 million metric tons of plastic, and that only 9% of it has been recycled. The remainder was either burnt (12%) or packed into landfill (79%).

Plastics, and the subsequent exposure of microplastics as a serious threat to human and animal health, have dominated the environmental headlines for the last few years. But the question of electronic waste - e-waste - has been relatively under-discussed. Electronic and digital infrastructure is often touted as the greener and more eco-friendly of any given option - banks often ask you to review your statement online, rather than print one on paper. But this ignores the immense damage that electronics cause, during their production and particularly during their disposal. The full list of chemicals and substances found within e-waste is vast, but some of the more potent include: brominated flame retardants, polybrominated diphenyl ethers, polybrominated biphenyls, polychlorinated biphenyls (PCBs), polychlorinated dibenzodioxins, polyaromatic hydrocarbons, lead, chromium, cadmium, mercury, lithium, arsenic and bismuth. The sheer volume of this waste has ballooned out of control; China alone was estimated to have produced 15 million metric tons in 2020. In general we can categorise e-waste into three main types - large household appliances (fridges, freezers etc), personal equipment (smartphones, tracker gadgets, TVs) and IT equipment (monitors, servers, fibre optic cables etc). All of these are set to increase as the costs of production have lowered for the average consumer and as more countries develop their digital infrastructure.

The movement and shipping of e-waste is, in principle, subject to control through the Basel Convention (in force since 1992). However, without the ratification of the United States and with precious little enforcement
mechanisms, the Convention has failed to prevent millions of tons of e-waste being transported and dumped across the world. One place in particular has garnered international attention - Agbogbloshie, Ghana - and is listed among the top ten most toxic places on earth. Despite some substantial hyperbole about illegal e-waste trafficking, the waste dump near the centre of Accra does pose a huge health risk, both to the adults and children working there, and the greater environment of the coast of the Gulf of Guinea. In particular the open fires used to melt the plastic from copper wiring and the subsequent extraction by hand of precious metals and electronic components without safety equipment causes horrific neurological and physical harm to the workers. Similarly, in Guangdong, China, the former rice village of Guiya was quickly established as the electronic graveyard of the world. In the early 2000's, over 60,000 people were employed under the most primitive conditions to harvest and extract valuable metals from e-waste, sent from all over the world. Burning plastic, soaking chips in acid baths, breathing in dioxin tainted ash; the workers were recovering gold, toner, copper and silver. The water became undrinkable and had to be brought from elsewhere, rice could not be grown, children were exposed to critical levels of lead, toxic dust saturated with chromium, nickel and zinc settled over the town. Since 2007 the area has been subject to state-led efforts to raise safety and health standards, but the pollution and contamination is likely permanent and has yet to be dealt with.
One major incentive to bring e-waste recycling back under

national controls is the growing problem of data security within e-waste. All those mobile phones, hard drives, servers and consumer gadgets are packed with passwords, personal data and in some cases even state secrets. Journalists reporting on Agbogbloshie went rummaging through the informal markets which surround the dump, they found a hard drive containing unencrypted sensitive US Government data:

> *A team of journalists investigating the global electronic waste business has unearthed a security problem too. In a Ghana market, they bought a computer hard drive containing sensitive documents belonging to U.S. government contractor Northrop Grumman… They were marked "competitive sensitive" and covered company contracts with the Defense Intelligence Agency, the National Aeronautics and Space Administration and the Transportation Security Agency.*

Organised crime in Ghana has realised the goldmine of information that Agbogbloshie represents and regularly purchases hard drives, looking for useful data:

> *The students take the hard drives to Regent University in the Ghanaian capital and ask computer scientist Enoch Kwesi Messiah to help read what is on them. Within minutes, he is scrolling through intimate details of people's lives, files left behind by the hard drives' original owners. There is private financial data, too: credit card numbers, account information, records of online transactions the original owners may not have realized were even there.*

> " *I can get your bank numbers and I retrieve all*

your money from your accounts," Messiah says. "If ever somebody gets your hard drive, he can get every information about you from the drive, no matter where it is hidden."

That's particularly a problem in a place like Ghana, which is listed by the U.S. State Department as one of the top sources of cyber crime in the world

Conclusions: The Return Of The State?

I selected the three problems addressed in this article - polymetallic nodule mining, sand extraction and e-waste - as good examples of the relationship between the environment, technology, health and the State. The 90's paradigm of globalisation outstripping the nation-state and rendering it obsolete has thankfully run its course, although some tone-deaf commentators and ideologues are still wedded to the 'market first' vision of humanity. What has come screeching back into the void of COVID-19, the retreat of US hegemony and the rise of China is the fundamental importance of national governance. Some, like the UK, are beginning to realise how withered their powers have become, others like China are confidently asserting their muscle. The control of national territory, especially in the ocean; the enforcement of national treaties; the ability to shut borders to the flow of material goods; the development of safety protocols and infrastructure for recycling critical technologies (eg batteries); the protection of ecological assets, and the ability to tackle organised and transnational crime are all fundamental tasks of the nation-state. While the left wing environmentalists are correct that pollution or biodiversity depletion doesn't magically stop at the border, what we must recognise is that handing over national autonomy to international organisations not only hasn't helped, but neuters the very tools needed to reign in the excesses of modernity. This is not to argue that national cooperation, treaties, international agreements and so forth can't be realised - they absolutely can, and they are best done through a strong national and territorial framework. I will finish here by reflecting on my opening remarks: technology changes the way humans relate to their environment, and leverages their capacities. Many technologies have huge downsides as well as enormous benefits, and the best way to retain an optimal asymmetry is for the different techno-complexes to be under the control of a sovereign state.

THE DOG THAT DEFIED DARWINISM

*The development of the Córdoba
Fighting Dog and its consequences*

T he domestication and development of dog breeds is a
fascinating subject, showing how biology and culture
overlap to create new kinds of life. Domestication is
often seen as 'unnatural' in some sense, as does selective
breeding, but we should remind ourselves that humans are
not the only species to domesticate others. Fish and insects
are well known for engaging in farming and domesticating
plants, fungi and other animals. One could argue that certain
ants enslave others, even controlling them through violence.
Despite our best efforts however, we have learnt that not all
species will cooperate to become domesticated. If Man could
tame deer and others in that family, it would have happened
a long time ago. The semi-domestication of reindeer is about
as close as it gets. Domestication itself is a specific biological
act, with a common set of processes across animals and plants,
although they are not fully understood even today.

The story I want to look at here is a unique example of selective
breeding which seemed to defy the basic commandments of

evolutionary biology - the compulsion or instinct to procreate. The tale is a sad one, of a dog species developed to become the ultimate fighting machine, at the expense of all the beauty of that creature. But it also should remind us that biology is a study dominated by exceptions, and even the most fundamental rules can be broken. Whether you see this as a natural or unnatural phenomena will probably depend on your own philosophical position about Life and what constitutes Life.

The domestication of the dog was a watershed moment for life on earth, transforming the capacities and extended phenotype of human cultures. The origins of the event are remote and somewhat blurry, since the archaeological distinction between a buried wolf and a buried dog is minimal to non-existent until specific breeds become established. The oldest definitive dog burial is the Bonn-Oberkassel dog, dated to 14,223 years ago in Germany. The juvenile animal was suffering from canine distemper when it died, which infers that its owners were caring for it until it expired and was buried with two people. Certain Mesolithic dogs were buried in human cemeteries, some even with grave goods, which has led to much speculation about how these foragers must have regarded the 'personhood' of particular animals. Somewhere around 20-30,000 years ago in Siberia is the generally accepted time and place for the beginnings of dog domestication, with a number of scenarios posited, including:

Migratory Wolves Theory - that humans essentially learnt how to be mobile pastoralists while observing and moving with wolf packs hunting reindeer herds

Overlapping Niches - that humans and wolves share a similar niche in behaviour and economy, leading to either conflict or cooperation.

Campfire Theory - the most famous, that wolves self-domesticated by becoming familiar with human encampments, eventually trading away autonomy for resources and protection.

Food Partitioning - that dogs were domesticated during the Ice Age since humans had huge amounts of excess protein that they were unable to metabolise, leading to mutual sharing of megafauna kills: fat and organs to the people, lean protein to the canids.

However it happened (details for another article), most dogs prior to the Victorian era came from only a handful of basal dog lineages: Afghan Hound, Akita, Alaskan Malamute, Basenji, Canaan, Chow Chow, Dingo, Finnish Spitz, New Guinea Singing Dog, Saluki, Samoyed, Shar-Pei, Shiba Inu, Siberian Husky·

Dogs appear south of the original wolf distribution in the Old and New Worlds almost always with the arrival of agriculture. For example, despite the fact that human remains are present in much older contexts at Coxcatlan Cave in Mexico, dogs first appear only ~ 5,200 B.P. alongside the appearance of agricultural communities (35). The same is true in sub-Saharan Africa, where dogs appear after the advent of the Sudanese Neolithic ~ 5600 B.P. (36), in Peninsular Southeast Asia ~ 4,200 B.P. (37), and in Island Southeast Asia ~ 3,500 B.P. (38). Dogs only arrived in South Africa ~ 1,400 y ago following the arrival of cows, sheep, and goats a few hundred years before (39), and in southern South America ~ 1,000 y ago with the arrival of sedentary societies (40).

-Rethinking dog domestication by integrating
genetics, archeology, and biogeography

The development of the more recognisable breeds of today is a very modern phenomenon. Several bottlenecks, including the Victorian love of breeding for aesthetics and function, and the world wars, left the global dog population looking unrecognisable:

> *Both World Wars had a major impact on the genetic diversity of the domestic dog. In the United Kingdom, English Mastiffs were reduced to 14 individuals (18), Sussex Spaniels to 10 (22), and Manchester Terriers to 11 (18). Bernese Mountain Dogs (18) and Italian Greyhounds (22) vanished completely and many other breeds suffered significant bottlenecks*

> *Even the basal breeds identified in this and other studies experienced recent and significant demographic change. The Shiba Inu faced extinction in World War II and the modern breed is an amalgamation of three isolated and distinct Japanese lineages (18). The Finnish Spitz, supposedly used for millennia by Finno-Ugric people, was nearly extinct by 1880. A single breeder, Hugo Roos, set out to rescue the type by travelling to remote villages and collecting the few remaining individuals least likely to have been crossed (accidentally or purposely) with other breeds (18). The fact that Finnish Spitzes retain a basal genetic signature is testament to the success of Roos's efforts to obtain uncrossed individuals.*

One dog however with a much more ancient lineage is

the cluster of breeds called Mastiffs, and latterly Bulldogs. Possibly originating in Asia with Tibetan Mastiffs, the breeds made excellent war dogs, attack dogs, guard dogs, protection animals, hunting and sport dogs. The Conquistadors brought legendary mastiff-type dogs with them to the New World, which became the terror of the local populations. One dog, Becerrillo, was owned by Ponce de León, and was infamous for sniffing out and killing Indians. Mastiffs may have been brought on the Mayflower, and were certainly present in the Americas by the 1800's.

Mastiffs are described as brachycephalic, or flat-faced, with a less pronounced jaw. Such dogs have a mechanical advantage when applying pressure with their teeth, and mastiffs can reportedly reach around 500 lb per square inch of force, which dwarfs many other breeds. This quality makes them ideal fighting dogs, asserting the greatest power over another canine with the least number of bites.

Dog fighting is still a huge underground industry all over the world, and dogs continue to be bred to become superior fighters. Alongside the breeds themselves the dogs are often given testosterone, dietary supplements to build weight, and are trained to fight with heavy weights and to hang on to objects while suspended to increase jaw strength. One city that was famous for dog fights was Córdoba in Argentina, in particular during the 19th century. The city's most famous canid became known as the Córdoba Fighting Dog.

The Córdoba Fighting Dog, or "viejo perro de pelea Cordobés", was the ultimate combat animal. A crossbred mastiff which descended from Spanish fighting dogs, mixed with some newly imported English Bullterriers, the Córdoba proved to not only be aggressive enough in the ring, but to have that quality which fighters prize in their animal - 'gameness'.

While few fights are to the death - their owners can call a halt by handling or picking up their dogs - most end with both dogs utterly exhausted and when one has no fight left. Dogs may die later of injuries like severed arteries, or they are put down if an obliging vet can't be found. A turn is called when a dog turns away from its opponent, refusing to fight. The dogs go back to their corner, if one refuses to come out - or "stands the line" - the fight is over. A cur - a dog that doesn't want to fight - can be a liability to owner and breeder and risks being destroyed.

-The shadowy, paranoid world of dogfighting

Gameness is the quality of willingness to fight, and to continue fighting despite exhaustion and injury. The Córdoba seems to have been exceptional in this regard, defying broken bones, deep bites, pain and tiredness to stay in the game. But it went further than this, these dogs were so aggressive that they couldn't be easily kept together in kennels, since they often turned on one another. They might turn on their siblings, or even their own puppies.

Most bizarre of all, the Córdobas became infamous for their unwillingness to mate. Male Córdobas seemed to regularly prefer to fight and kill any presented female, rather than copulate, which is an extraordinary level of aggression. This difficulty ultimately led to them being mated with other breeds, which caused their extinction (along with the outlawing of dog fighting in Argentina in 1954). What emerged from the Córdoba was a new breed - the Dogo Argentino - which was created by medical student Antonio Nores Martinez and his brother. The Dogo was a crossbreed between the Córdoba and other, more stable dogs:

Antonio Nores Martinez, inspired along with his brother Agustin, ingeniously conceived to turn that old fighting dog, now considered a native breed, into something more noble and useful – that is, a hound for "big game," able to hunt the wild boar, puma, jaguar, fox and other pests that invaded the Argentine fields, producing huge losses to the main agricultural activity of the time.

To implement their plan, they crossed the "perro de pelea" with other breeds that were already fixed in type and recognized by the international dog world, such as the Boxer, Pointer, Great Pyrenees, Dogue de Bordeaux, Bulldog, Bull Terrier, Irish Wolfhound and Great Dane.

All this was to attempt to give agility, strength, size, scenting ability, endurance and intelligence to this unique dog breed. It was a veritable cocktail replete with challenges – just think that they were combining molossoid dogs with those of Sighthound and Scenthound type.

-Cordoba's Creation: The evolution of
Argentina's famous white dog

The Dogo is a more reliable animal, although it remains a banned breed in many countries, including the UK and Australia, due to its underlying temperament. The story of the Córdoba is an extreme example of selective breeding and its consequences, in this case seemingly to defy the will to reproduce. There's an interesting question at the heart of this, about how we should understand Life and biology - was the Córdoba an unnatural phenomena? Or can nature create such single-minded monsters under the right conditions? If so, what other qualities and instincts could be bred into an animal?

BIOLOGICAL VITALISM, OR WHAT IS LIFE?

Teleology, animal behaviour
& neovitalism

A spectre has long haunted the field of biology, the spectre of vitalism. In our nominally rational age we are used to describing life as an epiphenomena, one which can be best explained in the language of the machine. Parts, components, software, circuits - these metaphors are a surface deep attempt to ensure biology remains wedded to the Cartesian principles that life, and everything else, can be reduced to its fundamental constituent elements. But this view, more scientism than scientific, has long been contested historically and creaks under the mounting weight of recent evidence. What remains, lurking in the background, is a philosophy of life that seeks to understand the forces, the drives, the will which organises and directs organic matter towards an end. This irreducible, teleological conception of biology can be called vitalism, and I shall attempt to outline the main problems and principles in this brief overview.

The Problem Of Biology

Aristotle knows through various observations that the embryonic parts are not all simultaneously present, but come successively into being; and thus, to use a modern term, we may call his theory "epigenetic". How then do these parts come into being: does the one form the other or do they simply arise one after the other?

-The History & Theory of Vitalism, Hans Driesch, 1914.

The ancient problem of biology is how to explain the difference between animate and inanimate matter? Whilst a simple explanation posits that life is simply stuff which is organised and directed by an external spirit or divine will, observation shows that living organisms 'unfold' or develop, from acorn to tree, with some kind of invisible will or direction. Something internal and indivisible. The Presocratic search for the 'arche', the underlying principle or substance, led to Thales and Anaximander positing water or fire as the governing element. Onto this Aristotle stamped his theory of hylomorphism - that living beings are composed of both matter and form. To illustrate, a human body after many decades contains none of the same molecules from its infancy, the body is constantly replacing itself. Yet it remains identifiably the same person. The form, the organising directive of the body, stays the same. Aristotle labels this the soul, that force which binds matter and points it towards an end.

The idea that life requires 'vital heat' and water underpinned 'spontaneous generation', a theory with remarkable longevity. From the ancient Greeks to Louis Pasteur, people have observed with their own eyes life emerging from mud, foam, decaying matter, stagnant water and even animals changing from one form to another, such as barnacles morphing into barnacle geese. In the most corrupt mediums, life is always present, new forms and shapes coming forth. Debates over spontaneous generation led to the modern hypothesis of 'abiogenesis', that life did indeed come from a non-living organic substrate. To paraphrase Georg Ernst Stahl, life is activity and not matter, which is indifferent and simply obeys the organising and governing laws of activity. This conundrum, of form or activity and matter, has not been fully resolved by modern biology.

The second great problem of biology is teleology. This sounds like a tedious undergraduate seminar topic, but it goes to the heart of why vitalism is still relevant. Under mechanistic and Darwinian principles we cannot say that living beings exist to fulfil a certain goal or end. To most laypeople, the question "what is an animal for?" may sound strange. Animals exist because God made them, they exist to be eaten, to be pets, they exist for themselves and their own mysterious reasons. To a standard biologist life has no reason, no goal, no end. Life is the product of natural and sexual selection, which blindly and coldly steers different species towards adaptation to their environment. Should that environment change, the 'blind watchmaker' pushes them down another path. But this exceptionally dull view of life rests on quicksand. In what has been dubbed 'irreducible teleology', the philosophy of biology has failed to jettison goal-driven behaviour from the field.

Questions over whether traits are selected by evolution because they have a certain function become cringingly tedious. Dawkins went so far as to call Darwinian adaptations 'designoid', rather than 'designed', such is his fear that the world be seen as alive and full of purposeful beings. Ernst Mayr showed the difference with two classic sentences:

"The Wood Thrush migrates in the fall in order to escape

the inclemency of the weather and the food shortages of
the northern climates."

"The Wood Thrush migrates in the fall and thereby
escapes the inclemency of the weather and the food
shortages of the northern climates."

The latter phrase, while perhaps relished by the more mechanistically minded, obliterates any sentience or intelligence in the thrush, and also fails to capture why the bird migrates. One might retort that the thrush is merely the survivor of those ancestors which initially migrated, but this pushes the problem backwards. Birds, like all organisms, don't perform random behaviours with the hope their descendents will be better adapted. They pursue their own inbuilt behaviours, innate to them, which always brings in the problem of teleology. As J.B.S Haldane quipped:

Teleology is like a mistress to a biologist: he cannot live
without her but he's unwilling to be seen with her in
public.

The Limits Of Modern Biology

Biology developed in the opposite way to physics. For biologists the 'Grand Narrative' of Darwinian evolution came first, and the huge expansion of genetics and molecular science has served to fill in the blanks later. Physics by contrast has no overarching theory. This has had the effect that new revelations in the biosciences have to be contextualised within an existing theoretical framework. The 'modern synthesis' of neo-Darwinism in the mid 20th century successfully integrated Mendelian thought of inheritance with Darwin's laws of natural selection, and then 'evo-devo' in the 1970's began linking specific genes to the process of organismal development, leading ultimately to the genomics revolution of the last few decades. Regardless of how much data has been produced however, the goal of understanding biology has remained elusive.

Every student of the life sciences is taught a basic axiom of biology, one referred to as the Central Dogma. Put simply - DNA makes RNA, RNA makes proteins. The more nuanced definition is about the flow of information in a biological system. Francis Crick, the originator of the dogma, tried to pin down an absolute law of biology, that information cannot pass backwards from a protein to the DNA. This has served to create the only stable anchor in a field dominated by exceptions to the rules, and yet, it too is wrong. Darwinism itself was the product of struggle and strife between competing theories of life and nature, one of which was Lamarckism. Lamarck (1744-1829) proposed that organisms gain useful traits throughout their lives which then be acquired by the next generation, classically the example of a giraffe's neck is used. As the giraffe stretched its neck and lengthened its muscles, so its offspring would be born with a longer neck. The 'Weissman Barrier', the separation between bodily cells and those germ cells which lead to embryo formation, squashed Lamarckism for generations (outside of the Soviet Union), but Lamarck has had something of a renaissance with the discovery of epigenetics.

Epigenetics is a complex and misunderstood term, but it refers to the system of biological mechanisms which control DNA expression and how changes to these mechanisms can be inherited. For example, the ability to digest the milk sugar lactose is dependent on the organism producing the enzyme lactase. Lactase production is controlled by a series of molecular 'switches' which 'turn on' lactase production during infancy and then 'turn off' production as the organism weans off milk onto other foods. In a famous 2013 study, mice were trained to fear a particular smell, the offspring of these mice also feared the same scent - a genetic memory attributable to epigenetic modifications. These heritable changes to the epigenome need not alter the DNA directly, but they can profoundly affect the resulting phenotype. To go further, epigenetic modifications can become assimilated into the genome under certain conditions. Similarly a whole host of proteins and transcriptional factors exist which make the causal determinism of the Central Dogma untenable - reverse transcriptase, RNA splicing proteins, prions, integrase enzymes and so on. Much of this sounds depressingly boring but the ramifications are immense.

Darwinian biology is predicated on the idea that information flows in one direction, that an organism is controlled by the expression of genes which are preserved as DNA sequences in the genome. How organisms adapt comes down to generational selection of traits which ultimately produce a fitter and better adapted individual. Central to this is the notion that traits arise from mutations and genetic diversity already present within the genome. What cannot be allowed is that the environment and organism itself self-direct the course of change, mutations are random, a pool of untapped potential which arises from chaos without guidance. The problem with this is that everything in the cell works against this premise. Intricate proofreading machinery guards DNA against mutations, damage can be repaired, and when mutations do appear they are overwhelmingly deleterious or lethal. The list of genetic diseases is vast, the list of genetic enhancements very small per generation. This matters because life is expressed through different, well defined species, and species are not defined by single mutations like lactase persistence, but rather by their form, their shape and body plan.

The problem of how species arise suddenly has been debated for decades, with biologists like Stephen Jay Gould proposing theories like 'punctuated equilibrium' to explain periods of rapid species diversification. Exactly how novel complex species appear in the fossil record is still argued over today - events like the Cambrian Explosion, the Devonian land plant or the Cretaceous flowering plant explosion seem to defy the idea of a regular, steady beat to evolution. The genetic developmental mechanism, the Hox genes, were well established prior to the Cambrian Explosion, and yet the vast bloom of different body plans occurred much later in a relatively short period of time. Body plan genes are immensely complex and seem to possess a 4-dimensional quality, allowing an embryo to develop a 3D structure, but also each gene seems to regulate another, unlocking a cascade of perfectly timed regulatory events which allow a blob of cells to differentiate into fingers, eyes, organs and limbs. Any mistake in this sequence can produce a serious flaw in the final overall form. The link between these developmental genes and natural selection doesn't appear obvious or straightforward, almost any tinkering within this 4D space would have deleterious effects. To quote from Simon Conway Morris in the excellent 2003 book Origination of Organismal Form Beyond the Gene in Developmental and Evolutionary Biology:

> But the reverse is also the case, whereby phenotypic diversity emerges from a conserved genomic framework. A striking example comes from the arthropods. Averof (1997) reminds us that the identical complement of Hox genes, which in arthropods underpins their axial reorganization, seems to have no obvious bearing on the widely varying degrees of tagmoses and segment organization. Thus, although genome arrangements

*and duplications must provide an important basis for
metazoan diversifications, the fundamental patterns
continue to elude us.*

Why Vitalism, Why Now?

Many readers may be thinking that these are all minor issues
which will surely be resolved in a few years, so why are
we talking about vitalism again? The answer is, as logical
positivist Rudolf Carnap admitted in 1934, that the laws
which govern natural phenomena seem insufficient to explain
biology.

Let us return to the migrating Wood Thrush. Migratory
behaviour is an instinct, a pattern of behaviour which is innate
to a species. Like the inborn fear of hawk silhouettes in rabbits
or the urge in a beaver to make a dam, these are not partial
drives or confused images, these are fully operational and help
guide an organism to food, mates and safety. But instincts are
not simple from the point of view of the biologist. The split
between bodily function and behaviour should be dismissed,
since instincts grab the entire body and direct it toward an end.
The physiology of the organism can be rearranged for a time
period, hierarchically managed by some governing pattern -
fear, attraction, hunger. But as Arguello & Benton state in their
2017 paper:

> *All of us have marvelled at the remarkable diversity of
> animal behaviors in nature. None of us has much idea
> of how these have evolved*

These patterns, the ability for matter to become organised
and directed, in a sense demarcate the difference between

living and non-living things. Biology seems to defy the basic laws of thermodynamics insofar as it moves towards greater complexity, greater levels of organisation, what Schrödinger called 'negentropy' or negative entropy. The Russian chemist Ilya Prigogine worked for decades on the question of how chemical systems can spontaneously produce order under conditions of non-equilibrium. Structures like crystals, tornadoes and snowflakes exhibit this property of self-assembly, even for short periods of time. Life itself seems to arise from the ability of matter to self organise into proteins, cell membranes and the bewildering complexity of DNA, a molecule which physically encodes the information needed to create shape, form and the higher processes of an organism. Even without ascribing an external spiritual force, it seems that the laws of physics allow for and even drive towards the development of complex structures. The mathematical biologist Stuart Kauffman argues in his 1993 book The Origins of Order Self-Organization and Selection in Evolution that this capacity for matter to self-organise should be considered a separate force in biological evolution, alongside natural selection, providing the underlying structure for life. In describing the patterns of the developing fruit fly embryo he says:

> *Therefore, it is terribly striking that a number of the maternal, gap, pair-rule, and segment-polarity genes do actually come to exhibit complex, multipeaked longitudinal patterns of RNA transcripts and protein abundance in the syncytial egg. Whatever the mechanism governing the patterns, the phenomena are truly beautiful*

He later notes that Darwinism as a foundation has major fractures in its base, saying:

We do not understand the sources of order on which natural selection was privileged to work

These sources of order seem to include beauty and symmetry in their deepest origins. No matter how much detailed work is done on the most foundational mathematical interfaces between chemistry and biology, some sort of elusive ghostly residue remains impossible to grasp. This is why vitalism and even animism will never be fully expelled from biology, something seems to 'will' order and form onto matter and even if these turn out to be straightforwardly mechanistic in principle, the question still remains of why the laws of physics allows such order to arise. The sceptical materialist will answer that we can only ask this question because we live in such a universe, thus rendering it moot, but this is highly unsatisfactory. Perhaps for some the use of mere language to brush away difficult questions is enough, but for many this type of rhetoric will never suffice. Biology seems haunted by something 'extra', some other almost demonic force which drives life to differentiate into species, each one a reflection and manifestation of this underlying Will to Life. The quality and types of life this produces is best left for another time, but hopefully this little introduction to what we could call 'neo-vitalism' has sparked in the reader some interest in the age-old basic question of 'What is Life'?

PART THREE - PREHISTORY

TRYING TO MAKE SENSE OF THE VENUS FIGURINES?

Race, goddesses, fertility, magic, obesity, motherhood, sex and death

In 1864 Paul Hurault, the 8th Marquis de Vibraye, was digging around in the cave systems of Laugerie-Basse, Dordogne. He had always been an amateur archaeologist, but soon his name would be immortalised. His discovery of a female figurine, a slender 8cm tall ivory creation, prompted comparisons with the Aphrodite of Knidos, and he named her La Vénus impudique - the 'immodest Venus'. She is dated to the Magdalenian period (~17-12kya), and she became the first of many similar female figurines to be uncovered during the archaeological rush of the late 19th century. Today we call these types of small portable figurines 'Venuses', although the meaning of the term has changed with intellectual fashions. Nobody is entirely sure how many there are, how to define them, or even what time period we are dealing with. Typically a Venus figurine refers to a statuette of the female form, often with large or exaggerated bodies, made between roughly 40-10 thousand years ago. But the Upper Palaeolithic Venus phenomenon was just the first, and a renaissance of the form appears during the Neolithic of the Near East and continues into the Bronze Age, where they become more stylised and linked with named female deities. Whether or not the Palaeolithic and Neolithic Venus moments are connected is an open question. Geographically we're focusing here on Europe and parts of wider Eurasia, since these have produced the majority of the artefacts. If the physical and chronological nature of these figurines is ambiguous, then their interpretation has been vastly more muddled. We'll work through them, from Victorian ideas about race to feminist theories of the Mother Goddess, from materialist ideas about obesity to recent thoughts about childbirth. Almost no other artefact type has produced so much controversy and speculation, and the 150 years or so of thought is a window onto the ever-changing landscape of archaeological theory.

Early Days: Race, Steatopygia And Primitivism (1864-1900)

Prehistory as a field was born in great strife. In 1823 the Reverend William Buckland had discovered the ochre-saturated bones of a Palaeolithic man in Paviland Cave on the Gower peninsula. Although he believed them to be the remains of a Roman prostitute, their true age is around 33,000 years old. He struggled to believe that any human could predate the Biblical flood, and he was not alone. In fact by the mid 19th century the nascent study of prehistory was divided into 'fixists' (E. Lartet, A. de Quatrefages, M. Sanson, L. Bourgeois and J. Delaunay) and those convinced of the reality of human evolution (Paul Broca, P. Topinard, T. Hamy, G. de Mortillet and M. Boule). Religious fixists insisted on the created form of human beings since their divine beginning, whilst positivists and materialists stressed the gradual development of human faculties and capacities. Artwork occupied a special place for both camps, since it was accepted that the European disinterested aesthetic experience represented a pinnacle of human achievement. For the religious man, artwork was a gift, present in the earliest of souls, whereas for the student of Lamarck and Huxley, art was one of the final developments of the advanced types.

The 'immodest Venus' arrived into a world which was wholly unprepared for the idea of Palaeolithic art. Not only was there no theoretical lens to make sense of it, many scholars outright rejected it. Forgeries, rivalries, theft, competition, ideologies and national squabbles produced an atmosphere of distrust. One prehistorian, Gabriel de Mortillet, even accused the Spanish clergy of faking the Altimira cave art in order to discredit the field. Lubbock and Mortillet denied that prehistoric people were religious at all, and thus any artwork was merely for amusement, contentment, simple pleasure - art-for-art's sake:

> that our earliest ancestors could have counted to ten is
> very improbable, considering that so many races now in
> existence cannot get beyond four

- Lubbock, 1865

Against this view came the ideas of E.B. Tylor, who posited one of the most influential ideas in archaeological thought. He argued that, far from being irreligious and simple, tribal peoples all over the world in fact had a highly developed sense of spirituality - one which attributed a soul and being to inanimate objects and natural forces. Animism, as it became known, was the default inner state of man, unencumbered by dogma or proscription. Not long afterwards McLennan introduced the concept of 'totemism', and then in 1890 came Frasier's The Golden Bough. Concern with the mental state of the 'primitive mind' was paramount, ushering in dozens of ethnographic and anthropological works focusing on language, mythology, religion, artwork and oral histories. The Age of Primitivism had begun. One man in particular stands out for us - Édouard Piette - a French archaeologist who became fascinated with Venus figurines. He represented the Rousseaun wing of the intellectual movement, believing that the harsh but simple life of savage man was more free and spiritually rich than modern civilisation, a view which still resonates with many people today:

> *Exercise and open-air life disseminated among the savages, whom we regard as miserable, a touch of morality, of strength and calm that labourers and office clerks will never know... Ingenious man, dedicated to the art of drawing and sculpture was, in his time, a pioneer of civilization; he left his mark in a stage of humankind on the road to progress. He was not a savage enclosed in the narrow circle of his forefather's ideas, he was a man of progress and he might still be so*

> - Piette, 1873

Piette was a thorough and methodical scientist, horrified by the sloppy work, theft and vandalism which accompanied many excavations of the time. He negotiated the return of many invaluable artefacts, and by around 1900 he owned almost every Palaeolithic Venus figurine in existence. These included: L'Ebauche; La Vénus de Brassempouy; Le Manche de poignard; La Fillette; La Dame à la capuche; La Figurine à la ceinture and La Figurine à la pèlerine. A few details in particular bothered Piette. One was the 'Egyptian' style of some of the figurines, especially their hair or hoods, and the other was the startling fat deposits on some of the hips and buttocks of the carvings.

Steatopygia is a condition whereby large amounts of adipose fat tissue accumulates on the hips, thighs and buttocks, found predominantly in women of Khoisan, African Pygmy and Andamanese descent. It was noted by European explorers to southern Africa, along with the extended labia of various groups of sub-Saharan African women. Most famously the Khoikhoi woman Saartjie (Sarah) Baartman (1789-1815) who was exhibited around Europe as a a kind of curious savage, and many people paid to look at her almost-naked body, even to poke her with a stick. She, and other similar women, were known as 'Hottentot Venuses'. Piette and other archaeologists some decades later made the link between her steatopygia and the curvy shape of the Venus figurines they had uncovered. Unlike Hurault's 'immodest Venus', the name was instead directly associated with the African Khoikhoi body.

Piette developed a theory of Palaeolithic Venus figurines which drew both on this racial physiological science and the primitivism which he believed accounted for the style of prehistoric art. In his reading two races of Palaeolithic humans lived in Europe, one which looked more 'African' and the other more 'Egyptian' or 'Greek'.

> *What troubles me is that there were two human races during the Eburnien, one with fatty protuberances, an enormous descending abdomen, ample thighs, prominent hips and, probably, buttocks that were correspondingly imposing. The enormous size of the abdomen was a result of concentrated fat deposits, held in place by fibrous tissue, which also accounts for the abundant hips and a sort of calf on the front of the thighs. This latter was not muscle. In this regard, there can be no doubt about the analogy with Bushman women. This race was also as hairy as Esau.*

The other race was without body hair, had flat abdomens, somewhat slender thighs, and hips and buttocks lacking the fatty outgrowths. The artists who represented them exaggerated the abdominal flattening, the slenderness of the buttocks and the lack of projecting hips; and this could have been out of hatred for the other race which at that time must have been a conquered people

-Piette to Reinach, 11 January, 1895

There was no question that these figurines could have been stylistic or artistic, since the primitive animistic mind could only copy nature, rather than import any imaginative license. This dualism between art and function, born out of the European experience of art as a disinterested medium, was retained in Palaeolithic art studies. Primitive man possessed the aesthetic impulse, but it was bound by the need for symbolic and magical functionality. The Venus figurines were perfectly naturalistic, but no doubt stored some deeper purpose. Only through the racial struggle for greatness had some people freed art from the baser needs of life, and although this could be glimpsed in the cave art masterpieces of the time, Palaeolithic man was still the infant of the species.

Making Sense Of The Palaeolithic (1900-1945)

Between 1900 and 1945, many more Venus or female figurines and artworks were discovered across Europe and further afield. These include the famous Venus of Willendorf (1908); Lespuge (1922); Dolni Vestonice (1925); Petersfels (1927-32); Moravany (1930); Mal'ta (1928) and Buret' (1936-40). The latter sites, in Siberia, were surprising, and indicate a cultural or group connection stretching from France deep into Eurasia.

Of course, these findings were not separated from the sites themselves, nor were they insulated from the developments in archaeological thought more broadly.

Trying to define the different eras of the deep past was a problem not just for the Palaeolithic, but for all of prehistory. These then had to reckon with the different 'stages' of civilisation found across the world. From the Arctic to South Africa, Polynesia to the Amazon, a whole constellation of different peoples had to be slotted into any general theory of human development. In 1816 Christian Thomsen had developed the 'three-stage' model we are still familiar with - a stone age, bronze age and iron age. Sir John Lubbock's 1865 work, Pre-Historic Times: As Illustrated by Ancient Remains, and the Manners and Customs of Modern Savages, had separated the stone age into an 'old' (Palaeolithic) and 'new' (Neolithic). Hodder Westropp proposed a 'middle' age, the Mesolithic, in 1866, which was immediately controversial. Analogies between prehistoric stone tools and Aboriginal or Andaman tools proved irresistable, and prehistorians began drawing lines of comparison between the shell middens of Denmark and the contemporary people of Tierra del Feugo. Terms like 'Mousterian' (1876), 'Magdalenian' (1885) and 'Aurignacian' (1906) became better defined, and the latter two came be characterised through craniometry, physical anthropology, ethnographic analogy and artwork as 'Caucasoid' and 'Negroid' respectively.

In 1911, the architect Emmanuel-Élisée Pontremoli and sculptor Constant-Ambroise Roux began work on the entrance structure to the new Institute of Human Paleontology in Paris. They chose two designs, one for each side. The first of which depicted a Caucasian Magdalenian man, wearing a primitive crown, drawing a bison on a cave wall. The second depicted a Negroid Aurignacian man sculpting a Venus figurine. This was a crucial symbolic moment, chiseling in stone the two racial phenotypes of Palaeolithic Europe, with the superior and sophisticated cave-art triumphing over the sensual and earthbound Venus. Reinforcing this was a series of busts, made by sculptor Louis Mascré and the prehistorian Aimé Rutot between 1909 and 1914. Again the Magdalenian man was a ruddy brown, vigorous individual, skillfully carving his art into reindeer antler, whilst the 'Negroid of Menton' Aurignacian was an African-looking man, sculpting the newly discovered Venus of Willendorf.

It should be noted however, that the interpretation of this racial schema was more nuanced than perhaps modern readers might expect. In linking the Aurignacian to the San Bushmen, which was the dominant consensus, there wasn't necessarily a universal judgement on what this meant. As William J. Sollas (1849–1936), professor of geology at Oxford University, wrote of Aurignacian art and sculpture in his 1911 work, Ancient Hunters and Their Modern Representatives:

> the best examples attain so high a pitch of excellence that enthusiastic discoverers have spoken of them as superior in some respects to the work of the Greeks... we cannot survey the series of pictures with which Aurignacian man has illustrated the animal life of his time without a feeling of delight, and the pleasure we feel in this glimpse of a vanished fauna is enhanced by the fact that we look at it through the eyes of the ancient hunter himself... although far from attaining to our standard of beauty, yet still there was something prepossessing about the Bushman to those who looked with a discerning eye, all that we learn about the Bushmen impresses us with their great intellectual ability

Waves Of Matriarchy: Mother Goddesses And Venus Figurines

Turning away from race as the explanatory framework, we now dive into the depths of another, more well-known, theory for the Venus figurines - their symbolic representation of female deities and female social power. The idea of a matriarchy, a female-led or centric society, is one of mankind's oldest enduring myths. Between 1864 - 1884 this myth was to undergo probably its most powerful revival, thanks to three books: Das Mutterrecht (Motherright) (1861) by Johann Jakob Bachofen; Primitive Marriage (1865) by John Ferguson McLennan, and Origin of the Family, Private Property, and the State (1884) by Friedrich Engels. Although very different in inspiration and conclusion, the groundwork was laid for first-wave feminists to draw on prehistory to make the case that the original human society was female-centred, largely peaceful and largely egalitarian. The American feminists Elizabeth Cady Stanton and Matilda Joslyn Gage argued in the 1880's that prehistory was a period of female supremacy and rule over men. Nobody could quite agree whether this golden age was one of free love and promiscuity or chaste sacred motherhood, but they were all convinced that the prehistoric evidence supported their position. The strange esoteric blend of eugenics, theosophy, moral exhortations to chastity, reverence for motherhood and recognition of the divine feminine all swirled around in the Edwardian gallop towards universal suffrage. Gage, and then the British activist Frances Swiney, pioneered the belief that early societies worshipped goddesses and were led by female priestesses. This enthusiasm largely disappeared with the wars and the right to vote secured, but it came back with a roar during the 1970's.

The intellectual passion for matriarchy within archaeology

and its related fields was not trivial however. Excavations at Knossos by Sir Arthur Evans and scholarly investigations into Hellenic religion by Jane Ellen Harrison drew on Bachofen to explain the presence of female 'goddess' figurines. Frazer and Harrison, along with the 'Cambridge Ritualists', helped maintain the matriarchal myth and embedded it into the Classics. Harrison's 1903 work, Prolegomena to the Study of Greek Religion, insisted that pre-Classical Greece was a goddess-worshipping matriarchy. The link continued throughout the 20th century, with Florence Mary Bennett's Religious Cults Associated with the Amazons (1912) and later works by J. H. Thiel (1931), George Thomson (1949) and E. A. S. Butterworth (1966), all shoring up the image of an archaic female-led society.

With the advent of second-wave feminism came an urgent need to understand the origins and development of patriarchy as an institution. Although it began its life largely outside of the academy, texts such as Simone de Beauvoir's The Second Sex, continued to rely on an account of prehistory which identified patriarchy as a later intrusion into a more female-friendly world. The 'Goddess Movement' began in earnest throughout the Western world during the 1970's. Carol P. Christ gave her influential speech 'Why Women Need The Goddess' in 1978, laying out the feminist critique of Christianity and patriarchy and defending the myth of the ancient Goddess as both real and necessary. Although mainstream archaeology had largely moved away from this narrative, it found its champion in the Lithuanian scholar Marija Gimbutas. Gimbutas had bucked the trend of grand meta-narratives by presenting the story of 'Old Europe', the earliest Neolithic agricultural communities, as one of peaceful egalitarian matriarchy. She interpreted Neolithic Venus figurines, artwork and spiral iconography as evidence for a Great Goddess religion. She also resurrected older ideas about the invasion of the Indo-Europeans from the Pontic-Caspian steppe through the 'Kurgan Hypothesis', pointing out that patriarchy and the diminishment of female-centric art seem to coincide with the appearance of kurgan burial mounds and the male dominance of the Bronze Age.

Along with most of 'civilization' in ancient times, they worshipped a goddess of fertility and abundance, and Earth Mother of creation and regeneration. They were a peaceful artistic community, enviably 'in-tune' with all that surrounded them. Nearly 6,000 years ago, these particular people took advantage of their environment and in the relative isolation of their islands advanced a style of spiritual expression unlike anything found elsewhere in the region. Successful for more than a thousand years they continue to develop and to thrive with no trace of conflict or war (...) As we know, not much survived of the early matrifocal people of mainland Europe once they were overrun and assimilated by aggressive Indo-European tribes identified by Archaeology and author Dr. Marija Gimbutas

-Linda C. Eneix 1997

Meanwhile, in Anatolia, the most potent symbol of this new Goddess movement was being constructed. The site of Çatalhöyük had been discovered in 1958 and was excavated during the 1960's by James Mellaart. This was to prove a most fruitful combination. Mellaart's discovery of Venus figurines on the site resulted in an outpouring of goddess literature. He and his acolytes were convinced that Çatalhöyük was a peaceful, egalitarian, matrilineal society, dedicated to the worship of the Great Goddess. His particular blend of Wicca, neopaganism and feminism resulted in Çatalhöyük becoming a pilgrimage site for the movement:

Perhaps more interesting and far reaching is the connection between goddess tours and the archaeological work at the site. As Hodder states (1997, 693),'at the site itself we are visited by bus-loads of people on Goddess Tours who are interested in a spiritual connection with the site, who may come to pray, or who are part of the New Age, Ecofeminist or Gaia Movements'. But it is not simply a matter of visiting the site or buying the T-shirt, many of these people want to adopt an interventionist role. Recently, a house has been bought in the nearby village which will operate as a base for goddess groups and this has led to local tensions amongst the conservative, largely Islamic township of Qumra. Additionally, some goddess groups want to build a shrine at the site. Increasingly as goddess groups contribute financially to the project, they will ask for something in return. Already they are dissatisfied with archaeological data freely available to them on the web. As Hodder remarks, the 'fact that these answers are insufficient was made clear in discussions with the New Age Women's Movements. When we told them that we would provide the data so that they could make their own less androcentric interpretations from the site, they complained that this was not enough 'because when you hand over the data to us, they have already been interpreted by you' (Hodder 1997, 693-4)

-Lynn Meskell, 'Oh My Goddess!'

Despite rigorous critiques of Mellaart's work and his falsifications of the evidence, Çatalhöyük has never shaken this legacy, and even today seems cocooned in a protective shell of interpretation. It continues, much like the Venus figurines, to be seen as a bastion of Neolithic, female-centric egalitarianism. Hopefully the next few generations of archaeologists will be able to lay the Goddess to rest.

Sex Magic & Fertility

After race and feminism comes sex. If archaeologists are less comfortable with the grandiloquence of the 'goddess', they do seem more at home with the neutrality of 'fertility'. One reason is that fertility and sexuality belong to the study of biology and evolutionary science, which naturally pays great attention to how mating and reproduction occurs across the animal world. It's good to be reminded that Gimbutas' and Mellaart's writings about great goddesses were deeply unfashionable throughout the 60's and 70's and beyond. In fact archaeology had pivoted towards a more rigorous scientific approach. The 'New Archaeology' or 'processual archaeology' wanted nothing to do with mythical golden ages or deities, it wanted a clear-eyed objectivity to be cast onto the material record, to blow away the cobwebs of cultural interpretation and to rely on hypotheses, logic, rationality and the creation of testable frameworks to explain cultural change.

In 1968 a fresh wind swept through figurine studies with the work of Peter Ucko. His 1968 dissertation monograph Anthropomorphic Figurines of Predynastic Egypt and Neolithic Crete took aim at the entirety of the Mother Goddess hypothesis, and his later works used an effective combination of empirical studies and anthropological analogies to open the door to alternative explanations. These figurines had no one explanation, he argued, they could easily be children's toys, initiation tools, magical items or burial aides.

> On the basis of the suggested lines of investigation above (1-4), it is possible that the figurine material of Knossos may include figurines made for the following

categories of reasons: those made by, and for, children to play with; others as some sort of initiation figures used as teaching devices to accompany songs or tales, and thrown away after use; still others as vehicles for sympathetic magic, carried and cared for by mothers desirous of offspring and kept in the house until the birth of a child

-Peter Ucko - The Interpretation of Prehistoric
Anthropomorphic Figurines (1962)

As we saw in the earlier development of Palaeolithic art studies, the question still lurks - what were the figurines for? Removing the Goddess did not reveal an answer, so much as provide new possibilities. The carry-over from the 19th century was the magico-functional paradigm, more easily expressed as 'sympathetic magic'. In 1899 two Australian anthropologists, Walter Baldwin Spencer and Francis Gillen, had provided one of the most powerful analogies in prehistoric art theory. Their work on the Arrernte or Arunta Aboriginal peoples revealed that cave art was connected to fertility - in that the Arunta people would draw images of animals in the hope that they would multiply. This idea was picked up by two giants of the field - Salomon Reinach (1858-1932) and Abbé Henri Breuil (1877-1961) - and extended to other domains of Palaeolithic life, including hunting and human fertility.

Fertility was of course a preoccupation for the Goddess theorists, and the notion of a Mother Earth rests on the fecundity of women and their abilities to reproduce and nourish. The other side of this argument is about control, a topic feminists have long critiqued, and a major point of debate surrounding the later domestication of plants and animals. If there was no matriarchy, then fertility was presumably under the control of men? A host of new ideas started to spill out from archaeologists: figurines were prehistoric porn (Guthrie 1979); representations of prostitutes or after-life sex slaves (Orphanides 1983; Karageorghis 1981) and totems of fertility. In fact no less than 10 surveys of prehistoric figurines between 1975 and 1987 suggest fertility as the most likely motivating factor behind their creation. Of those that disagreed or rejected the fertility argument, only one also excluded eroticism or pornography as a function (Pfieffer 1985). To quote from Sarah Nelson's 1990 article Diversity of the Upper Paleolithic 'Venus' Figurines and Archeological Mythology:

> If the figurines are assumed to have been made by men, then it follows that they were created for male purposes. Even when they were first discovered, the Abbe Breuil (1954, cited in Ucko and Rosenfeld 1973:119) said they were for "pleasure to Paleolithic man during his meals". Berenguer (1973:52) focuses on reproductivity: "we may deduce man's obsessive need for women who would bear him lots of children to offset the high mortality rate caused by the harsh living conditions." Von Konigswald worried about other possessions, "It certainly is an old problem: how could man protect his property, mark a place as 'his home', 'his living site' so that others would recognize and respect it, especially in a period where there were no houses, just abris and caves?" He concludes that men made the "grotesque" figurines to guard their property, and scare off intruders!

Whilst certain scholars do seem curiously obsessed with seeing sex everywhere during the Palaeolithic, Guthrie in particular (over 60 pages in his 2005 book on Palaeolithic Art is spent describing hip-to-waist ratios, erotic fat, sex toys and more) the counter-arguments needed little more than good objective observation. The type-casting of the Venus of Willendorf as the 'typical' expression of Palaeolithic and other figurines hid a more complex reality. Simple descriptions of each of the figurines would in fact reveal that obesity and exaggerated sexual characteristics were not the dominant feature, and as figurine discoveries from Magdalenian Germany during the 60's-80's showed, there could be great differences across space and time. As Rice's 1981 breakdown of 188 Venus figurines revealed, of those that could be identified as female, the full age range from pre-pubescent to grandmother were represented almost equally. Almost none of them could be described as pregnant. Sadly this basic point, that many of the figurines look nothing like the swollen Willendorf, has been lost. Even today as we'll see, the majority of studies on the Venuses focus on their supposedly exaggerated physiques.

Palaeolithic Obesity?

Amongst these articles was a cutting from the Life section of an edition of USA Today containing a report on FAT!SO?, an American organisation concerned with raising public awareness of issues of 'fat acceptance' (Hainer 1996: 1-2). The article describes the adoption of the Venus of Willendorf as their mascot, and places the figure in a thoroughly contemporary frame of reference by characterising her as "a short, squat, faceless figurine with prodigious love handles. And breasts so large that- well, let's just say she doesn't need the Wonderbra"

-Lander, Louise Muriel (2005) From artifact to icon: an analysis of the Venus figurines in archaeological literature and contemporary culture

A point of contention amongst Palaeolithic researchers is whether the Venus figurines are supposed to be pregnant or obese? We've seen how the enlarged buttocks gave support to racial classifications, but as academia turned away from the concept of race other explanations were needed. The Goddess argument saw the enlarged breasts, hips, buttocks and stomachs as stylisations and reflective of the essential female nature, while the male-focused fertility cult saw these aspects as similarly feminine or through an erotic lens. As critiques of all these came and went there is still no good proposal for why many figurines look fat. One simple explanation was that some Palaeolithic women were in fact obese, an idea which runs counter to our image of mammoth hunters permanently at the edge of starvation. We can separate out the later Neolithic figurines here and say they are more plausibly representations of obese people - agriculture providing the excess calories in this model.

This is what we could call a form of realism, looking at the figurines as accurate depictions of real people at the time. As a general theory it has prompted some interesting ideas, and continues to do so: In 1976 J.R Harding wrote a brief article entitled Certain Upper Palaeolithic 'Venus' Statuettes Considered in Relation to the Pathological Condition Known as Massive Hypertrophy of the Breasts, where he considers the Venus figurines to be depictions of a medical condition, rather than an ideal; numerous papers studying fatty tissue deposition, iodine deficiency, fatty liver syndrome and more all refer back to the Venus, in particular the Venus of Willendorf. Jean-Pierre Duhard described the shape of Pleistocene women in general based on the proportions and measurements of the figurines. Using different fat deposition markers - "steatopygia (deposits round the buttocks), steatocoxia (round the hips), steatotrochanteria (femoral deposit) or steatomeria (crural deposit)" - he was able to characterise each figurine in turn and draw some conclusions:

> *In our far distant ancestresses there existed the same morphological diversity as today, as is shown by sculpture, with a realism more physiological than anatomical, showing subjects of varying ages and at different phases of their functional life. One particularly important point is their adiposity, or the location of the fatty deposits. These have specific sex-related functions, which obviously have not changed since that period, and undergo identical changes in physical appearance following the same laws of physiology: it was therefore of interest to discover whether, despite different climatic conditions, way of life and different food resources, the same clinical forms of adiposity would be observed.*

- Duhard, J. (1991). The shape of Pleistocene women

That the figurines display physiologically accurate placements of fat suggest that these were not stylistic imaginary fancies, but rather a close replication of what people saw in their everyday lives, much like the animals drawn in the caves. In this archaeology had returned to the 19th century understanding of Palaeolithic art, that it was imitative. However, the obvious shift was the move away from racial categorisations towards a broader 'human' or 'female physiology'. This has been further explored in research looking into adaptations to the coldest point of the last ice age, when many figurines were made. Even in the 1960's this point was confusing, how could Gravettian ice age hunters be familiar with female body fat when they lived as active mobile hunter-gatherers in freezing conditions? A 2020 paper published in the Obesity Journal by Richard J Johnson and colleagues ran with this idea. They mapped out the location of figurines in comparison to the known glacial maximum line in Europe, and then compared the hip-to-waist and shoulder-to-waist ratios of the various Venus figurines. They argue that a correlation exists between the most obese figurines and their proximity to the coldest parts of the continent, making them either accurate representations of real people, or ideal body types for women to survive in those conditions.

The final analysis to note here has become relatively well known outside of academia. This is the original idea that the Venus figurines look the way they do because they represent women drawing themselves. Pioneered by LeRoy McDermott in 1996, the self-representation theory, in my experience at least, has convinced a lot of people. It neatly explains why so many figurines seem exaggerated, but also lack faces and often feet. In the absence of mirrors women needed to look down at themselves and carve what they saw, unsurprisingly focusing on their breasts and hips. Impossible to refute or prove, McDermott's argument will probably always remain popular as a partial explanation for the figurines, even if it can't explain their greater meaning and purpose.

Clothing & Motherhood

As we move through the 90's and into the 000's, the original question asked 150 years earlier continues to perplex scholars, and new examples of the figurines keep appearing. In 2005 ivory Venuses were found in Zaraysk, Russia, and in 2008 a classic figurine was found at Hohle Fels cave in Germany. This turned out to be between 40,000-35,000 years old, putting it at the start of the Aurignacian period, likely one of the earliest Venuses ever made. Discussions about gender and sex in the Palaeolithic also continued to flow, bringing some of the third-wave feminist critiques about gender performance and creation into archaeology. In 2000 a paper entitled The "Venus" Figurines: Textiles, Basketry, Gender, and Status in the Upper Paleolithic, brought forward a number of arguments to make the case that the Venus figurines were almost certainly dressed, both in their sculpted form as well as possible miniature clothing being placed on them. This new focus on the individual hairstyles, patterns, grooves, symbols, dots and so on echoed some of the original questions posed by Piette in the late 19th century. It was certainly a fruitful line of enquiry and matched ethnographic understandings of dolls and figurines in other cultures, which are often dressed up like people, adorned with objects and given hairstyles made of organic materials.

New advances in archaeological science, combined with this focus on the clothing of the figurines produced one of the most interesting hypotheses about their function. A 28,000 year old female skeleton from Italy, dubbed 'La Donna di Ostuni', was discovered to have preserved a perfect 8 month old fetus inside of her. Researchers working on their remains are confident that the evidence points to the mother having died from a condition known as eclampsia. This causes severe convulsions and seizures, strong headaches, blurred vision and other visual distortions and can result in death. What makes this case so interesting for us is that she was buried wearing a headcap made from hundreds of small seashells, which looks very similar to the 'bobbled' cap found on a number of Venus figurines, including the Venus of Willendorf. As the researchers state:

> Many of these statuettes were very small and light probably used as necklace amulets. Eclampsia (again a specific human feature among mammals), occurring at the end of pregnancy in young primiparae has probably terrorised our ancestors. Certainly, seizures were

recognised to start from the head (muscle contractions, visual disturbances, unusual head or eye movements, mouth alteration, loss of consciousness); therefore, we may propose the hypothesis that the headdress that pregnant women wore was probably a protective artefact against these ominous events like death at birth and convulsions.

To my mind this represents one of the first papers where concrete contextual evidence has managed to be used to explain the function of the figurines - a protective female amulet of sorts. Doubtless they had other uses, nothing stays semantically static for 30,000 years, but being able to show something like a death during pregnancy is light years ahead of speculations about sex slaves or abstract 'fertility cults'.

Putting It All Together

Having covered over a century's worth of research, are we able to say anything meaningful about the Venus figurine phenomenon? Well we have roughly four basic hypotheses to show for it all:

Realism: the figurines are accurate representations of Palaeolithic and Neolithic people. This can be looked at sexually, racially (not a popular or likely productive take) or physiologically, in particular the focus on obesity and age.

The Goddess: the figurines are representations of a general female deity, still a popular view amongst some feminists and environmentalists, but generally seen as anachronistic now.

Magico-Functional: the figurines are some kind of magical

object relating to protection, luck, motherhood, pregnancy, fertility, ancestors, dead spouses, shamanic or religious activity or something else.

Mundane: this would include art-for-art's sake, children's toys, dolls, throwaway objects, teaching or visual aides, or some other less exotic function.

Personally I think the figurines should be considered more realistic than stylistic or idealistic, and any proposed function needs evidence stronger than just ideas like 'fertility'. I haven't had the space here to consider the figurines in the wider context of Palaeolithic art, nor to look at whether the Palaeolithic and Neolithic figurines represent one unbroken tradition, or two separate creations. It is interesting in the light of genetic studies that the figurines seem to continue to be made, despite population turnovers and disappearances. I lean towards them being for personal use, with most of them being small and portable, and likely connected to pregnancy and protection. Hopefully future work can integrate wider lines of evidence, rather than speculation, but we must always be prepared to admit in the final analysis that we simply don't know.

I leave you with a portion of Camille Paglia's superlative description of the Venus figurines from her 1990 magnum opus Sexual Personae: Art and Decadence from Nefertiti to Emily Dickinson:

> Venus of Willendorf carries her cave with her. She is blind, masked. Her ropes of corn-row hair look forward to the invention of agriculture. She has a furrowed brow. Her facelessness is the impersonality of primitive sex and religion. There is no psychology or identity yet, because there is no society, no cohesion. Men cower and scatter at the blast of the elements. Venus of Willendorf

is eyeless because nature can be seen but not known. She is remote even as she kills and creates. The statuette, so overflowing and protuberant, is ritually invisible. She stifles the eye. She is the cloud of nature. She is eternally pregnant. She broods, in all senses. She is hen, nest, egg. The Latin *mater* and *materia*, mother and matter, are etymologically connected. Venus of Willendorf is the nature-mother as primeval muck, oozing into infant forms. She is female but not feminine. She is turgid with primal force, swollen with great expectations. She has no feet. Placed on end, she would topple over. Woman is immobile, weighed down by her inflated mounds of breast, belly, and buttock. Like Venus de Milo, Venus of Willendorf has no arms. They are flat flippers scratched on the stone, unevolved, useless. She has no thumbs and therefore no tools. Unlike man, she can neither roam nor build. She is a mountain that can be climbed but can never move. The braided cap of Venus of Willendorf is hivelike—prefiguring the provocative beehives of French court wigs and shellacked swinging-Sixties towers. Venus buzzes to herself, queen for all days, woman for all seasons. She sleeps. She is hibernation and harvest, the turning wheel of the year. Female jiggle is the ducklike waddle of our wallowing Willendorf, who swims in the underground river of liquid nature. Sex is probings, plumbing, secretions, gushings. Venus is drowsing and dowsing, hearkening to the stirring in her sac of waters. Is the Venus of Willendorf just to female experience? Yes. Woman is trapped in her wavy, watery body. She must listen and learn from something beyond and yet within her. The Venus of Willendorf, blind, tongueless, brainless, armless, knock-kneed, seems a depressing model of gender. Yet woman is depressed, pressed down, by earth's gravitation, calling us back to her bosom. We will see that malign magnetism at work in Michelangelo, one of his great themes and obsessions.

In the west, art is a hacking away at nature's excess. The western mind makes definitions. Life always begins and ends in squalor. The Venus of Willendorf, slumping, slovenly, sluttish, is in a rut, the womb-tomb of mother nature. Never send to know for whom the belle tolls. She tolls for thee.

THE NEOLITHIC SKULL CULTS OF THE NEAR EAST - PART ONE

The Epipalaeolithic, Natufians, Jericho & the Agricultural Revolution, Göbekli Tepe and early Anatolia

> *"Besides the group of plastered skulls, a single example was encountered of the skull of an elderly man, without any of the other bones of the body, carefully set beneath the floor in the angle of a room. The earlier phase of the Pre-pottery Neolithic at Jericho also had a cult of skulls, which are found separated from the bodies and arranged in groups in various ways. To this phase also belongs a collection of infant skulls buried with the neck vertebrae attached, showing that the head had been cut off and not collected from skeletons. This find recalls the nests of severed heads found in a pre-Neolithic stratum at Ofnet Cave in Bavaria..."*

> *- L. H. WELLS, 1959*

The quotation above comes from a short paper published

in the South African Archaeological Bulletin, entitled From Jericho to Wessex? A Neolithic Enigma. The question concerns the curious phenomenon of the prehistoric obsession with the skull, a subject which Wells tackles by covering graves and excavations from Mesolithic Germany to Mycenaean Greece. What is it that so attracts man to curating and displaying the human head? What Wells could not have anticipated was the uncovering of many more plastered skulls, not just at Jericho, but across the whole Levant and Anatolia. We now know that this area, the ground zero for the Neolithic agricultural revolution, had a deep fixation with heads - cutting them off, dangling them from pillars, stacking them, burying them, tenderly covering them with gypsum and lime, and living with them staring out the very walls and floors of their domestic living spaces. To my knowledge no-one has comprehensively tackled the question of why this is so. Despite the mounting genetic and archaeological evidence for the complex shifts of people and culture within the Fertile Crescent, Anatolian and Levantine archaeology is a labyrinth, wrapped in centuries of speculation, but I will attempt to follow the thread back to its source, and see if any sense can be made of the Neolithic Skull Cult.

The Epipalaeolithic & The Dawn Of Agriculture

Around 15,000 years ago, a group of hunters made their way towards a series of imposing limestone hills, overshadowed by a huge volcanic mountain. Their task was grisly but simple - locate and retrieve the head of a buried man. As they gently shovelled and scooped the dirt away, they came across a mouldering body, its teeth falling out. Retrieving the head, ensuring the jaw was intact, they replaced the earth and made their way home, pausing perhaps to make an offering, or light a purifying fire. This was Pınarbaşı, one of the only sites we have for the post-glacial period in Anatolia, before the advent of farming. It is also amongst the earliest records for the practice of 'post-burial cranium retrieval' - burying someone, only to return later and take the head.

3,000 years later, in western Galilee, a group of farmer-foragers began to dig into the circular stone burial mounds at Hayonim Cave. They had returned to an old haunt, a site known to their ancestors out of mind and time. As they dug, they found the bones, and then they laid their own dead amongst them. They shifted the old ones aside, mixed up long bones and ribs, offered pendants and teeth. But this time, unlike their forebears, they came back again to take the heads. This muddled grave site, of 48 people in 16 graves, shows a clear pattern. The earliest bodies kept their heads, but their descendants did not. We know this culture as the Natufians, perhaps the world's first farmers. At some point in their millennia-long journey of domesticating grasses and animals, they began to retrieve the heads of their dead, often without the jawbone.

This region, from the Anatolian highlands, across to the Zagros mountains and the Persian Gulf, and down to the Sinai, has been dubbed the 'Fertile Crescent' since 1914. It was here, during the wild temperature swings that characterised the end of the Ice Age, that the Neolithic Revolution began, and agriculture emerged as a new mode of human subsistence. The Natufians are often credited with this innovation, a Levantine people with mysterious origins. Although the power of modern archaeogenetics has succeeded in uncovering all manner of group dynamics, as we will see, we are still reliant on traditional methods of flint tool classification to carve up the Palaeolithic cultures which flourished in the Levant - names like the Emiran, Ahmarian, Aurignacian, Mushabian and Kebaran cultures. The Natufians are likely to be partial ancestors to a group known as 'Basal Eurasians', a branch of Eurasian humans which split earliest and possess little Neanderthal admixture. This is still contentious, and much work remains to be done to understand the Natufians, but it has long been clear that they were the first hunter-gatherers to domesticate wild grasses and legumes, between 10-13,000 years ago.

If we picture the Fertile Crescent at the dawn of agriculture as made up of three main gene pools, the southern Levantine Natufians, the Central Anatolians and the Iranian/Zagrosians, then we can begin to map the cultural influences which then played out in the later Neolithic. The Central Anatolians are also an enigmatic genetic group, with some evidence suggesting that they partially derived from European hunter-gatherers who fled the advancing ice sheets down into the Aegean. Work on this comes from mitochondrial haplogroups and whole genome analysis from both Pınarbaşı and Girmeler. These two people, intriguingly, can be modelled as 45-48% Balkan Hunter-Gatherer, which suggests a deep connection likely dating back to those foragers escaping the ice around 20,000 years ago.

Head and skull treatments during this immense span of time do suggest special attention was paid to the cranium. Roughly 50% of all Epipalaeolithic sites possess headless skeletons. Along with Pınarbaşı and the later phases of Hayonim Cave, we also have headless skeletons at el-Wad Terrace and Hilazon Tachtit. The even earlier Kebaran site of 'Uyun al-Hammam shows a skull removal burial, suggesting the practice came before the Natufians. A cache of skulls was found at Erq el-Ahmar and the deliberate burning of skulls seems to have occurred as well, such as at Wadi Hammeh 27. Headdresses, adornments and red ochre staining rounds out the evidence, which points clearly towards the intentional modification and movement of heads.

The Early Neolithic, Without Pots, Without Heads

I don't want to dwell on how and when agriculture appeared, since that would take several articles itself, but we move from what is called the Epipalaeolithic into the Neolithic when that threshold is crossed. The division of time in the Near East has been decided through extensive investigations and looks something like this:

Pre-Pottery Neolithic A: 10,000–8,800 BC
Pre-Pottery Neolithic B: 8800–6500 BC
Late / Pottery Neolithic: 7000-4500 BC

The rather dull names of Pre-Pottery Neolithic A and B (PPNA/B) originate with the archaeologist Kathleen Kenyon (1906-1978), a pioneer of careful ceramic excavation methods and leading authority on the famous Neolithic city of Jericho. Jericho became the 'type site' for the division of PPNA & B, meaning it came to define those classifications, which have largely held up to the present day. The difference between the two is profound, with PPNA being a mixed foraging and farming culture living in circular houses, and PPNB relying solely on domesticated plants and animals, living in rectangular houses, using lime plaster and different stone tools. The introduction of pottery at the end of the Neolithic period represents yet another cultural shift.

It was Kenyon herself who first depicted Jericho as having a 'Cult of Skulls' in her 1957 book on the excavation. She, and her contemporary Ian Wolfran Cornwall, initially toyed with the idea that buried and ornamented skulls were 'trophy heads', before settling on the more familiar theory that this was an 'ancestor cult'. Around 280 individual skull burials are known for the Natufian and PPN period, and half of all Levantine examples were recovered from Jericho. The city was founded around 9000 BC and was protected from the world by a massive stone wall and imposing tower. To describe the PPNA inhabitants of Jericho as 'living with their dead' would be an understatement. Over 270 bodies were discovered during excavations - under floors, crammed into foundations, squashed between walls. Heads separated and piled together, including five infant skulls, decapitated and placed in some kind of plastered altar basin at the base of a building.

Continuity with the Natufian past seems to be present, not only in the burial styles, but in some cases the people of the PPNA interred skulls and bodies with those of earlier individuals. Caches of skulls also appear as far afield as Iraq (Qermez Dere), Jordan (Erq el-Ahmar) and Israel (Netiv Hagdud). If a pattern does emerge during the PPNA then it could be characterised as 'decreasing mobility'. Heads taken from burials don't seem to move as far, and the connection between architecture and skulls/decapitation becomes much clearer. At Jerf el-Ahmar, a headless female skeleton was found splayed on the floor of a building which had burnt down. The most plausible interpretation is that the individual was decapitated, and the house deliberately set ablaze, the two acts of ritual death combining into one.

Göbekli Tepe: Predation & Headhunting

Göbekli Tepe is one of the greatest archaeological enigmas of all time. A site without precedent which continues to vex archaeologists. What we do know about it is vastly outweighed by its mysteries, in particular, who built it, and why? This puzzling quality has attracted attention from a much wider range of thinkers and writers than most archaeological sites do, and countless videos and books cite

Göbekli Tepe as evidence for extra-terrestrial activity, lost or hidden civilisations or the secret origin of cultic religions. Even staying within the bounds of conventional explanation leads us to some unsettling conclusions - in defiance of the academic desire for liberal interpretations, Göbekli Tepe points towards a cosmological vision based on bold and blatant masculine archetypes, of predatory and dangerous animals, of blood, violence, decapitation and the celebration of aggression and death. Whether or not this is true, all lines of available evidence point in this direction, as we shall see.

Göbekli Tepe is a site located in southeastern Anatolia, predominantly consisting of 20 enclosed circles, each with limestone pillars. Only four of these circles, or temene, have been excavated. The characteristic pillars, over 200 in total, are shaped like a 'T', with many sporting human motifs, such as hands, arms, loincloths and in one case, an erect phallus. The general consensus is that the pillars are abstract representations of people, and they appear across the region at similar sites. Of the four circular structures - A, B, C and D, the largest is enclosure D, sporting a huge pair of 'male' coded T-pillars. In addition to the human carvings, what strikes anyone who looks at this site is the rich and wide range of animal carvings across the pillars. Most prominent are snakes, but boar, scorpions, vultures, aurochs, gazelle, ducks, onagers, foxes, various birds and large carnivores are numerous. Many of these are snarling or show aggressive posturing. Between the pillars are stone walls, entrances, stone benches and rectangular enclosures. Interestingly the images are not random, but carefully patterned. In circle A snakes are the dominating species, in B foxes are more frequent, in C boars, while Enclosure D is more varied, with birds leading the numbers. This had led some researchers to suggest that Göbekli Tepe was a communal structure built and maintained by different groups, or clans, with each one represented by a different animal 'totem'.

What is missing from Göbekli Tepe is equally as interesting. Many domestic tools and objects, such as awls and craft working artefacts, are absent. Fireplaces and hearths are also missing, which helps reinforce that the site was not a normal living area. Although some domestic structures have been excavated nearby recently, the overall impression is that Göbekli Tepe was a cultic or religious centre, used for ritual, political and spiritual purposes that we can only hint at.

In terms of construction dates, Göbekli Tepe spans both the PPNA and PPNB. The earliest dates place the initial buildings around 9500-9000 BC, making it roughly contemporaneous with Jericho. The site was used past 8000 BC before it fell into ruin, and some recent work shows that small groups lived amongst the rubble for a while. The PPNB occupation shows a marked reduction in pillar size and frequency, but great effort was expended in producing a waterproof flooring, made of crushed and burnt lime, mixed with clay and red ochre, before being polished. There is speculation that the pillar structures supported some kind of wooden roof, or possibly a second floor or platform. Either way, Göbekli Tepe at its peak must have been an awe-inspiring and perhaps terrifying spectacle, with flickering torches illuminating the dreadful sight of predators, snakes and vultures, headless men as you walked from the outside into the inner sanctum of rings. Although no agriculture has been recorded in the area, the inhabitants of Göbekli Tepe likely had communal feasts and gatherings. Large quantities of meat, grain and possibly alcohol were consumed on site, probably brought from somewhere else, given the lack of hearths

As interesting as this is, why are we talking about Göbekli Tepe? We have reason to believe that the site was integrated into a number of southern Anatolian sites, linked by a common skull cult. To quote from Graeber & Wengrow's 2021 book, The Dawn of Everything:

> In both medium and message, Göbekli Tepe could hardly be more different from the world of early farming communities. Its standing remains were wrought from stone, a material little used for construction in the Euphrates and Jordan valleys. Carved on these stone pillars is an imagery dominated by wild and venomous animals; scavengers and predators, almost exclusively sexed male. On a limestone pillar a lion rears up in high relief, teeth gnashing, claws outstretched, penis and scrotum on show. Elsewhere lurks a malevolent boar, its male sex also displayed. The most often repeated images depict raptors taking human heads. One remarkable sculpture, resembling a totem pole, comprises superimposed pairings of victims and predators: disembodied skulls and sharp-eyed birds of prey. Elsewhere, flesh-eating birds and other carnivores are shown grasping, tossing about or otherwise playing with their catch of human crania; carved below one such figure on a monumental pillar is the image of a headless man with an erect penis (conceivably this depicts the kind of immediate post-mortem erection or 'priapism' that occurs in victims of hanging or beheading as a result of massive trauma to the spinal cord)

In addition to the imagery of decapitation and head-hunting, there are several skull fragments from the site which give a chilling insight into how the place must have looked. Three skulls so far have shown a particular modification shortly after death, a hole drilled into the top of the skull and grooves carved down the bone. The most easily explainable scenario for these is that the skulls were being hung with cord or string, supported by the grooves to prevent slippage. Thus, we can add dangling skulls to the list of cranial activity at Göbekli Tepe.

To state that Göbekli Tepe was a place concerned with predators, male energy and human heads would be an understatement. Almost every aspect of the site presents us with images of aggression, hunting, violence, decapitation and even perhaps a fear, terror or mingled respect for the dangerous forces of wild nature. The people who carved these images focused on the most lethal species they knew of - snakes, scorpions, felines, bulls. They focused on predators, scavengers and hunters, they were fixated on human heads being tossed around by wild beasts, torn off by raptors. But in the wider context of Anatolia, this is just the tip of the iceberg.

Welcome To The House Of Skulls

Even out here in this upland Eden of steppe and forest, with running gazelle and quiet glades, there were horrors perhaps greater than Göbekli Tepe. Göbekli is just one of many 'tepes' scattered around the southern Anatolian uplands, we have Kocanizam Tepe, Taşlı Tepe, İnanlı Tepe, Karahan Tepe, Hamzan Tepe, and countless more waiting to be discovered and excavated. Many show similar features to Göbekli Tepe, such as stone heads, T-shaped pillars, carvings of wild animals and an absence of agricultural domestic life. Exactly who built all these is still a mystery, but most likely the descendants of the Central Anatolian hunter-gatherers, who had adopted some herding practices, and who were in contact with communities to the south and north through trade of obsidian, shells and foodstuffs. Isolated they were not, but certainly they had developed what seems to be a hyper-masculine culture focused on the practice of predation, perhaps a spiritual extension of hunting, in which they saw themselves as the apex hunters, not only of animals, but also of other humans.

We start our tour around this region with Körtik Tepe. This site lies to the east of Göbekli Tepe, a settlement made up of circular houses, hunting debris and the paraphernalia associated with collecting and grinding wild grains. Remarkably, this unassuming site contains the most human remains of any contemporary Middle Eastern settlement - 743 graves, with over 800 identified bodies. This alone makes it unusual, but a not insignificant number show signs of violence before death, and another group bear marks of 'de-fleshing', a nice euphemism for hacking and slicing away the meat from the head and face of a person, including detaching the jawbone in some instances. Cut marks to the rest of the body follow the major joints, and a rough pattern on the head looks similar to marks found on scalping victims. There is no consensus about what these marks represent - cannibalism, de-fleshing to create clean bones as part of the burial process, trophy scalping, manipulation of the dead to prevent spiritual attack from the deceased, the humiliation of enemies... the list goes on. What is clear is that the head was singled out for special treatment, consistent with the wider fascination with the skull we've seen so far.

Moving onto another major Neolithic site - Çayönü Tepesi - which is dated to between 8,630 to 6,800 BC, we again see an overwhelming preoccupation with the human head. Çayönü is a complex site, which shows evidence for a wide range of foodstuffs. The people here were not only gathering wild plants and hunting wild boars and deer, but also making use of domesticated and semi-domesticated plants and animals. Some researchers believe that the pig was first domesticated at Çayönü, but this remains to be seen. Also amongst the material artefacts were the region's oldest copper objects - beads, hooks, pins and awls. Most striking however is the two types of burial found across the site, the first a more typical domestic-related burial, the second a far more disturbing practice found only in a building known to us as the House of Skulls. This unassuming structure, rebuilt several times, consists of a main room with many smaller shelf-like vaults or niches at the back. At the centre of the main room lay a huge one-tonne cut and polished stone slab, along with a large black flint knife. Analysis of the stone and knife has revealed crystallised haemoglobin from aurochs, sheep and humans. Within the building itself, over 450 human bodies were uncovered, including 90 skulls, some with the vertebrae still attached. The bones indicate that the majority were young adults, with some children. A mounted aurochs skull on the exterior of the building completes the picture of a temple of death.

The identification and diet of the people at Çayönü Tepesi has been of considerable interest to archaeologists. Bone isotope studies of both the inhabitants and the House of Skulls victims shows that not only did men and women eat different diets (meat and cereals for men, more legumes for women), but the people deposited in the House had a different diet to the people of the settlement, indicating they were from somewhere else, or treated very differently during their lives. A recent genetic study of the inhabitants shows that they were a mixture of central Anatolian and eastern Zagros peoples, consistent with the ancestral profiles we've seen so far. The paper also highlights a child with artificial cranial deformation - head binding - a topic we'll return to in Part Two.

Describing all of southern Anatolian cultic practices and buildings would take a book, but in general they have the following features, found at the three sites just described: a specialised room or building, often semi-circular and half-sunken, with a special, labour intensive floor of terazzo or tiles, containing pillars, monoliths and stelae, decorated with images and paints, and with no trace of domestic or agricultural life. As archaeologist Tatiana Kornienko states:

The world of sculptures and reliefs at Göbekli Tepe is diverse and unusual. In a way, however, it repeats and adds to the representative picture already known from Nemrik IX, Bouqraz, Hallan Çemi, Körtik Tepe, Jerf el-Ahmar, Tell ʿAbr 3, Nevali Çori, Çayönü Tepesi, and other early Neolithic settlements. The most popular images found at the sites—the objects of worship— are anthropomorphic and mixed-type creatures; female and male, figures and symbols; heads of people; bucrania; and images of birds, feline predators, snakes, scorpions, and turtles. In Göbekli Tepe's iconography there are also images of a wild boar, a lion, a spider, and a fox. These motifs are characteristic for sites dating to the PPN period in general; however, in Upper Mesopotamia they are similar in meaning, style, and manner and are clearly concentrated in buildings having a special purpose.

End Of Part One

Unfortunately, we've only scratched the surface of the Neolithic skull cults in the Near East, and a second article will be necessary to cover crucial sites like Çatalhöyük and ʿAin Ghazal. We've raced through the Palaeolithic transformation to agriculture, the Natufians, early Neolithic cities and the cult centres of Anatolia, but we have yet to look at PPNB sites, the phenomenon of plastered skulls, artwork and figurines and really try and tie together some conclusions. Broadly speaking we've seen how the Neolithic skull cults drew on Epipalaeolithic and Natufian traditions of skull retrieval and associations between buildings and bodies, but the transformation and differentiation through the Neolithic is crucial to understanding how the skull cult fully emerges.

THE NEOLITHIC SKULL CULTS OF THE NEAR EAST - PART TWO

Plastered skulls, Çatalhöyük, stone masks, statues and conclusions

"In the later phase of this period, Miss Kenyon has described the remarkable 'Skull Cult' characterized by the modelling of a life-like head in plaster over an actual skull, sometimes with but usually without its lower jaw. Beneath the floor of the house from which these modelled heads were recovered, an assemblage of about thirty skeletons was excavated. 'From many of these bodies the skull had been removed, often leaving a displaced lower jaw. In some cases, where the bodies were very tightly packed, the bones seem literally to have been ransacked to remove the skulls, at a stage when the bodies were sufficiently decayed to allow of the separation of limbs from the trunk, but the ligaments were still sufficiently intact for the individual bones of the limbs to remain in articulation'"

- L. H. WELLS, 1959

This is the second article looking at the 'skull cults' of

the Neolithic across the Levant and Anatolia, a phenomenon which has intrigued and baffled researchers since Jericho was excavated in the 1950's. Last time we covered an immense span of time, from the Pleistocene migrations of people into the region, the Natufian origins of agriculture, the earliest Neolithic settlements and cities, and finishing with an in-depth look at Göbekli Tepe and the cultic sites of the Anatolian highlands. This time we will slow the pace down and examine the Pre-Pottery Neolithic B in closer detail, casting some light on the spectral plastered skulls and the enigmatic settlement of Çatalhöyük. There can be no one answer to the riddle of why the earliest Neolithic farmers focused so much attention on the human head, but I will try to draw on a number of interpretations to sketch some interesting hypotheses. People in all times and places consider the head to be powerful - spiritually, romantically, artistically, for purposes of adornment, display, prestige, for healing, magic, the concentration of energy, consciousness and a thousand more reasons. But even with this in mind we today feel perhaps shock or revulsion at the thought of carving up and decorating a loved one's skull, to be encased in plaster for eternity. The very alien world of the Neolithic Near East can only be glimpsed at, and what we do see is an unfathomable gulf of incomprehension. Hopefully these two articles go some way to making sense of this abyss.

Plastered Skulls, Ancestors & Intimacy

Plaster and skulls were two important materials in the Levant and Anatolia circa 8800-6500 BC. I've written before about the development of lime and gypsum plaster during this period, but the significance of plaster extends beyond the utilitarian and into the ethereal. We saw at Göbekli Tepe and other highland sites that ritual rooms or centres often possessed a special plaster based flooring, highly polished and routinely maintained. Given the almost magical quality of fizzing hot quicklime, perhaps this is understandable. But here we see the combination of plaster with human skulls. Around 80 have been recovered from the Levatine sites of Jericho, Tell Ramad, Beisamoun, Kfar Hahoresh, Tell-Aswad, 'Ain Ghazal, and Nahal Hemar, and from two Anatolian sites - Çatalhöyük and Köşk Höyük. Interestingly the Anatolian practice emerged later, when it had ceased in the Levant, a chronology we will return to.

But what is a plastered skull? The term refers to the end process of preserving a human head. In general it seems that a person was buried and then dug up again, something we saw dating back to hunter-gatherers just after the Ice Age ended. The head was retrieved and cleaned, the jaw removed and often the teeth extracted. Afterwards a plaster mixture was spread over the skull, in particular the face, and life-like features were sculpted. Sometimes shells were used to imitate eyes. What makes this complex though is that each skull is slightly different - at 'Ain Ghazal one skull was covered in pink plaster, another in white. Some have closed eyes, others open. Some use reeds to help keep the plaster from slipping, most do not. Some have bitumen added to the eyelids, others have red/black stripes or were painted red, One plastered skull of a child from Köşk Höyük showed a green stain on the forehead, which has been interpreted as some kind of copper ornament placed on the head at death. At Yiftahel several skulls appeared to have been coloured afterwards and then a kind of headdress placed on top.

What is striking is how much effort was expended to make the faces appear realistic, one of the earliest examples of artistic naturalism. Earlobes, nostrils, eyelids, eyebrows, cheeks and other features are often captured in great detail with the plaster. Alongside the plastered skulls are other forms of 'ornamented skulls', which we shouldn't ignore when thinking about skull cults in general. At Nahal Hemar we have a skull with criss crossed lines of a bitumen/collagen mixture adorning the hairline. 'Ain Ghazal has a number of cached skulls which were painted with some kind of ochre crayon and charcoal, producing a vivid red-and-black striped pattern. Given that we also see groups of skulls buried without any decoration or plaster, we can infer that plastering was just one of many treatments available to a skull after death.

So who were these people? This is a question that continues to puzzle archaeologists, since finding any kind of pattern would help with interpreting what the skulls were used for. It seems that men, women and children all underwent plastering after death, although since we only have 70 over a two thousand year period, it is likely they were 'special' in some way. Interpretations have ranged from war trophies to an ancestor cult, which is the general consensus today. Since these appear with the advent of the PPNB era, many have inferred that they represent a response to increasing populations and gathering social complexity. Researcher Ian Kuijt states:

> Neolithic secondary mortuary practices are a form of bodily recirculation. There are at least two dimensions of the physical circulation of objects: reuse and modification. In the recirculation of objects in ritual practice, the power of the performance comes from the reenacting of events or stories. While plastered skulls may have served as stationary ritual relics, it is also possible that they were passed around during performances, displayed, and actively reused. There is strong evidence for the reuse of human skulls and plastered skulls in ritual events. Reflecting on the differential wear on the plastered skulls of Kfar HaHoresh cache L1304, Goring-Morris says, "At least one was plastered, and it appeared to have symbolically 'died' when the outer plaster layer began to deteriorate,

at which time it was ritually reburied a second time."
Although the specific use-life remains elusive, it is
reasonable to assume that ritual objects would have
been displayed, used, and recirculated within various
village social networks.

Some have suggested that the faces all trend towards a general archetype, rather than preserving individuality. With the exception of Jericho, the other Levantine sites favoured half-closed or closed eyes, with heavy eyelids and an almost dreamy expression, perhaps the sleep of death. This of course stands in stark contrast to the Anatolian highland cultic sites, where skulls were roughly decapitated, suspended on strings or haphazardly thrown into rooms. In the Levant we see intimacy and great care taken over their preservation, a marked distinction between two genetically different populations and culture-areas. The Anatolian zone was a place of hunting, with some domesticates, but full of stylised imagery of dangerous wild animals. The Levantine zone was almost totally agricultural by this point, where bones and skulls were passed around and intentionally cached.

In general the skulls are associated with domestic settings, being buried under the floors of houses, sometimes under a layer of plaster. This suggests familial and kinship ties with the dead, living on top of their ancestors. That said, some cultic sites are known - at Nahal Hemar, the plastered skulls were found in a cave, along with other ritual objects and no evidence of domestic life. Stone masks were also found in the cave and we'll look at these terrifying visages when we turn to artwork. The typically domestic and household burial scenario, combined with the rise in population density has led some researchers to argue that plastered skulls were a 'levelling mechanism', designed to help reinforce and foster a general egalitarian outlook amongst the Levantine farmers. To quote from a 2017 thesis paper by Catherine Maier:

The lack of evidence of obvious material differentiation among individual burials in the PPNB suggests an overall egalitarian social organization, while still incorporating competitive differences between individuals and households. The lack of clear material differentiation could be associated with a deliberate homogenization of community members after they are deceased, and, by extension, the existence of social and ritual mechanisms designed to minimize real and perceived differences within and between households and communities.

Kuijt has argued elsewhere that the skulls form part of a series of social technologies which try to strengthen community, rather than kinship bonds. As the numbers of people increase, nepotistic webs of family and clan can easily destabilise an egalitarian society, unless some way is found to bind everyone together, rather than just blood ties. Creating cults of common community ancestors who represent everyone, rather than specific lineages, could be one such method.

Çatalhöyük: Kinship, Heads & Vultures

Çatalhöyük is one of those major world heritage sites which has attracted all manner of theories and speculations, owing to the confusing and sometimes contradictory nature of the evidence. A proto-city that flourished between 7500 - 5900 BC in southern Anatolia, built on two mounds with a now extinct river separating them, Çatalhöyük was a majority-agricultural, semi-hunting based society. Due to the fantastic preservation and excavation skills of James Melaart and Ian Hodder, we know more about Çatalhöyük than almost any other prehistoric site. We know that people lived in a hive-like maze of mudbrick houses, with plastered interior walls. The settlement is noticeably clean and tidy, with rubbish and sewage dumps found outside the city limits. Almost no public or communal buildings have been found, the inhabitants mostly focused around family rooms and hearths. Storage units of peas, barley, wheat, almonds, pistachios and fruit have been found, sometimes with female 'goddess' figurines placed into them. The dead were wrapped and bound and placed under floors, beds, hearths, small platforms and other domestic areas. Famously the city appears to have been far more egalitarian than previously anticipated, with little indication of either hierarchical organisations nor patriarchal institutions. That said, various lines of evidence point towards patrilocal family structures and an increase in violence towards women as Çatalhöyük came to an end.

Much like Levantine burial practices, Çatalhöyük shows a similar intimacy and familiarity with skull retrieval, digging up and moving around older bones and curating skulls above ground until they essentially disintegrated. To give just one example, Room 129, located in the North Area of the settlement, has been nicknamed the 'Skull Retrieval Pit'. Here at least ten individuals were found, five of whom were disturbed and had their skulls removed after decomposition. No evidence of decapitation was found, which matches the general pattern in Çatalhöyük and Levantine sites, contrasting with the earlier Anatolian highland sites. At least one plastered skull has been recovered so far, cradled in the arms of another buried person, and a number of ochre-stained or decorated skulls. Unlike in the Levant though, Çatalhöyük has no skull caches and retrieved skulls often retained the mandible. We have a strange pattern here: Çatalhöyük is an Anatolian site, but primarily based around agriculture. It carried on a tradition of intimate familial skull retrieval and decoration which was disappearing in the Levant around the same time. The artwork of the city shows many examples of bulls and leopards, depictions more common to the highland Anatolian cultic sites, and used plastering for both domestic and mortuary practices.

Population movements between the Levant, Anatolia, Mesopotamia, the Zagros region and the Aegean have been extensively studied in the last few years, ostensibly with the aim of understanding how Neolithic farmers migrated into Greece and the Balkans. Two points of note stand out for us: one is that kinship relationships within Çatalhöyük appear to be distinctly non-biological, the other is that Levantine ancestry in Anatolia during the PPNB period is very low, but increases at Çatalhöyük during the subsequent Pottery Neolithic era. I wouldn't be the first to suggest that Çatalhöyük was born of the mingling of two peoples, separated by a river but building kinship networks that overcame simple tribalism. Jacques Cauvin, in his book The Birth of the Gods and the Origins of Agriculture, outlines how the Levantine 'skull cult' was introduced into Anatolia through an emigration of people heading north. Hodder succinctly describes his argument:

> *Cauvin treated at some length the spread of the PPNB. He saw this as a movement of people from the middle Euphrates, sometimes integrating into local cultures, and introducing rectangular architecture, herding, and the 'skull cult' into, for example, Anatolia and the central and southern Levant between 8600 BC and 7000 BC. He then discussed a further spread of the Neolithic in the later PPNB and Pottery Neolithic between 7500 BC and 6300 BC. This was seen as a 'great exodus' of people who now moved into semi-arid landscapes and into Cyprus. He described the spread as a colonisation, even messianic in tone.*

If the intimate 'skull cult' was introduced from the Levant, a different Anatolian tradition may have been combined with it. Depictions of vultures and other raptors eating and attacking humans are common at Göbekli Tepe, Nevalı Çori and other sites. Bones of griffins indicate exploitation for feathers. During the earliest excavations at Çatalhöyük, James Mellaart proposed that bodies were eaten by vultures, based on murals depicting vultures hovering over headless corpses. While this hasn't been a popular theory, other researchers have tentatively supported this argument, relying on distinctive V-shaped marks on skeletal remains. We know from modern Tibetan and Zoroastrian 'sky burials' that vultures can strip a body of flesh within hours, leaving a skeleton that can be more easily manipulated and buried. It is therefore entirely plausible that this form of 'sky burial' was combined with the 'skull cult' to create a co-ethnic mortuary practice at Çatalhöyük.

Artwork: Statues, Masks And Figurines

To round out this long series we turn to skull and head based artwork across the Near East during the Neolithic. A number of different forms and materials present themselves - clay figurines, plaster and clay statues, stone masks and sculptures. In a similar way to the plastered skulls, these are often naturalistic and represent no specific person in particular. They are simple enough to have been made by anyone and there doesn't seem to be a specialist craft working tradition during the PPNB for these forms of art. At 'Ain Gazhal we have one of the earliest statue making cultures. These almost alien looking figures are around 1m in height at the tallest, almost sexless, with the occasional breast or enlarged belly, made from limestone plaster over a reed frame. 15 statues and 15 busts were uncovered in two caches during excavations at 'Ain Gazhal in 1983/5 and they remain some of the strangest objects from the period. Some of the feet possess six toes, a curious feature which appears in numerous sacred art forms throughout the Middle East. The Biblical reference to a man of great stature, Gath, in 2 Samuel 21:20, describes the man as having six fingers and six toes. But it is the head which received the most attention. Unlike the plastered skulls, the eyes of the statues are wide open, with a bitumen iris which even today stares blankly out at the observer. An impassive and frankly unsettling face completes the look. Given that they were deliberately buried it seems likely that they were of spiritual or religious importance to the community.

The stone masks of this period are probably the most disturbing artefacts of them all. Only a handful have been recovered, the majority now in private hands. Finds from the cultic Nahal Hemar cave and from around Hebron in the modern West Bank point to perhaps one major production site, and they were taken to other places for ritualistic purposes. Made from smooth stone, with symmetrical features, cut-out eye sockets and grinning toothed mouths, these look distinct from the calm faces of other Levantine 'head-art'. Menacing, snarling, threatening, predatory. They show traces of having been painted and perhaps decorated with headdresses or other headgear. It's unclear if they were meant to be worn or mounted in some way. Unlike the more communal, ancestral skulls and statues that we've seen, these look more like masks of a ritual specialist or secret society, indicating some kind of hierarchy. This might not be true of course, but they don't fit into the general Levantine pattern and their use remains subject to current research.

Many examples of plaster figurines exist from all over the sites we've covered - sadly this isn't the place to look at the 'bull cult' which is another feature of the PPNB and later, nor do we have space to look at the so-called 'goddess' figurines from Çatalhöyük and elsewhere. Instead we finish with the Anatolian tradition of miniature stone masks and human heads, found at Nevalı Çori and Göbekli Tepe. These fit into the more violent schema we've come to expect from PPNB Anatolia - screaming expressions or absent mouths, many having been decapitated by forceful blows, breaking them off the 'body' of stone, leaving behind jagged necks. The contrast between these and the relaxed plastered skulls and statues could not be greater.

Are There Any Conclusions?

Over two articles I've attempted to show how the different 'skull cults' of the Near East Neolithic developed through time and space. We can broadly point to two great 'culture-zones' - the Levant and Anatolia. Both the Levantine Natufians and Pleistocene Anatolians shared a common ritual of skull retrieval, possibly from the same source, or from two convergent origins. Whatever the case may be, as agriculture developed in the Levant in the wake of the Younger Dryas, two modes or approaches to the human head came to flourish. The first was more egalitarian and ancestral, with the people of the PPNA living with and amongst their dead in domestic settings, eventually finding its greatest expression in ornamented and plastered skulls, statues and artworks, collectively interested in communal ancestors. These objects were produced without specialisation and eventually buried, often around their descendant's houses. The second was something else entirely. The highland Anatolians rejected the logic of domesticity, structuring their societies around hunting, herding and foraging, with some supplemental agriculture. They built cultic centres which glorified violent death, decapitation, the danger of wild animals and masculine predatory behaviour. They roughly severed heads on ceremonial altars, dangled skulls from huge pillars and smashed off the faces and crania of statues. These two distinct cultures produced something new when they collided at Çatalhöyük, pouring both of their traditional practices into one mould, casting a mixed product which simultaneously revered the wild and worshipped their forebears. Perhaps something of this violent Anatolian culture was passed on to the ancient Sumerians and Assyrians, who conceived of decapitation and skeletal disarticulation as the worst of punishments? The images of skull mountains being eaten by vultures would certainly resonate with someone from Göbekli Tepe.

Is this an oversimplified narrative? Of course. Entire books have been written on this subject and many more will undoubtedly follow. My aim, as always, is to unearth the evidence which is often hidden in academic papers and textbooks, and to bring it to a general readership with a story. Academics shy away from grand narratives, partly since they are often wrong, but narratives help us orient ourselves when we encounter new facts. Maybe what I've crafted here will help you anchor yourself into the world of the Near East Neolithic, a framework on which to hang new information. How people treat their dead can tell you a great deal about their culture, and the cultures of the earliest farmers will never stop being interesting.

THE FIRST HUMANS IN EUROPE

Hominins, Neanderthals and the humans before the Aurignacians

W here to begin with the topic of who were the first humans in Europe? Even to ask the question is to invite the response, 'who counts as human?', and there's some truth here, where do we draw the line between the different stages of human evolution? I'll make it simple, lets start at the very beginning. Who inhabited Europe and when? Traditionally the sequence has usually run something like: unknown humans > Neanderthals > Aurignacian Homo sapiens. But we know now that the Aurignacians were not the first modern humans to set foot in Europe, and the growing body of evidence for multiple incursions deserves looking at in detail. So let's jump in, who was the first human ancestor on the continent?

Apes, Monkeys & Migrations

In each great region of the world the living mammals are closely related to the extinct species of the same region. It is therefore probable that Africa was formerly inhabited by extinct apes closely allied to the gorilla and chimpanzee; and as these two species are now man's nearest allies, it is somewhat more probable that our early progenitors lived on the African continent than elsewhere. But it is useless to speculate on this subject, for an ape nearly as large as a man, namely the Dryopithecus of Lartet, which was closely allied to the anthropomorphous Hylobates, existed in Europe during the Upper Miocene period; and since so remote a period the earth has certainly undergone many great revolutions, and there has been ample time for migration on the largest scale

-Darwin, 1871, The Descent of Man

Darwin's discussion of human origins notes a mystery which is still with us today, where did the earliest Great Apes originate? Our nearest relatives, the Hominidae family group, contains the chimpanzee, the orangutan, the gorilla, the bonobo and every type of human. Classifying the various human sub-species is a challenge for this century, and there's new material turning up by the day. At first glance it would seem logical that the Great Apes also evolved in Africa, but a growing body of evidence points towards Europe as the cradle of the family.

The Miocene period is where we begin, somewhere between 23 and 5 million years ago. This epoch saw Africa join Eurasia; the Mediterranean evaporate and refill again, and apes evolve into their modern forms. By the end of the timeline we see the ancestors of chimps and humans finally split, opening the evolutionary path for modern humans to develop and diverge. The earliest known ape species in Eurasia is the Griphopithecus, a thick-enamelled creature discovered in Germany, and dated to around 17 million years ago. He had arrived with many others of his kind from Africa, such as the Kenyapithecus, Equatorius and Nacholapithecus, all species with thick enamel, spread out from Kenya to Turkey to Germany. After another 5 million years the split between the orangutans and the rest of the apes becomes visible, with the former moving towards Southeast Asia. In Europe this new species of ape is collectively called the Dryopithecines - fruit-eating quadrupeds with a stiff back, thinner enamel, a broad thorax and powerful grasp. They were something like a modern ape, a vital part of the transition towards later hominins.

The earliest hominines are European and there are no fossil hominines in Africa for at least two million years after they first appeared in Spain and France...

The best-known samples of late Miocene European hominines are about 10 to 9.5 Ma in age (Rudabánya, Can Llobateres, Ravin de la Pluie). By this time hominines had diversified substantially and in some ways mimic the diversity that existed among Pliocene hominins. Ouranopithecus was substantially larger, with much more robust jaws, thickly enameled teeth, and many other adaptations to a diet that must have emphasized the consumption of hard or tough food objects, like australopithecines. Rudapithecus and Hispanopithecus were highly suspensory, arboreal soft fruit frugivores, with cheek teeth closely resembling those of living chimpanzees. The brain of Rudapithecus is known to have been as large as that of modern chimpanzees, and it is possible that this fossil ape had cognitive capabilities similar to those of chimpanzees

-Miocene Hominids and the Origins of the
African Apes and Humans, Begun, 2010

What seems clear, after all this time, is that Darwin's suspicions were correct. Although the later ancestors of modern humans emerged in Africa, their forebears in turn had evolved in Europe, before leaving as the climate began to dry out.

> *Indeed, there is another possibility, which is that the large range, diversity, and density of Miocene hominines in Europe point to a European origin, with a subsequent dispersal into Africa in the late Miocene. There is strong evidence for the latter hypothesis in data from the morphology, geochronology, and paleobiogeography of European hominines and other land mammals.8, 23. Hominines occurred in Europe at least two million years before they appeared in Africa.17*

-European Miocene Hominids and the Origin of the
African Ape and Human Clade, Begun et al, 2012

The number of features shared between Dryopiths and later hominins is quite large, including facial, nasal, sinoid and skull modifications and rearrangements. Their effect on later developments leading up to the final split between ancestral chimps and humans seems to have been profound.

The Great Apes were however, forced out of Europe, and many went extinct. What they brought back to Africa with them, along with their new physiology, was a more flexible and adaptive set of behavioral strategies, to manage the increased seasonality and ecological change. The next time their descendants set foot in Europe, the story would be very different.

Back-To-Europe: Homo Antecessor And Their Kin

The first hints of something happening in Europe come from a controversial set of fossil fragments and teeth found in Greece and Bulgaria. Dubbed Graecopithecus freybergi, the remains were the centre of an academic controversy in 2017, when a paper published in PLOS One tentatively argued that Graecopithecus could be the first example of the hominin family after the break with ancestral chimpanzees. Dated to 7.2 million years ago, the media declared that Europe and not Africa was the birthplace of the human species. Other academics have responded, ultimately leading to both camps accepting that we don't have the evidence yet to support Graecopithecus's inclusion into the hominin group.

The first accepted appearance of the newly evolved Homo species in Europe was recently discovered in Spain. The archaeological site of Sima de los Heusos, Atapuerca, is amongst the most important in the world, having yielded tools and bones of numerous human species, including Neanderthals. The genetic and skeletal data from the site has been invaluable in building family relationships between different human species. The oldest to date are between 1.4 and 1.2 million years old, which include teeth, a finger bone and two jawbones. They could belong to either Homo erectus or antecessor. The consensus leans towards them being Homo antecessor, which makes sense, since this sub-species of human has only been found in Spain.

Antecessor, or 'pioneer man', is one of the many mysterious branches of the human tree that we don't fully understand. They seem to be an offshoot of the species that would evolve into Homo heidelbergensis, the common ancestor to both modern humans and Neanderthals. What is particularly eerie though is that antecessor appears to have developed very similar skeletal characteristics as modern humans, including a gracile, flatter face and similar spinal and shoulder anatomy. Almost like a dry-run for modern humans. However, the fate for hominids is never usually good, and antecessor appears to have gone extinct. Their legacy seems to have been a voracious taste for hunting down juvenile members of their own kind and cannibalising them.

This period of time, between the evolution of the Homo genus and the more familiar later species has always been an awkward muddle. Numerous species and subspecies have been named, classified, re-classified and dropped, and the debates over whether a single tooth represents a new hominin or an existing one are dull. So we shall proceed with the most straightforward of narratives as I see it, but you may disagree. Around 1.5 million years ago, we have an offshoot species living in Spain, likely the first to arrive back from Africa, but they don't contribute to any later surviving population. Instead we see the advance and much wider spread of a different human species - Homo heidelbergensis. This thickly-browed, fire-using species has left evidence in the form of skeletons, artefacts and even footprints as far north as Britain. From what limited evidence we have, they must have inherited the Acheulean handaxe tradition from their Homo erectus forebears and made limited forays into Europe as the weather permitted. The dates for this colonisation are all over the place, but after about 800,000 years ago, we begin to see the coalescence of adaptive behaviours which allowed humans to live in much colder climates. The use of fire, hafted weapons, handaxes and a diverse set of strategies for hunting different animals and foraging for plant foods all contributed to the later appearance of Europe's longest lived inhabitants - the Neanderthals.

A Neanderthal World

In comparison to the feeble evidence we have for Europe's humans over the hundreds of thousands of years that antecessor and heidelbergensis lived and died, evidence for Neanderthals seems plentiful. Exactly when they split from the rest of the human family is not clear, somewhere between 400 and 800 thousand years ago, but they flourished in Europe until around 40,000 years ago - meaning they may have inhabited the continent for ten times longer than modern Homo sapiens. Their exploits have become better known in recent decades, rising from their poor early PR as primitive savages to being respected as an inventive, creative species - capable of sailing, making fire, distilling tar, making art, hunting huge animals, producing clothes, potentially venerating eagles and identifying medicinal plants. We also know a great deal more about their genetics, and when and where they interbred with modern humans and Denisovans.

The details of how Neanderthals lived, their hunting strategies, tool production, domestic settings and so on have been well documented in many recent books and articles. What is often missing from academic archaeology is any kind of meta-narrative, how populations formed, moved and disappeared. From this vantage Neanderthals are still somewhat mysterious, and they seem to behave very differently in their wider social relations than modern humans. Their evolution from Homo heidelbergensis seems the most likely origin story, with small groups being isolated as successive waves of glaciation hit Europe, over time forming the distinctive Neanderthal features in at least Western Europe, before they went east, all the way to Siberia. By 120,000 years ago there were at least two deeply divergent Neanderthal populations, generally defined by 'western' and 'eastern' titles.

The deepest divergence among Neanderthal genomes sequenced to date is found between eastern and western Eurasian Neanderthal populations represented by the ~120 ka Altai Neanderthal from Denisova Cave7 and the >44 ka Vindija 33.19 individual from Croatia. Genomic data of all other available Neanderthal remains, the earliest in western Europe being ~120 ka (Scladina and Hohlenstein-Stadel (HST)), while the latest being ~40 ka, suggest genetic continuity in western Eurasia for ~80 ka. Recent results obtained from sedimentary DNA suggest that the genetic landscape was significantly altered by expansions of Neanderthal populations ~105 ka. This gave rise to lineages in western Europe represented by samples from Central Europe (Vindija), the Caucasus (Mezmaiskaya Cave), and Siberia (Chagyrskaya cave 8), the latter likely replacing the earlier Altai-like population. The genomes of late (<50 ka) European Neanderthals, including an individual from the Caucasus (Mezmaiskaya 2), were all found to be more similar to Vindija than to other known lineages, indicating further population turnover towards the last stages of Neanderthal history in the Caucasus or western Europe.

However, even within these broad lineages and turnovers, Neanderthals seem to differ from modern humans in their extremely low inter-group mixing and higher instances of inbreeding. A recent discovery of a well-preserved Neanderthal male from southern France, nicknamed 'Thorin', revealed that Europe possessed a number of small, isolated groups, which kept to themselves for millennia.

Our results nevertheless suggest a minimum of two distinct Neanderthal lineages present in Europe during the late Neanderthal period. In the absence of any detectable gene flow between Thorin and other Neanderthal lineages after its divergence, we conclude that Thorin represents a lineage that has stayed isolated for ~50 ka... Our results thus also shed light onto the social organization of Neanderthals, suggesting that small isolated populations with limited, and potentially without, inter-group exchange as a possibly more general feature of Neanderthal social structure.

The divergence of Thorin's lineage also matches another discovery from northern Spain, where an almost total Neanderthal population replacement occurred around 100,000 years ago. Clearly over a very long time span, Neanderthals were also separating, remaining separate and moving into one another's territory. Evidently they also preferred to live and mate amongst their own groups. One has to imagine that isolation for tens of thousands of millennia would produce huge language differences, assuming language development worked in the same way for Neanderthals as modern humans.

Waves Of Humans

Dating the entrance of Homo sapiens into Europe has always been a topic of great interest amongst archaeologists, especially since examples dating back around 180,000 years have been found at Misliya Cave in Israel. Debates continue to be had over the identity of a pair of skulls found at Apidima Cave in Greece, one of which has been suggested to be an early Homo sapien, but could equally be Homo erectus with early Neanderthal features. Given that these date back around

210,000 years, we are looking at potentially multiple waves of modern humans either within Europe or on her borders.

If Thorin was an exceptional find for archaeology, his burial place might enter the top ten sites for all of prehistory. The cave of Grotte Mandrin is set to rewrite the human story, and provides the best and most detailed sequence of events surrounding the first attempts of modern humans to colonise Europe. The limestone cave system is perched high above the Rhône valley, providing superlative views of the landscape, access to river systems and good quality flint. The cave provides an almost perfect set of stratigraphic layers which document not only the lives of its resident Neanderthals from 100kya to their extinction 42 kya, but also astonishing glimpses into the earliest Homo sapien visits into the continent. Around 120,000 flint tools and animal bones have been painstakingly recovered, along with millions of micro flint chips, and many human remains. As I've written before, deep prehistory tends to be defined by types of stone tool industry, in this case the Mousterian being the style associated with Neanderthal sites and skeletal remains.

The final series of phases from 54 kya to 42 kya seems to run thus:

Mousterian style stone tools – Neanderthal

Short transition period dubbed 'Neronian' - modern humans

Two post-Neronian phases with Mousterian tools - Neanderthal re-occupation

First Upper Palaeolithic layer - 'proto Aurignacian' modern humans

The distinguishing features here are the styles of stone tools. To the layman, this might sound a bit vague, but the contrast between the Mousterian tools, which are large flakes, and the Neronian is huge. We can look not only at the final form of the tools, which are nothing alike, but also the manufacturing methods required. The Neronian toolkit is dominated by excessively small micro or nano points, which have no precedent in the hundreds of millennia in Europe before then. These tiny crafted weapons point in one direction - the first use of the bow-and-arrow.

Not only do comparative studies of these points against experimental flint arrowheads further support this hypothesis, but they hint that the Neronian arrows may have been tipped with poison. Incredibly the researchers working on the cave have been able to use trapped layers of soot in the interior to date the sequence of occupations, akin to dating a tree by its rings. In an astonishing set of results, archaeologists were able to determine that no more than one or two years passed between the Neanderthals and the first human Neronians. These were no mere scouts, a child's tooth was discovered in the Neronian layer, and they maintained a presence for around forty years before disappearing, the cave falling back into the hands of the Rhône valley Neanderthals.

What happened next is just as remarkable. The controversial tool industry known as the Châtelperronian has been argued to be either a Neanderthal innovation based on contact with modern humans, or an early intrusion of humans into Neanderthal Europe. Recent arguments for the Châtelperronian sites in Franco-Iberia as a second wave of sapiens has to be considered alongside the reoccupation of the Rhône:

If the Châtelperronian effectively corresponds to a second migratory phase by H. sapiens, and originated from the same Levantine cultural substrate, the absence of chronological and geographical overlap between phase I (IUP / Neronian) and phase II (NEA / Châtelperronian) is all the more remarkable, as the territorial expansion of this phase II affected large territories- Atlantic, continental, and Mediterranean- which remain quite geographically disjointed. Over this same period, the Rhône valley was occupied by Neandertal groups that carried the Post-Neronian II traditions [1]. Could it be that in the same geographical space that saw the first migrations of H. sapiens into Europe, Neanderthal groups no longer allowed access to their previous territory? This would be remarkable, since the Post-Neronian I and Post-Neronian II, which mark a return of Neandertal populations to a large territory around Mandrin, also indicate a persistence of Neandertal populations in one of the main migratory arteries of Western Europe [1]. This could well indicate a refusal or a resistance from the aboriginal populations against a return of H. sapiens at the very moment when, according to this hypothesis, these latter populations would manifest their first real colonization by way of settlements, not only numerous, but also over vast territories across Western Europe.

What we have to postulate then is that modern humans had established a strong maritime presence along the Mediterranean shorelines, and were finding major river systems blocked off by Neanderthals. They were forced to instead move up through northern Iberia and the Balkans.

The final proto Aurignacian expansions, circa 42 kya, are visible within Grotte Mandrin. Again soot deposits reveal the overlap to be a few years at most, perhaps shorter. This wave of colonisation was to be the last time Neanderthals lived in the valley, their ancestral home taken over by the new arrivals. It is entirely possible that these last Neanderthals were using small point weaponry, having inherited the tradition from a long forgotten Neronian population over ten thousand years prior.

The Last Neanderthals

We still have a long way to go to understand these pre-Aurignacian human groups. One of the only sets of human remains from this period, dated to 45,000 years ago, is the Zlatý kůň skull from the Czech Republic. Her genome showed similar levels of Neanderthal introgression, but the sequences were much longer, and she did not pass on her ancestry to the later Aurignacians and Gravettians. As for the Neronians and Châtelperronians, we are currently blind. Hopefully DNA can be extracted from those found at Grotte Mandrin, which would give us much more information about who was arriving on the shores of Europe over 50kya.

The Neanderthals themselves suffered not only the colonisation of their lands by the sapiens, but were also hit with a major climatic downturn around 42,000 years ago. The abandonment of inner Iberia, coincided with the Protoaurignacian ascendency. The reasons for the Neanderthal's demise are beyond what I can write here, but likely a combination of genetic fitness, social flexibility and adaptability, higher birth rates, use of dogs and multiple niche exploitation all counted. Aggression and violence seem a given, over the millennia of interactions, and since the Neanderthals seemed to have avoided each other, they likely shunned the newcomers as well for the most part.

As to their survival, it is possible that some clung on past 40,000 years ago. A number of disputed sites exist within Spain, and a controversial skeleton of a young boy found at Lagar Velho 1 in Portugal hints at some longevity. Dated to 24,500ya, the boy reportedly shows facial features and anatomical structures consistent with being a Neanderthal hybrid, but other researchers have argued this is a preservation issue. At least one paper argues for an Iberian holdout up until 28 kya, and the Croatian Vindija Cave Neanderthals have been redated to around 32 kya. Probably the best site comes from the Polar Urals, at a site called Byzovaya, where Mousterian tools were tentatively dated to around 33,000 years ago. The site contains butchered mammoths and reindeer, with contemporary Upper Palaeolithic stone tool sites close by. Along with the Russian Mezmaiskaya Cave Neanderthal bone dates of 35 kya, it is looking more and more like Neanderthals retreated into two refugia - one in southernmost Iberia and one towards the Russian Arctic. Since no Mousterian tools have been associated with modern humans, this doesn't seem a far-fetched hypothesis.

Conclusions

So we come to the end of this long tale, one which has seen various stages of human evolution take place within Europe. The time scales are of course staggering, and we can't really imagine what 50k years of isolation looks like, let alone 500k or a million. What we can see are broad trends, supplemented by amazing snapshots of moments in time. The slow domination by hominins who possess greater adaptability, both biological and cultural, seems to be the story of Europe's various human branches. The latest developments in building something of a narrative to understand the arrival of H. sapiens has to be amongst the most exciting topics in archaeology today - to be able to see in soot depositions just a few years in a person's life is mind-blowing, and being able to deduce from pieces of stone that the first intruders carried a new and deadly projectile weapon is fodder for the imagination. The story of Europe's Neanderthals, melting away as the sapien trail is blazed, is also poignant. Surviving either on the extremities of Iberia, perhaps looking to Africa to escape, or butchering mammoth in the chill dark of the long polar night, their backs turned to their sapien neighbours just over the hill. Hopefully we find more of these stories to tell, the deep time of Europe's first humans.

THE ROAD TO METALLURGY - FIRE & ROCKS

The long story of how humans mastered fire, pigments and minerals

How, when and why humans began to master metals is one of those great questions of archaeology and world history, the long slow story of controlling fire and experimenting with different rocks, pigments and ores. Too often though it is presented as an ex nihilo breakthrough, a revolution without precedent. In fact, humans had been tinkering with both fire and inorganic chemistry for tens of millennia, starting with cooking, creating paints, manufacturing glue, ceramics, weapons and artwork. In this brief piece I want to bring that story alive and lead you through these earliest glimpses of chemical experimentation, starting with the deep Palaeolithic, and finishing with the dawn of metallurgy. We'll see by the end that smelting ores was not a breakthrough act from scratch, but the product of a perfect combination of developed experience, insight and location.

Fire & Rock - Humble Beginnings

There are surely many ways to tackle the problem of metalworking, but I want to make it simple. There are two key technologies which need to be controlled before metallurgy can begin - the ability to make, direct and manipulate fire and heat, and the ability to locate, identify, manipulate and exploit inorganic materials. By inorganic I mean materials as diverse as clay, ores, minerals, different rocks, crystals and geological features. To smelt metals you must have a good idea of how to create the right temperature and conditions and how to select the right ore and heat it in the right way. These two technologies have exceptionally archaic roots, starting with the invention and use of fire and the discovery of colourful stones, powders and pigments.

Locating the first use of fire has proved to be a classically impossible problem for archaeology. Broadly speaking we have two lines of evidence, which unhelpfully don't quite line up. First is identifying features on sites and artefacts that conclusively prove the controlled use of fire, the second is the physiological adaptations of humans to cooked food. The earliest traces of fire appear around 1.5-1 million years ago, which points to Homo erectus as the first masters of the flame. Two sites, one in Koobi Fora, Kenya, and the other in Wonderwerk Cave, Northern Cape province, South Africa, have fairly solid evidence of heating from micro changes to the surroundings sediments. Other similar sites, from Chesowanja, GnJi1/6E, Kenya; Gadeb, Ethiopia and Swartkrans, South Africa, show the limited use of fire through this time period. Though what is strange is that Homo erectus didn't seem to use fire as a 'base camp' at this point. The surrounding Kuruman Hills near Wonderwerk Cave have turned up tens of millions of stone tools, dating to the contemporary Acheulean, but show no evidence of fire.

Despite this, plenty of archaeologists disagree with the trace evidence and instead prefer much later periods for more reliable signatures of controlled fire, but here we run into a dilemma. Both Homo erectus and sapiens show intense physiological adaptations towards cooked food. In fact, it goes further than this, we are obliged to eat cooked food. As Richard Wrangham neatly summarises:

> *Key evidence comes from research on raw foodists, that is, people who live for long periods on all-raw diets. Raw-foodist groups typically live in industrial societies on store-bought foods. Even though raw foodists take little exercise compared with hunter-gatherers and have fewer disease challenges, on average they experience chronic energy shortage leading to low body mass index (BMI). In the only study of reproductive performance, incompetent or absent ovulation left more than 50% of women on an all-raw diet unable to reproduce (Koebnick et al. 1999).*

> *These physiological detriments are striking because the diet eaten by raw foodists is extremely high quality compared with any known hunter-gatherer diet (if their diet were eaten raw). Most of the raw foodists' diet is rich in digestible energy and low in structural fiber because it comes from domesticated species. Furthermore, raw foodists typically process the food extensively by nonthermal means (such as by blending) and (in spite of their supposed adherence to raw) often use heat to lightly cook (up to around 114°F). In addition, raw foodists experience no important*

seasonal energy shortages (because they buy from globally connected markets; Wrangham 2009).

This obligation, a product of our shortened digestive tracts, smaller teeth, larger brains and lowered tolerance for meat-borne pathogens, points to a very early use of cooked foods in the Homo diet, freeing up calories to feed the hungry brain. At least, this is the 'Cooked Food Hypothesis'. It infers that sometime during the Lower Palaeolithic, different hominins like Homo erectus and their ancestors began regularly using fire to chemically alter their food. How they made these fires and how they fitted into their social lives is uncertain, perhaps far more sporadically and more remotely than we like to imagine.

The second revolution in human technology that concerns us during the Palaeolithic is the appreciation of colour and the deliberate sourcing and manufacture of inorganic pigments, primarily from an iron-rich clay called red ochre. If any material can claim to have been our constant, common companion, it would either be flint or red ochre. Found in artwork and particularly in burials the world over, red ochre is the colour of cave paintings, of early textiles and jewellery, of graves and death and likely of skin painting or coverings. Ochre also has many other interesting uses, aside from its colour, including being worn as an insect repellent and sunscreen, as a binder in early adhesives, and as an ingredient in leather preservation. This wonderful little snippet from Alexander Marshack's 1981 paper on ochre gives a sense of the time depth involved here:

At the Homo erectus shelter of Bečov, Czechoslovakia, J. Fridrich excavated a piece of red ochre that was striated on two faces with the marks of abrasion, and here on flat rubbing stone with a granular crystallised surface

that had been abraded in the centre, clearly in the
preparation of ochre powder. On the floor of the shelter,
at the side where the piece of ochre was found, there
was a wide area of ochre powder. Seating himself on a
rock against the wall of the shelter to study the ochre,
Fridrich found that his feet accidentally fitted the only
two areas without ochre powder. Homo erectus had sat
on this stone, away from other activities in the site,
while he made his red powder.

The evolutionary development of symbolic thought and behaviour is believed to occur at the threshold of sapien emergence as a species. Ochre pieces from Blombos Cave in South Africa, dated to 350,000 years ago, and the Olorgesailie basin in Kenya, dated to 307,000 years ago, appear to bear this out. Olorgesailie also shows long distance procurement of obsidian and even manganese dioxide, again for grinding to make pigments.

Neanderthals - Fire, Glue And Art

Speeding into the Middle Palaeolithic and the Neanderthals in particular, we come to another internal academic crossroads. The question at this point is not whether Neanderthals used fire, they absolutely did, but whether they were capable of creating fire on demand. If this sounds ridiculous its because it is, but I will be fair and give the sceptics their due.

The proposal that Neanderthals were unable to make fire when and where they liked is probably best defended by the archaeologist Dennis M Sandgathe. Across two papers (here and here) he outlines his case based on the frequency and timing of Neanderthal hearths and burnt artefacts (flint, bone etc) at a number of well excavated sites, particularly Pech de l'Azé IV and Roc de Marsal (Dordogne, France). In these papers he shows that fire use is strongly associated with the warmest climates and seasons, and appear infrequently or are absent during the coldest. This is something of a paradox, which Sandgathe explains as Neanderthals exploiting lightning strikes and wildfires, rather than creating fires themselves. This model has been thoroughly demolished, in my mind at least, by several detailed and complex papers which draw together palaeoclimatology, archaeology and geology to make the opposite case. Readers are welcome to follow the paper trails of arguments in the literature themselves, but I think with the following evidence we can be confident that Neanderthals had a superb grasp on fire production and control.

Neanderthal hand axes, those large pear-shaped flint tools, characteristic of their species, have been analysed closely under microscopes and many display a pattern of scratches and striations which look very similar to flint tools striking against iron pyrites ('fool's gold'). This combination has been well documented ethnographically, which is not a surprise since pyrite striking on flint produces a visible spark. Other evidence for Neanderthal fire skills come from well-preserved wooden spears, where the points have been fire-hardened, as well as from their careful selection of firewood, as attested from Abric Romaní in Spain. But probably the best display of fire technology comes from the Neanderthal production of glues - specifically tar created from heating birch-bark. This procedure can only be done at a certain temperature and oxygen has to be excluded from the process, indicating that Neanderthals had a fine-tuned mastery of heat.

Finally, the existence of Neanderthal artwork, long dismissed as a possibility, has been amply demonstrated over the last ten years or so. Red ochre, manganese oxide and dioxide, shell beads and feathers have all been discovered in Neanderthal contexts. Taken together, we should be satisfied that Neanderthals not only had superb control over fire production and use, but also that they understood the visible and working properties of different minerals - pyrite, flint, manganese ores and red ochre. All crucial steps towards metalworking.

The Upper Palaeolithic - Ceramics, Cave Art & Fossil Fuels

If I'm focusing heavily on the European archaeological record, it's because that is where the best archaeological work has been done. The cold climate of the Palaeolithic, combined with the birth of archaeological science in Europe, has meant preservation and focus here is unparalleled, but I will expand to other parts of the world as we go on.

The Upper Palaeolithic in Europe, roughly from 50 - 12,000 years ago, saw a tremendous explosion in human creativity and inventiveness. Here we see the first ceramics appear in the human record, during the Pavlovian/Gravettian period (33-21,000 years ago). The site of Dolní Věstonice in the Czech Republic is astonishing for many reasons - earliest evidence for textiles, incredible figurine artwork, rich burials and so on - but the invention of ceramics counts amongst the world's breakthrough technologies. However, unlike the utilitarian ceramic containers of later times, the Gravettian taste was far more cultic and religiously oriented. Thousands of fragments of animal figurines are known from Dolní Věstonice, all displaying signs of thermal shock. Combined with the discovery of limestone kilns in strange structures some way from the camp, we have a fascinating glimpse into the Upper Palaeolithic mind.

Careful analysis of the chemical composition of both the kilns and the figurines suggests that the people of Dolní Věstonice were gathering a kind of clay-like material called 'loess', which was wetted and pressed or sculpted, before being placed into a hot fire. The deliberate overloading of water and rapid temperature gain meant the figurines exploded, with glowing glassy fragments launching themselves from the hearths. The temperature inside the kiln was enough for the limestone to form lime (calcium oxide), a material we'll see again soon. This intentional manipulation of chemistry, on a dark night by a glowing fire, paints a picture of people leaving their camp, gathered around a special kiln, to observe animal models glowing and exploding with great noise and visual effects. A magical performance.

Alongside such pyrotechnics came a profusion of cave art, mostly during the later Magdalenian period (17-12,000 years ago). This was the time of the most famous cave paintings, of Lascaux and Altamira - herds of animals, strange shamanic hybrid men, hand-prints and the careful exploitation of the cave surface to make bulls and horses appear like they were emerging from the very rocks themselves. The symbolism and meanings of these paintings will be debated forever, but what is often overlooked is the technical production. Alongside scaffolding to reach high areas of the cave, we see crayons, feather quills, blowpipes, brushes and special applicators. The pigment palette of red ochre and charcoal was expanded with crushed calcite, kaolin, umber, sienna and manganese. Binders, such as animal fats, marrow, albumen, saliva, urine, blood, vegetable juice and calcium carbonate-rich cave water were used. Extenders and preservatives such as crushed bone, biotite, feldspar and ground quartz were also added to the pigments, displaying a stunning level of ingenuity and experimentation on the part of these artists.

Finally, to complete the growing story of fire and fuel

management, the Upper Palaeolithic and beyond also saw the first exploitation of fossil fuels, as well as superb control over heating stones. Lignite fragments appear in certain hearths, such as at Les Canalettes and Les Usclades at Causse du Larzac (France). Adding flint into the fire to alter its working properties really comes into its own during the Palaeolithic Solutrean period (22-17,000 years ago). Solutrean tools are famously outstanding amongst the technological advances of the Palaeolithic, displaying skills and techniques not seen before. Remarkably, the method required to heat chert and other tool-stones to make them easier to work requires controlling the temperature in a narrow band between 250 °C and 300 °C. This is an astonishing level of control for an outdoor campfire and suggestions for how this was achieved has included a 'sand bath' made under a fire, or some kind of earth oven or kiln. Work still continues to understand how the Solutreans were able to do this, but it should tell us that sophisticated pyrotechnology was feasible during the Palaeolithic.

End Of The Ice Age - Global Revolutions

The end of the ice age saw the world fragment and coalesce around a number of different economic strategies - complex hunter-fisher societies, early agriculture in the Near East, animal domestication, the introduction of forager and farmer ceramics, intensive proto-farming of different plants and stone/brick architecture. Within these revolutions there was an expansion of technologies involving heating different materials.

Plaster quickly became an invaluable material amongst Near Eastern Neolithic societies - as I've outlined in a previous article, many cultic buildings and mortuary treatments of skulls required the production of gypsum and lime plasters. To quote from The Beginnings of Pyrotechnology, Part II: Production and Use of Lime and Gypsum Plaster in the Pre-Pottery Neolithic Near East:

> *Gypsum plaster is made by heating alabaster or gypsum rock ($CaSO4:2H2O$) at a temperature of 150-400°C to form the hemihydrate which, when mixed with water, reacts to reform the dihydrate …. The mix tends to set quickly and the resulting product is relatively soft and susceptible to chipping; it absorbs water, and can only be used for exterior purposes in dry climates. Lime technology is a good deal more complicated. Lime plaster is made by heating limestone ($CaCO3$) for an extended period at bright heat, 800-900°C, to form quicklime (CaO), which must be soaked in water to form slaked lime ($Ca(OHh)$, a process in which considerable heat is generated. The slaked lime paste can be stored for some time before use, but after drying and standing in air, the product reacts with the atmosphere to form the carbonate, $CaCO3$.*

What is often forgotten about these plasters is how energy and resource intensive they would have been to make. A limestone kiln circa 1850's Britain required 1.8 tonnes of limestone and two tonnes of wood for every tonne of quicklime. Neolithic production kilns were likely less efficient, sucking up huge quantities of wood, charcoal, stone and manpower. On top of this is the danger involved in quicklime production - unlike many small scale technologies we've seen so far, kilns of burning limestone have the potential to seriously injure or kill their workers, anticipating the increased risk of metallurgy from heat and toxic fumes.

In a similar vein we see Neolithic salt production beginning to emerge across Europe, using wooden wells, charcoal burners and ceramic vessels to drive off the water and condense the salt. One of the best examples with preserved oak trunk wells comes from Fontaines Salées in Saint-Père-sous-Vézelay (Yonne, France). The production of charcoal itself, long a topic of speculation amongst Mesolithic archaeologists, should also be considered here. To my knowledge no early charcoal production sites have been located for Holocene Europe, but this is likely due to the charcoal being removed and the presumed earth oven 'clamp' being unidentifiable in the record.

Neolithic mining expanded from its proto-form and became a serious and organised activity in multiple regions. The Gavà Neolithic Mining Complex (GNMC) near Barcelona possessed five levels of activity, galleries and chambers, with the aim of acquiring varlscite, a green phosphate mineral similar to turquoise that can be easily cut and polished to make ornaments such as necklaces or bracelets. Red cinnabar (mercury sulphide-HgS) began to be sought after for its vibrant pigmentation - in places like Almadén (Ciudad Real, Spain) and Vinča, on the right bank of the River Danube. Widespread cinnabar use led to mercury poisoning, as documented in the bones of Neolithic people from Perdigões, Portugal. Geological and mineralogical knowledge began to be accumulated across Europe, the Near East and wider Eurasia. As the researchers studying the Gavà Complex conclude:

The present study suggests that the Neolithic miners recognized simple three-dimensional geological structures (tabular bodies, as fractures and the stratigraphic discordance between the Silurian gray shales and the Quaternary caliches, clay deposits and debris), and used these observations to plan new mines and/or to search for new resources. There is sufficient evidence that the Neolithic miners formed their own ideas about which rocks were favorable to find variscite bearing veinlets (gray shales) and which were not (brown and multicoloured shales). We have found no evidence that the miners dug indiscriminately into the rocks

Cold Forging - The Dawn Of Metals

As we draw towards the end of the story, we need to finish on the last rung of the technological ladder - cold forging, or cold working. This refers to manipulating metals without the use of heat, or at least using very low temperatures. Cold forging appears all over the world, from the high Arctic to Anatolia, and even without the later sophisticated metalworking methods, it provides useful cutting edges, points and durable tools.

Typically cold forging refers to copper, although meteoric iron can be cold worked, as the Inuit of Greenland discovered. Native copper, the fortunate occurrence of a metal unbound to other minerals, can be easily worked wherever it is found. Around the North American Great Lakes, the Old Copper Complex cultures made use of native copper possibly as early as 9,500 years ago, which makes them amongst the earliest metal working peoples. The area around the Levant and Anatolia saw an obvious transition from Epipalaeolithic peoples using malachite for green pigments, to early Neolithic worked copper (Aşıklı Höyük, Nevali Çori), followed by annealed copper beads and pieces around Çayönü Tepesi and Çan Hassan (6000 BC) and then a smelted and cast copper awl at Tel Tsaf, Jordan Valley, Israel around 5,000 BC. Copper extraction and working developments in the Balkans follow a similar pattern.

Without heading into metallurgy proper, this seems the right place to stop in a potted history of pre-metallurgical fire and mineral technologies. We've seen how the first developments of fire and pigmentation grew from their simple and sporadic roots, through increasingly complex and surprisingly early methods of heat control and mineral use, to the first stirrings of copper working across different parts of the world. I've necessarily left out many places and examples to make the article manageable, but hopefully you'll agree that this is a fascinating story of human creativity and innovation, and that metal working was the end result of millennia of tinkering and experimentation, both for utilitarian tools and more esoteric and artistic endeavours.

PARANTHROPUS - THE EARLIEST TOOL MAKERS?

*Who made the first stone tools,
and what did they eat?*

The earliest phase of prehistory is a mess. A thick fog-of-war full of numerous hominin species, none of which can be genetically analysed and are often just crumbling fragments or portions of skulls and teeth. The surest guide we have is the ever faithful stone tool, which represents the most crude and basic approach to lithic production, named the 'Oldowan industry', after Olduvai Gorge in Tanzania. Of course, other species make use of tools, including those made of stone - capuchin tools can be confused for early human tools, and some researchers have even identified a 'Chimpanzee Stone Age' around Côte d'Ivoire. Primates making tools does of course raise questions about how we identify those made by early humans, rather than other branches of the family tree. A 2021 paper embarrassingly reported that horses and donkeys can unintentionally create stone tools just through the action of their hooves:

> we show that equids can sometimes also produce equally complex cores with conchoidal breakages that exhibit the characteristics of intentionally-flaked hominin artefacts by bipolar technique and methods. As a result, sharp edged flakes with percussion platforms, previous scars and bulbs, which can easily be mistaken with hominin-made flakes, are also produced by equid self-trimming. Given the ubiquitous presence of equids in landscapes inhabited by hominins, this imposes caution when interpreting isolated flaked rocks and urges some degree of revision of the criteria to identify strictly hominin-made tools.

Given these qualifications it is no surprise that a huge cloud of uncertainty hangs over everything in this field - which hominin species is the direct ancestor of Homo sapiens? Which species made the first stone tools? Did our earliest forebears eat meat or just plants? Could these archaic people talk to one another? The questions never end.

Resolving the problem of how the Homo genus arose is one of the biggest and most difficult questions across all the sciences. We can narrow down the primate family into four categories: the New World monkeys, the Old World monkeys, the Great Apes and the strange Prosimians (lemurs, tarsiers etc). The Great Apes can be, very simply, subdivided again into chimps (Pan), gorillas, orangutans (Pongo) and 'humans' (Homo), which itself contains all our weird and wonderful ancestors. The human-chimp split was the last of this group, and exactly when and how it occurred is still debated. One semi-plausible scenario holds that the ancestors of humans, chimps and gorillas were separated into three regions by the Zaire River and the Rift Valley, perhaps 7-10 million years ago. I'm not including the Asian branches of the primate family here, those mysteries will need another article.

This new family branch immediately produces some fascinating species - around 7 million years ago we get Sahelanthropus tchadensis, then at 6 million we see Orrorin tugenensis, around 5 million Ardipithecus ramidus, and at 4 million Australopithecus arrives. The Australopithecines are assumed to be the ancestral species to our own, specifically Australopithecus afarensis. These guys leave fossilised tracks and appear to be the first 'toolmakers', creating the first 'pebble choppers' and mastering the techniques of striking a core to produce a deliberate flake of stone.

But like all these species, the boundaries and names are relatively arbitrary, and researchers are constantly re-defining the groups and how they can be classified. If you work in the field you'll know that the tendency is either towards 'lumping' or 'splitting' - lumping different fossils together under one name, or splitting different fossils into new species. One such debated group is Paranthropus.

Paranthropus is an outlier in an already crowded field. A robust creature, somewhere between a gorilla and a human, with extremely powerful jaws. The muscles for grinding dense foods were connected to a crest on their skull for extra power, and they likely combined walking upright with the ability to climb. Three identified sub-species existed: P. aethiopicus, P. boisei and P. robustus, spread out from east to south Africa. The huge jaws of Paranthropus have typically coloured every interpretation of their diet, pushing them towards a grinding-chewing plant eater. Something like a migratory leaf, bulb, root and fruit eater, complemented with honey and insects, has been the general impression. But the reason to write this article is a new paper from Science which potentially changes much about what we know of Paranthropus.

The paper, entitled Expanded geographic distribution and dietary strategies of the earliest Oldowan hominins and Paranthropus, was published in early February this year in Science. The authors present findings from excavations at Nyayanga, Kenya, many of which are remarkable. In summary:

Oldowan stone tools were found in contexts dating to 3.032 to 2.581 million years ago.
1776 bones were recovered in good condition. Two hippos display evidence for butchery, in some cases with the stone tools associated and even touching the bones.

Teeth from a Paranthropus species were found in close association with the tools and butchered bones.

Use-wear analysis of the tools revealed evidence for both plant pounding/grinding and butchering animal remains.

> The behaviors preserved at Nyayanga are at least 600,000 years older than prior evidence of megafaunal carcass and plant processing and substantially predate the increase in absolute brain size documented in the genus Homo after 2 Ma (24). The late Pliocene expanded geography of the earliest Oldowan, and new evidence of its use in diverse tasks amplifies our understanding of the adaptive advantage of early stone technology in hominin diet and foraging ecology.

What this means is that, if these results are accurate, the Oldowan stone tool industry was not confined to Ethiopia's Afar Triangle as often believed. It also means that Paranthropus ate a much wider diet and potentially had the capacity to produce stone tools, maybe even the earliest.

There are qualifications of course, and other 'firsts' have been published before. In 2015 a paper announcing an Oldowan site dating back 3.3 million years seemed to place Kenya again as ground-zero for the industry, and Kenyanthropus platyops as the suspected manufacturer. But in 2016 a response paper raised questions about the evidence and conclusions drawn. Suggestions that Paranthropus might have been the original tool-maker also date back decades, such as from this 1991 paper Who Made the Oldowan Tools? Fossil Evidence for Tool Behavior in Plio-Pleistocene Hominids:

> The most parsimonious interpretation of all present evidence, including geochronological, archaeological, and diagnostic fossil evidence of the hands of Australopithecus spp., Paranthropus robustus, and Homo habilis, indicates that Paranthropus and Homo habilis were both early toolmakers. Paranthropus may have been the first maker of stone tools, and these "robust" australopithecines may have relied heavily on lithic and bone technology to procure (and process) plant foods.

A quick divergence into plant biology - photosynthesis can be split into two main phases, the 'light' and 'dark' reactions. During the dark period, the plant uses the energy captured from light to create sugars. It does this by converting carbon dioxide from the air into a 3-carbon sugar, in a process called the Calvin cycle. At least, 95% of all plants do this. The remainder use a different process, which ends up with a 4-carbon sugar. These are called C3 and C4 plants respectively. Why this is important is because C4 plants are a very particular group, which contains grasses. C4 plants take up more carbon than C3, which means they have a different ratio of the carbon-13 isotope. Animals which feed on C4 foods are therefore identifiable through isotope analysis of their remains. In the story of early humans this is important, since around 3.5 million years ago the isotopic evidence shows a shift from a predominantly C3 to a more C4 enriched diet. Paranthropus has long been presented as an example of a C4 specialist, moving to grasslands and more open, temperate environments to exploit those plants. But we now have the possibility in front of us that meat played an important role in their diet, meat from animals which fed on C4 plants. It is therefore possible that some of this C4 enriched signature came from animals, rather than plant foods.

The results from Nyayanga confirm that both plants and meat were prepared by Paranthropus using stone tools, so we're not ruling out that they ate a lot of fibrous plant material. But we must now expand our range of habitat, species and diets away from earlier assumptions. Other hominin species, in other places, were using stone tools to eat an omnivorous diet. Given that Paranthropus is likely not a direct ancestor to modern humans, we can't claim that meat and tool use were the reasons for our success.

Lots of questions remain - did Paranthropus simply steal or scavenge the tools? Did they hunt or stumble upon the hippos? How widespread and how old was the Oldowan industry? Who else could have been using that toolkit?

I've always been a believer that apparent revolutions in human development are always older than they appear - fire, hunting, tools, language and so on. My hunch is that we'll see both the Oldowan tools and meat eating pushed back further in time in the coming years.

THE BALTIC CORDED WARE: WHEN THE HERDER MET THE HUNTER

Is this the first known case of European farmer-herders 'going native'?

In general, farmers eventually win against hunters. It's a dynamic we've seen play out on every continent, and with the exception of marginal and inhospitable geographies, farmers either push out or convert hunter-gatherers to agriculture. But the process isn't linear nor inevitable in the short-term, and the strange interactions of the borders in between still fascinate us - the Wild West, the frontier, the explorer entering the jungle. When Neolithic farmers first encountered European foragers, a whole range of relationships occurred, from warfare to peaceful co-mingling, and as the static farmers gave way to the incoming steppe herders yet more complex societies arose. One of these was the massive Corded Ware Culture, a huge territory of different subgroups which practised a mixed farming-pastoralist economy. Despite millennia of agricultural spread however, there were still pockets of hunter-gatherers in Europe, particularly on the northern coastlines. The story I want to outline here is the curious tale of when the Corded Ware moved into the eastern Baltic, encountering the amber-trading fisher-foragers, whose culture and customs dated back far beyond the Corded Ware, with echoes of the archaic Palaeolithic. But they were not eradicated, nor did the Corded Ware leave. Instead something new temporarily emerged, a hybrid society which we are only just beginning to understand.

Ceramic Foragers - Setting The Scene

Lithuania, Latvia and Estonia occupy a unique geographical position in prehistory. A rich productive environment, situated on a sea which readily connects Sweden, Finland and northern Europe, and with easy access to the eastern grasslands and major river systems. The inhabitants of the eastern Baltic received pottery before the first farmers arrived, a forager technology which had slowly diffused across Eurasia, most likely with women marrying into neighbouring groups, bringing their ceramic-making skills to new people. Around the 6th millennium BC life was changing in this region. Much of the Baltic and Finnish/Karelian peoples had adapted to life with precious little flint, making use of slate, quartz, bones and other materials to make tools. As a result, long-distance trade routes had opened up down into northern Europe, bringing coveted amber and Polish 'chocolate flint', as well as red and green slates from northern Scandinavia and Lake Onega. Two broad cultures appear to develop between 5200-4200 BC - the Baltic Narva Culture and the larger Comb Ceramic Culture, which stretched from the eastern Baltic to the Urals. Genetically these were a mixture of Eastern and Western Hunter-Gatherers, although the ratios were different: about 70% Western and 30% Eastern for the Narva, and 65% Eastern and 15% Western for the Comb Ceramic, with an intriguing 20% Steppe Herder ancestry as well. Alongside these were a host of other smaller Mesolithic/Neolithic cultures - the Zedmar, the Neman - but we'll try and keep things simple.

The Narva were one of those hunter-gatherer cultures that don't make sense to modern ears. They were largely sedentary, made pottery and buried their dead in cemeteries. They constructed stone and wooden pit-houses, with indoor fireplaces that used large stones to keep the inside warm during the night. They fished, hunted seals, tracked deer, gathered wild fruits and traded amber for flint. Their world was one of rivers, marshes, coastlines, lagoons and small islands. It was into this watery scene that the Corded Ware and Globular Amphorae cultures arrived.

The term 'Neolithic' is worth highlighting for a moment. To western archaeologists the word refers to the novel package of people, technology and foods which arrived in Europe from Anatolia around the 7th millennium BC. To an archaeologist from eastern Europe the word means something else - thanks to the legacy of Soviet archaeological theory, 'Neolithic' refers to the process of a hunter-gatherer tribe becoming sedentary and eventually adopting agriculture, which starts with ceramics. For this reason we have a muddle of terms now for ceramic foragers in northern Europe - Mesolithic, sub-Neolithic, Neolithic - which describe largely sedentary, pottery-using hunter-gatherer-fishers.

When Did Farming Reach The Eastern Baltic?

If the Neolithic was traditionally defined as the emergence of sedentary, pottery-using farmers and pastoralists, how do we know when the Neolithic reached the Baltic? The Narva and other fisher-forager peoples were already stationary and already using ceramics. According to conventional wisdom, some kinds of domestic animals reached Lithuania around 5900 BC, their bones and teeth appearing in settlements, in graves and personal ornaments. But upon closer inspection, we can safely say this is nonsense. In a pretty damning paper from 2016 called Deconstructing the concept of Subneolithic farming in the southeastern Baltic, researchers got access to the archives of these supposed domestic animal remains and thoroughly debunked them:

> An investigation proved that most of, or possibly all, the early farming "evidence" came from the wrong identification of the plant and animal species and incorrect dating of crop remains and domestic animal bones. The errors of dating were caused by the fresh water reservoir effect being ignored when dating the bulk lacustrine sediment samples, by the failure to evaluate the impact of the palimpsest and bioturbation phenomena on the formation of an archaeological layer, and by insufficient attention to stratigraphy and spatial documentation of the finds during very extensive archaeological excavations in the second half of the 20th century

This sounds very technical, but essentially it boils down to sloppy work. Teeth were incorrectly identified, animal bones which had been buried inside older layers were labelled Neolithic, when direct dating revealed them to be millennia younger. Despite excavators noting that Iron Age and Mesolithic pottery sherds were all mixed together, they still referred to the goats, sheep and cattle bones as Neolithic. When farmers plough, or dig ditches, or dig waste pits, it is easy for older objects to become tangled up with new. The earliest dates the 2016 paper could find for domesticated animals and crops was between 3200-2700 BC.

Fortunately these dates correspond fairly precisely with waves of pottery coming from the outside. Around 3200 BC ceramics from a culture called the Rzucewo turn up at Nida, Lithuania. Globular Amphora remains start appearing at Šventoji in 2700 BC and somewhere between 2800-2400 the Corded Ware emerges into the eastern Baltic. The Globular Amphorae descend from a mixture of Mesolithic hunter-gatherers and Anatolian Neolithic farmers, whilst the Corded Ware shows a more complex mixture of Globular Amphorae and a connection to the Yamnaya-derived steppe herders who moved into central and western Europe around 3000 BC. The Rzucewo are a strange culture, and we'll discuss them more as we go on.

It seems to be the case that the Narva maintained their culture and way of life after contact with the Globular Amphora people, perhaps exchanging amber for vessels of dairy or cereals. The neighbouring Neman Culture in Poland/Belarus shows that the Narva swapped pottery for good flint, and that the Rzucewo people also traded in the mixed agricultural-foraging borderlands. But until the arrival of the Corded Ware proper, the Narva seem independent - carving elk head figurines, producing pottery with their distinctive crushed shell temper and hunting and fishing as they always had done.

Enter The Corded Ware

This isn't the place to provide a detailed overview of the Corded Ware Culture, but suffice to say they were one of the most pivotal in European history - transmitting the Indo-European cultural and linguistic substrate which forms the foundation of European identity and her languages. The vast Corded Ware area can be subdivided into smaller, more regional peoples - the Battle Axe, Single Grave and so on. Based around pastoralism and some agriculture, the economy of the Corded Ware was bound to come into conflict with local hunter-gatherers and settled dense agricultural zones.

Studies into Corded Ware diet and mobility indicate that they ate more protein enriched foods than the earlier Neolithic - potentially coming from dairy or from manuring their crops. Women had a more varied diet, ate more vegetable and grain-based foods and moved around more, a combination best explained by females travelling to marry into new groups. Corded Ware settlements are more rare than for previous Neolithic societies, which is often explained by their pastoralist lifestyle, and the eastern Baltic is no exception. Both human remains and habitation sites are unusual, in part due to the acidic soils of the Finnic-Baltic regions. Typically Corded Ware presence is identified by their distinctive pottery and stone battleaxes, as well as distinctive burial styles and grave goods. This was certainly a movement of new people into a new area, perhaps sons looking for new pasture land to accommodate growing herds. What they found was a mosaic landscape of rivers, dense oak forests, island chain coastlines and wetlands.

From what we can tell through pottery styles, the Baltic coastline underwent some profound cultural mixing. Looking at the two sites of Nida and Šventoji (Lithuania), we see that the Narva people of Nida seem to culturally blend with their Globular Amphora neighbours to form the Rzucewo, who in turn adopt more Corded Ware elements as time goes on. At Šventoji there is no Rzucewo, just the appearance of Globular ceramics and then the intrusion of the Corded Ware. If this is confusing to readers, it is no less clear to the archaeologists paid to study it. It looks as though western Lithuania and northern Poland morphed into a shared agricultural-foraging zone, which was then occupied by the Corded Ware, who in turn pushed east and north. Evidence of violence on the few Rzucewo and Corded Ware skeletons we have show increased traumatic lesions, a man from Duonkalnis looks like someone attempted to scalp him, but he survived it. The time difference between Globular Amphora pottery arriving at Nida and then Šventoji is about 500 years, an incredible length of time for a mere 55 mile difference.

The Corded Ware 'Going Native'

My interest in this topic came from a line in a 2020 paper: Fishers of the Corded Ware Culture in the Eastern Baltic:

> Here, we present new AMS radiocarbon (14C) measurements, pollen and macrobotanical data from sediment samples and a portable fish screen, as well as technological, molecular and isotopic data obtained from ceramic vessels from three CWC sites in the eastern Baltic. Overall, our results indicate a de-Neolithisation process undergone by some CWC groups, particularly in lacustrine and coastal ecotones, and a shift to hunting, gathering and fishing.

De-Neolithisation means the process of agro-pastoralists 'returning' or changing their economies to hunting and gathering, a phenomenon which has happened many times in many places. For the Corded Ware it seems that the ecology of the eastern Baltic was initially not all that welcoming to their way of life - feeding herds in open fields and growing crops on rich soils. Instead they switched to fishing, hunting and combining their dairy and cereal produce with the fruits of the land. But there is more to this story than meets the eye.

In studying the diet of the eastern Baltic Corded Ware we have two main sources of data - firstly the food residues which have been absorbed into their pottery, and secondly the different isotope ratios in their bones. If the Corded Ware switched their diets from cattle, pigs, cereals and milk to wild fruits, deer, elk and fish, then we could expect to see that reflected in both their pottery and their bone collagen. But we don't.

> *The isotope and molecular evidence combined show that the Early Neolithic ceramics from all cultures (i.e. RC, GAC and CWC) were used for the processing of aquatic resources, regardless of location or vessel type, compelling evidence for continuity in pottery use beyond the Neolithic transition. Except for the RC wares, the youngest samples, dating to the Late Neolithic and Early Bronze Age, had the highest frequency of aquatic biomarkers compared to the other Early Neolithic ceramics. In the majority of cases, the isotope data suggest these were organisms from either freshwater or brackish environments that characterise the region. Here, there is no evidence that pottery use radically changed with the introduction of domesticated animals. Intriguingly, the human stable isotope record shows dietary shift in the Neolithic period away from aquatic resources.*

This, taken from a 2019 article looking at Corded Ware ceramics, paints a confusing picture. The Corded Ware did not adopt Narva ceramics, but their own pots match the Narva cultural signal of processing fish and seafood. Their bones clearly show that they ate domesticated animals and drank milk, but why then do their vessels say otherwise?

One likely possibility is that the Corded Ware bodies we have found reflect a particular type of person from that community - someone of a higher rank or caste, an elite - someone who fed on their traditional foods. This implies that Corded Ware pottery was being made to serve more people than just these elites, mimicking in effect the diet and habits of the local Narva. Did Corded Ware males marry Narva women who continued their traditions but with a different ceramic style?

Looking wider than just the Baltic coast, the Corded Ware in fact spread out across the sea, making connections and moving into Sweden and Finland, from where they traded different styles of ceramics, using different materials. Did they inherit a sailing tradition and sea-lanes from the coastal Narva and other ceramic foragers, did they rely on them to do the trading and sailing? We know that the foraging Comb Ceramic culture expanded from the Baltic coast to visit the Åland islands sometime in the 6th millennium BC. Clearly the Baltic sea was no impediment to these maritime peoples.

Genetic studies of these foragers and the incoming Corded Ware show that there was little to no Anatolian farmer admixture, suggesting the Globular Amphora people did not marry into the Baltic Mesolithic peoples. In fact, one paper goes so far as to call the eastern Baltic a 'genetic refugium' for Mesolithic hunter-gatherers, those who were being driven north by the arrival of the Corded Ware? Ultimately the modern Baltic populations still carry the highest amount of Mesolithic Western Hunter-Gatherer ancestry today, indicating that the Narva and other forager-fisher peoples maintained a strong presence amongst the dominant Corded Ware culture.

How did the Corded Ware change when it moved into the eastern Baltic then? We've seen that their diet seemed to shift, at least for some. The Corded Ware settlements at first fall into a periphery-centre model, where the inland mobile Corded Ware differed from the coastal sedentary foragers. A Rzucewo double-burial indicates that both local and pastoralist customs were blending together as time went on.

Corded Ware burials still largely maintained their individualistic nature, rather than communal, but barrows seem to disappear as a traditional practice. The inclusion of horses and wagons decreases and amber artefacts increase - all commensurate with a mobile people having to adapt to new conditions. It's likely that the settled communities around the coastline, with their skill at collecting and producing amber objects for trade and links with overseas groups, drew the Corded Ware from their inland comfort zone to the edge of the Baltic and then beyond. In the process of mastering this new civilisational zone, the Corded Ware switched to harvesting the rich and plentiful foods on offer, whilst maintaining their own distinctive way of life. In turn the Narva and other foragers were attracted by the prestige of new animals and crops, but steadfastly refused to become agriculturalists, preferring to maintain their old customs. I'll leave this here with some thoughts from Christian Lindqvist (1987):

The late agricultural activities in north-eastern Europe as well as other Baltic Sea areas are probably due to the fact that the Corded Ware culture expanded into vast areas with dense forests and woodlands with fairly rich large-game fauna, and coasts with extremely rich aquatic resources, supporting a comparatively dense population of more or less permanently settled, pottery-using hunters, fishers and gatherers... The spread of domesticated animals to northeast Europe was nevertheless inhibited for thousands of years, probably due to the fact that this environment was not suitable for the Mediterranean domesticates, and that there still existed a comparatively rich fauna and flora, which was utilized by a hunting and gathering population.

DIONYSUS, REWILDING & THE INVENTION OF WINE

The interesting parallels between the god of the vine and the domestication of the grape

T he line between domestic and wild often seems more visible from the other side, a feeling of loss and restriction of freedom. Amongst the various Greek deities, Dionysus stands out for this feeling or sentiment of a 'foreign madness', a divine intrusion into the mundane, bringing revelry and disorder. In Nietzsche's work The Birth of Tragedy, he associates the Dionysian with this instinct to escape the dreariness of settled and squalid existence. It seems an essential component of a 'rewilding' vision that one is already tame, but looking for an exit, chafing at the bit. Myths have real foundations, in my opinion, regardless of whether they emerge from historical fact or as psychological impulses peculiar to the characteristics of a people. Dionysus is the god of wine, and wine is a product of domestication. In a strange way the discovery of wild grapes and their fermentation is a story which mirrors the academic debates over Dionysus himself - did wine come from outside of Greece, or was there a local tradition of wild grape wine? Did Dionysus appear in Greece as a foreigner, or was he too an invention of that world. And what of the orgiastic rituals and madness which accompanied him - did that cult invent something new, or were they mimicking something much older than themselves, a half-forgotten whisper of the wilderness?

Making Wine And Growing Grapes

Where to begin with a topic as vast as this? The wild grape - Vitis vinifera sylvestris. Humans have eaten this plant since the Palaeolithic, as one of the many freely available fruiting vines and edible species, but it wasn't until the Neolithic that something approaching controlled management appears in the record. Legions of archaeologists, botanists, plant geneticists and viticulturalists have tried and failed to understand exactly when and where the Vitus vine was first domesticated. Not only is distinguishing a wild grape seed from a domestic one an extreme test of patience, but there is no genetic boundary between wild and tame. Introgressions and admixtures between wild, feral and cultivated varieties have occurred countless times, both by accident and deliberately, and on top of this we aren't sure if there was just one point of domestication, or multiple independent points. As one research paper summarises:

> *Whether the grapevine was domesticated only once, or whether some varieties were domesticated independently, is a mystery hotly debated and different scenarios are proposed. The main hypothesis defined as the "Noah hypothesis", so named in honour of the biblical patriarch who planted the first vineyard on Mount Ararat after the flood, proposes that grapevine*

domestication processes took place in a well-defined restricted area (Single-origin model). In addition, a multiple-origin hypothesis that provides for the foundation of independent lineages originating from wild progenitors spread some place along the entire distribution range has been proposed (Multi-origin model).

Viticulture lore for the past few decades has placed the single origin of grape domestication somewhere between the Black Sea and Iran, the Transcaucasian belt, and Georgia is often touted as the centre of this event. But other work suggests that secondary, parallel or independent domestication events occurred elsewhere, especially in Greece and her sphere of influence. If grape domestication is one problem, the next to tackle is when and where wine production first occurred. Logically one can make wine from wild grapes, and people still do. Simply crushing the fruit and leaving it in a vessel to spontaneously ferment is enough. Therefore domestication and vinification need two separate explanations.

The fermentation of grapes produces complex flavour molecules, including malic, pyruvic, succinic and tartaric acids. These, in particular the latter, can now be extracted from sherds of pottery, pointing to wine production on Neolithic sites. At Dikili Tash, a large settlement in east Greek Macedonia, chemical evidence for wine making points back to 4,500 BC. Grape pips and grape vine charcoal (associated with pruning and vine management) also appear during the early and middle Greek Neolithic, suggesting that intensive viticulture was developing and the skills being passed along through generations. Similar chemical analysis of potsherds points to wine production in southern Armenia around 4,000 BC. Most likely these represent wild grape cultivation and use - grape pips are fairly unreliable as markers of domestication, but a 'proto-domesticated' grape is not unreasonable.

Pine resin seems to appear throughout the Neolithic as an additive to wine, perhaps stemming from its use as a preservative or waterproofing agent, and people found the taste pleasant. Retsina, wine with pine resin, is still produced in Greece today. Beer, mead and wine, along with other alcoholic beverages emerged across the Old World between the middle Neolithic and the Iron Age. Sumerian cereal beer, Egyptian barley wine, Bell Beaker vessels full of mead and flavoured with lime blossom and meadowsweet, Iberian drinks containing nightshade alkaloids, and the use of opium, cannabis and other intoxicants all start to flourish throughout Europe and the wider Eurasian zone. The bizarre 'Nordic Grog' is a case of mixing the local with the foreign:

> *In general, Nordic peoples preferred a hybrid beverage or 'grog,' in which many ingredients were fermented together, including locally available honey, local fruit (e.g., bog cranberry, and lingonberry) and cereals (wheat, rye, and/or barley), and sometimes grape wine imported from farther south in Europe. Local herbs/ spices, such as bog myrtle, yarrow and juniper, and birch tree resin rounded out the concoction and provide the earliest chemical attestations for their use in Nordic fermented beverages.*

> *The importation of grape wine from southern or central Europe as early as ca. 1100 BC, again chemically attested here for the first time... It also points to an active trading network across Europe as early as the Bronze Age in which amber might have been the principle good exchanged for wine. The presence of pine resin in the beverages likely derives from the imported*

wine, added as a preservative for its long journey northward.

Alcohol, and intoxicating plants in general, were clearly big business and of major social importance. Linear B texts listing wine exports are well documented, and the association between wine consumption and cultic activities in the palaces of Pylos and Knossos have been discussed for over a century in the literature. What does seem to shift however, in the move from a more communal Neolithic culture to the early Bronze Age, is the rise of a warrior class which focused on violence, feasting and alcohol. In a 2012 paper, Feasting and the consuming body in Bronze Age Crete and Early Iron Age Cyprus, researchers observe:

> *It is in the Bronze Age that alcohol acquired an immense power and role in social interaction. Within the Bronze Age, however, we observe a significant diversity. Consumption of alcohol, most probably wine, was a major factor in the rituals of commensality... Day and Wilson have argued from their work at Knossos that within the EBA we see a shift from a mode of communal consumption, where people used to pass round drinking vessels such as the chalice, to forms of communal individualism, with the adoption of the smaller individual drinking vessels such as goblets and cups*

Wine in particular came to acquire a prestige which other drinks did not. Throughout the Near East Bronze Age, wine was the drink of elites, listed on Linear B tablets along with meat, cheese and honey. It was the drink of banquets, feasts and those who did not work the land or toil for their daily bread. It seems likely that later Greeks adopted the social custom of diluting wine with water, in part to distinguish themselves from other barbaric peoples who engaged in similar bouts of competitive drinking.

Enter Dionysus - Thrace & Crete

Dionysus is one of the most elusive deities of the Classical world, and tracking down hints of his origins is like walking into quicksand. Much has been made of the psychological and religious qualities of his cult, and how this might point towards his genesis. From William Cassidy's 1991 paper, Dionysos, Ecstasy, and The Forbidden:

> The myths of Dionysos present him as a god in conflict with the ruling values of the polis. The maenadic ritual complex, whether civic or private, is closely attached to these myths; the priority of one form of expression or the other need not concern us...

> Thus the Dionysiac freedom is an intolerable outrage to the king, who represents not the wisdom of the Greek cultural system, but a one-sided and all too common perversion of it...

> In the topsy-turvy realm of Dionysos, excess becomes balance. These qualities of paradox and reversal lie at the heart of the Dionysiac world. In the myths, those who oppose Dionysos on the law-and-order platform set the stage for their own lynching. The theme of opposition to Dionysos cannot be connected to a specific period of Greek history; indeed the opposition seems rather to be a collective matter, both psychological

The oft-repeated claim that Dionysian values were in conflict with Greek social orthodoxy appears in all sorts of tropes, including Dionysus' disdain for beer drinking. Famously Lycurgus of Thrace banned the Dionysian cult, chopped down his vines and refused to drink his wine. His punishments were cruel and suitably Bacchic. But if Dionysus was a foreign god, and his ways were hostile to the civilised Greeks, where did he come from?

One possibility comes to us from Soviet archaeology, and while I highly doubt the conclusions, there are nonetheless some interesting arguments here. Around 4,000 BC on the shores of the Black Sea, there was a crossroads culture situated between the Danube and the Dniester Rivers - the Usatove or Usatovo. These people were likely a Cucuteni-Trypillia derived farming society who had been partially overrun by early steppe herders, but still preserved something of their culture. In 1980 the Russian archaeologist Evgenii Yarovoi excavated an Usatovo burial site near the village of Purcari. Within tumulus 1/21 he apparently uncovered the skeleton of a man who was easily 7ft tall (215cm), who possessed a healed traumatic thigh wound. The grave itself was furnished with many high status and cultic objects, including a wooden staff, unusual ceramics, sacrificed animals, rare metal tools and weapons and evidence of feasting. The ceramics were found to contain wormwood, tarragon, thistle, barley and teasel pollen. In the opinion of one researcher, Henry Shephard, this is the origin of the Dionysus cult - the limping giant matches the depiction of Zeus bearing Dionysus from his thigh; the wooden staff matches the thyrsus of Dionysus and also bears the older name for the Dniester

River, the Tiras; the wine and feasting match the orgiastic cultic activity. Its all a little too neatly wrapped up for my liking, but maybe others will find it persuasive. Certainly Thrace and perhaps further north have long been connected to Dionysus, not least through the Balto-Slavic origins of Semele, the mother of Dionysus in some stories.

Maybe what we can take from this argument is the following: Dionysus did not come from the Anatolian or Egyptian world, but rather from a combined farmer-steppe cosmology? This, in my opinion, accounts for the 'rewilding' aspect of his cult, the tension between the inside and out, the wild and civilised. But how can we test this? Are other versions available?

The Minoan civilisation is now known to have its roots in the Neolithic farming cultures of Europe, despite earlier generations arguing for a North African or another point of genesis. We know from Mycenaean Linear B texts that Dionysus was important enough to have had his name inscribed for the ages, but did his cult predate the Mycenaeans in Crete? Minoan religion has fascinated scholars and artists for centuries, with frescoes of bull-leaping, goddess-like women and serpents. An unpublished report on finds from the temple of Anemospilia point to the presence of human sacrifice - a young man bound and trussed on an altar, with a bronze dagger close by and heavy blood discoloration on his bones. The remains of butchered and dismembered children at Knossos also point to the famous Minotaur story. The Eleusinian Mystery Cult has been argued to derive from Minoan agricultural rites, and philologist Karl Kerényi explicitly connected Dionysus with Cretan rituals:

> *The overall Dionysian impression made by Minoan art*
> *can be broken down into concrete elements which are*
> *present in the same combination only in the Dionysian*

religion of known, historic times. To the Greeks, Dionysus was pre-eiminently a wine god, a bull god and a god of women. A fourth element, the snake, was born by the bacchantes, as it was by less agitated goddesses or priestesses in the Minoan culture. Wine and bull, women and snakes even form special, lesser, 'syndromes' - to employ a medical expression deriving from the Greek physicians. They are the symptoms, as it were, of an acute Dionysian state which zoe created for itself. For Greek culture, this was the Dionysus myth; for the Minoan culture, before the arrival of the Greeks, it was the myth of a god called by another name...

If we approach one aspect of Dionysus, the motif of the 'dying-and-rising' god, we can see perhaps that there is a grain of truth to the older connection between Dionysus and the 'Earth Mother' cult. The Greek Demeter and Persephone, the Anatolian Cybele, the Minoan Rhea - these all appear to have their roots in the Çatalhöyük depiction of a plump female deity flanked by lionesses. As much as I shy away from connecting a Neolithic Anatolian figurine, separated by maybe 6,000 years from our point of focus, to the Minoan world - the temptation is strong. Phrygian and Hellenic agricultural festivals share many common features, and Dionysus, as the child of Persephone, is intimately connected to this widespread cosmology. The Minoan chthonic rituals, held in caves, and their golden rings and images of a Persephone-like woman, point to Crete as a stronghold of this agri-cult. Dionysus is often linked with the 'divine child', born on Crete, and who promotes not the childbirth and nursing side of women, but their ecstatic passionate madness. Sparagmos - the act of dismembering and then eating a person or animal in a wild frenzy - is part of the Dionysian and Orphic canon, with potential evidence coming from the sliced-up remains found at Knossos.

So, far from Dionysus emerging amongst steppe-herder-farmers on the Danube plains, we have here a totally different birthplace for the mad god. An island race, connected to the Anatolian, Egyptian and Greek worlds, incubating a long-lost Neolithic religion involving snake-haired women, human sacrifice, deities perishing like wheat stalks and rising again, sunlight pouring into caves and a magical child, all wound around with ivy, bulls and serpents.

The Greek Dionysus

In parallel to the story of grape and wine domestication, Dionysus has possible roots everywhere. But like the vine, we should also consider the possibility that he was the product of the Greeks themselves, refreshed and strengthened with impregnations from abroad. To build this argument we must first acknowledge that Dionysus was for the longest time considered a foreign deity, and the counter-evidence has been a long time in the making - more may yet be found. Beginning with his name, the theonym Dionysus is one of the most contested in the field, with -dio being easily connected to Zeus, but -nysus spawning dozens of theories. Mount Nysa, trees, nymphs, daughters, brides, sacred rivers, sons, magical children, wine and many more have been proposed, but it seems likely that his name pre-dates any Indo-European derivative. Leading from this, the earliest reference to Dionysus appears on Mycenaean Linear B tablets, which is important. This indicates that Dionysus was an established deity prior to the Archaic and Classical Greek periods. According to Mycenologist Thomas G Palaima:

> The Linear B tablets do not include detailed prescriptions for ritual practice that might illuminate the nature of Dionysiac worship during the formative prehistoric stage of Greek religion. However, when

interpreted carefully using all the scholarly approaches that have been developed by Mycenologists during the last half-century, they establish that:

Dionysos was associated with Zeus and the sanctuary of Zeus in the region of Khania in western Crete. Both received offerings of honey.

The cult of Dionysos was widely enough known so that a central Cretan shepherd and an individual in service to the Pylian lawugeta.< were named after him....

A Cretan shepherd named after Dionysos on a tablet from Knossos might date to as early as ca. 1225 B.C.E. and an earlier tablet at Pylos (god or theophoric?) might date this early, but it definitely dates before the final destruction at Pylos in ca. 1200 B.C.E.

No longer can we deny Dionysos a Mycenaean pedigree. How and at what stages and from what sources, regions or cultures the various elements and characteristics of his later cult came to be are topics for historians of post-Mycenaean religion . But they must begin now with the Linear B evidence.

After names we have images. Dionysus may well be the oldest god in figurative art - Cycladic kraters from the end of the 7th century BC show Dionysus as an older bearded man, along with Hermes, Artemis, Apollo and Herakles, indicating his importance and status. The Attic vase painter

Sophilos decorated a majestic dinos with a picture of Dionysus between 580-570 BC. As Cornelia Isler-Kerényi, daughter of aforementioned Karl Kerényi, notes in her work on Dionysian iconography:

> *The idea that Dionysos did not originally belong to that pantheon and was inserted into it against the will of the representatives of constituted order is solely due to the dominating influence exerted by the Euripidean and generally tragic image of Dionysos on 19th century classicists... Dionysos himself and the dancers are explicitly connected with wine. In addition, the dancers, like the proto-satyrs, are attributed to the wild sphere of the cosmos, the antithesis of the civilised world. Thus, wine is closely linked with the division of the cosmos into two parts, which is clearly felt to be fundamental: 'inside' and 'outside'; culture and nature. In fact, in these first images wine has opposite values that, however, paradoxically, do not seem to be mutually exclusive: in the krater it is a symbol of civic life; in the drinking-horn it is a symbol of a primitive phase; in the wine-skin, used for transporting wine, it is a symbol of the transition from 'outside' to 'inside*

The point made here is that Dionysus may seem foreign to the highly cultured and patriarchal Greeks, both before and after the Dark Age period, but this actually tells us something very interesting about their religious and cultural life. To go back to Cassidy:

> *It is fruitless, given the frustrating silences of the ancient sources, to continue to attempt to establish that Dionysos was originally a deity foreign to Greece. He is as native as Zeus and Apollo, indeed his nature may be*

far more native to the Aegean world than that of his Greek father. As we find him, Dionysos is a Greek god; while his myths present him with foreign associations, and while he is clearly related to foreign deities and rituals of similar nature and perhaps even common origin, his form as we know it from Hellenic sources is Greek. His foreignness, as this paper has argued, is to aspects of Greek society, indeed the ruling aspects, but not to Greek culture as a whole

Nietzsche divides different civilisations into masculine and feminine types. The label is not meant as an attack, but rather he means to describe those cultures which have an instinct for receiving and creating culture, and those which seek to expand and broaden their own. To the Greek he labels feminine, their genius being to take up and incubate all those influences of the Bronze Age world - Thrace, Phrygia, Anatolia, Egypt. Dionysus looks, much like his liquor, to be a product of that Hellenic genius. His origins may be remote and elsewhere, but it took the Greeks to fully develop all those complex aspects of his nature into a powerful god.

Civilised Cities & Ecstatic Orgies

We've seen in the opinions of various scholars, the tension between the orthodox and conservative Greek polis and the crazed cultic behaviour of Dionysus' acolytes. In particular Dionysus attracts women - literally drives them insane, inflames their passions and turns them over to madness. His portal is wine, and his most devoted followers leave the city and head into the wilderness, to cavort with satyrs, dangerous animals and spirits. Euripides and others describe or hint at all manner of deviant activities. Nursing baby animals at the breast, ripping apart a fawn or calf with their bare hands and eating it raw, perhaps even killing and eating humans; dressing in goatskins, drinking milk, honey and wine; handling snakes, ritualised dancing and forbidden sexual activities, amongst others. Male followers might cross-dress as women, an activity strongly associated with Dionysus himself. A Macedonian epithet calls him 'Pseudanor' - 'false man'. The power of his maenads was immortalised in many stories, perhaps most famously when they ripped apart Orpheus and Pentheus, although for very different reasons.

None of this suggests though that Dionysus was a foreigner to Greek soil. On the contrary his personality and mythology are tightly bound to the fabric of their world. From his birth and parentage to his associations with Delphi and Apollo, his dismemberment by the Titans and resurrection, and his patronage to that most Greek of products - wine. His nature is transgressive and anarchic, he upturns the order and sows divine madness, but such was Greek reverence for all parts of the human experience that he was a vital god - dark, cruel, savage, intoxicating, chthonic, frenzied, barbaric and yet keeper of many essential mysteries. Much like the grape and the vine, he is a product of both the wild and the domesticated, and the resulting ferment is a temporary escape into a divine world.

PART FOUR- HISTORY

THE LOST BUSHMEN OF THE DRAKENSBERG: THE SAN, THE BANTU & THE MOUNTAIN

A tale of rock art, cattle-raiding,
warrior kingdoms and secret tribes

A running theme of interest to me is the interaction between farmers and hunter-gatherers. We've looked before at an archaeological case in the Baltic, where incoming Corded Ware pastoralist-farmers adopted some of the characteristics of the forager-fishers who lived on the shore. This time we will look at a very different scenario, the so-called 'Mountain Bushmen' of the South African Drakensberg region. As stories go this one has it all - horse riding cattle rustlers, poison arrow wielding guerrillas, Zulu warriors and ancient artwork, buried in deep caves on the mountain. We'll look at the Khoisan people and their origins, the Bantu expansions and the difficult question of how to define the 'barbarian'. The conflicts between the various pastoralists, farmers, hunters and soldiers around the mountain range produced several mixed groups of different genetic and cultural backgrounds, who banded together for survival. How do we define the 'San' and the 'Bantu' when they mix together, and what can this story tell us about how farmer-forager dynamics play out?

Setting The Scene

South Africa is one of the nurseries of human evolution. Numerous archaic human species have been identified here since the 19th century, including Homo ergaster, Homo habilis, the mysterious Homo naledi and, somewhere around 200,000 years ago, one of the earliest branches of the sapien family. These first modern humans are thought to be the ancestors of a distinct grouping known collectively as the Khoisan. While the name has sort of stuck, it is fundamentally misleading. The name gathers together some different elements, including the use of click consonant languages (Khoe-Kwadi, Tuu and Kx'a); a distinct phenotype of reddish-sienna skin, epicanthal folds and a short, gracile stature; a pastoral or forager lifestyle and the mitochondrial haplogroup L0. Within this however there are many differences, and the historical grouping is in part based on how both Europeans and black African Bantu groups defined non-agricultural peoples. The names 'San' and 'bushmen' are exonyms, imposed terms from the outside, much as we've seen with Imperial Chinese categorisations of 'raw' and 'cooked' barbarians. To split up the phrase Khoi-San, we have the Khoikhoi and the San. The San are considered the oldest and 'purest' group, descendants from the first humans to live in southern Africa. They don't consider themselves to be one collective people, preferring their own nations such as the !Kung, the Khwe, the Ju/'hoansi and the Ncoakhoe. The Khoikhoi, or Khoekhoen, (called the Hottentots in older literature), are pastoralist peoples, who possess the ability to digest lactose due to their partial roots in East African cattle-herders.

The San in particular have become anthropological celebrities, often viewed as living relics of the stone age. Post-war ethnography has striven to expel the racial science from the discipline, but still ends up replicating its own form of primitivism, reading into the San a kind of 'eternal egalitarianism', which has found expressions in popular science books with sentiments like "our ancestors only worked four hours a day" or "humans are naturally peaceful and cooperative, designed to live in small kinship bands". As the Guardian succinctly puts it:

> The Ju/'hoansi people of the Kalahari have always been fiercely egalitarian. They hate inequality or showing off, and shun formal leadership institutions. It's what made them part of the most successful, sustainable civilisation in human history

We can recognise that this is a politically motivated caricature, whilst also acknowledging that the San nations are typically more egalitarian than most other cultures on Earth (although even the San believe in a gendered division of labour). Sharing and socially enforced reciprocity/gift exchanges help build social capital which will withstand hunger or conflict; the bonds between people are the main form of institution.

Geographically the modern San are restricted to Namibia, Botswana and South Africa, with a handful living in Zimbabwe, Zambia, Eswatini, Lesotho and Angola. Historically however their range was almost certainly much larger. Although a topic of much academic dispute, hints exist in the form of ambiguous skeletal remains, tool typologies, proto-ethnographic descriptions and the existence of click-consonants amongst the Hadza and Sandawe peoples of Tanzania.

The area of focus in this article though is the eastern portion of South Africa's Great Escarpment, known as the Drakensberg or uKhahlamba/Maluti, meaning either 'dragon's mountains' in Afrikaans or 'barrier of up-pointed spears' in Zulu and Sotho respectively. Alongside its impressive range of birds, snakes, plants and the famous white rhino, sections of the Drakensberg are also packed with cave and rock art, the majority made by the different San peoples. Something like 20,000 paintings scattered across hundreds of caves are testament to creativity and mythologies of the San nations, some potentially dating back thousands of years.

A Brief History Of The San

If there is one popular fact known about the deep history of the Khoisan peoples it is this - their ancestors represented the earliest differentiated branch of the human family. Numerous studies sampling modern San nations such as the Ju/'hoansi, Nama and Taa broadly agree that a deep divergence occurred somewhere around 160-300,000 years ago (see Fan et al, Lorente-Galdos et al, Bergström et al and Schlebusch et al). However, this has often been taken to mean that the ancestral Khoisan were some kind of homogeneous group and that Homo sapiens as a species evolved into their current modern form in southern Africa. Neither of these claims exactly line up with the evidence. Genetically the Khoisan are extremely diverse, and studies focused on Khoisan population structures reveal a potential tripartite division into a northern, middle and southern set of groups. A well known paper from 2019 reported that, using mitochondrial DNA variation, the oldest cluster (the maternal L0 branch) indicated that southern Africa was the sapien homeland circa 200,000 years ago.

However, we have skulls consistent with anatomically modern humans in Morocco dated to over 300,000 years ago, and a study looking at Y-chromosome paternal DNA variation found the oldest variant (A00 haplogroup) centred around the Mbo people of western Cameroon (a non Khoisan group). Clearly there is much more to be discovered about prehistoric African populations and their evolution.

One point that has become increasingly clear however, is the size and decline of the ancestral Khoisan populations. It has been estimated that when the Khoisan split, they were the largest demographic on the planet. This means that all non-Khoisan, i.e all other humans on the planet, are the descendants of the smaller human group which separated itself around 200,000 years ago.

The next major demographic event for the Khoisan nations, skipping over the Holocene pastoralist migrations which introduced lactase persistence, was the coming of agriculturalists from the north, in a process called the 'Bantu Expansion'. The term Bantu is really a short-hand for Bantu-speaking peoples, since they are not an ethnic group per se. Like all major migratory events, there has been substantial debate over whether the Bantu Expansion was real or not, but just like other migration periods, it has been confirmed through the use of genetics.

> *The Bantu-expansion began around ~ 5–4 kya in West Africa, however, the initial phases of this expansion (5–2.6 kya) were slow and confined to West-Central Africa. Most hypotheses about the Bantu-expansion routes are based on linguistics and archeology, however, archeological and linguistic inferences do not agree on several aspects... After migrating south of the rainforest (probably somewhere around present-day Eastern DRC or Angola), the Bantu-speakers separated into two*

groups. One of these groups expanded eastward, whereas the other moved directly south giving rise to the genetically and linguistically distinguishable South-Eastern Bantu-speaker (SEB) and South-Western Bantu-speaker (SWB) populations, respectively. The SEB group that migrated eastward, after reaching present day Zambia, probably again split into two branches, one continued eastward while the other moved South–East... The first arrival of Bantu-speaking agro-pastoralists in southern Africa is estimated to be around 2 kya.

This study confirmed large-scale population replacement in southern Africa, where Later Stone Age ancestors of the Khoe-San hunter-gatherers were replaced by incoming Bantu-speaking farmer groups of West African genetic ancestry, introducing the Iron Age into the region

The mitochondrial and Y chromosome proportions in SEB have shown the interaction among the Khoe-San and Bantu-speakers to be female biased for the former and male biased for the latter

-Bantu-speaker migration and admixture
in southern Africa 2021

Of immense scholarly interest has been the phenomenon of linguistic influence in the direction of the Khoisan to the Bantu, famously the adoption of click-consonants amongst southern African Bantu languages. One study of the Nguni branch of the Bantu languages argues that proto-Nguni included a now extinct palatal click, indicating that Nguni speakers were amongst the first to make contact with the Khoisan. Indeed a great many studies conclude that Nguni Bantu groups arrived in southern Africa around AD 300, marking the end of a millennia long expansion, which resulted in Bantu languages dominating Sub-Saharan Africa. Expansions of these kind also include the Indo-European, Austronesian and Pama-Nyungan.

The process of expansion and contact between the incoming Bantu farmers and the different Khoisan (and Pygmy) peoples was not homogeneous. In some places a total replacement seems to have occurred, and in others substantial admixture. In this way it mirrors other agricultural-forager dynamics, perhaps where conflict over prime farming land drives foragers away and intermixing occurs where the environment favours mutual reciprocity:

> There are no historically known Khoisan-speaking groups in either Zambia or Malawi or further northeast, and modern-day populations of Malawi show no traces of Khoisan-related ancestry. It is thus clear that the incoming Bantu-speaking populations must have replaced the Khoisan-related autochthonous populations with hardly any admixture... This is in contrast to populations such as the Kgalagadi and Tswana from Botswana with 33–39% and 22–24% Khoisan-related ancestry, respectively, or the Sotho, Xhosa and Zulu from South Africa with between ~10–24% Khoisan-related ancestry

> Analyses of uniparental data show a strongly sex-biased signal of gene flow in southern Africa, with Khoisan-speaking populations receiving paternal lineages from food-producers, whereas Bantu-speaking

groups incorporated mainly Khoisan-related maternal lineages. The intensity of this sex bias increases from North to South, possibly indicating changes in social interactions between immigrating groups and autochthonous peoples over time

-The genomic prehistory of peoples speaking Khoisan languages 2021

It is difficult to say today that either group possesses any real 'purity', both the modern Khoisan and modern Bantu peoples are still separate and still phenotypically identifiable, but genetically, linguistically and ancestrally they are mixtures of both groups. The branching separation that began 200,000 years ago suddenly came back together, rapidly. Added to this were the incoming Europeans to southern Africa, bringing new technologies, religions, languages, animals and so on. Having looked at the Khoisan, we can finally turn to our story proper.

Kingdoms, Colonies And Caves

The Drakensberg must have been a haven for hunter-gatherers, rich in eland, hartebeest, zebra and wildebeest during the summer, and full of sheltered caves and crags. The ancestral San had been living around the modern KwaZulu-Natal area for probably 20,000 years at least, largely without interruption. But now there were newcomers in the valleys - around 1700 years ago the first Nguni farmers crossed the Limpopo River - bringing millet, beans, dogs, cattle, sheep, goats and iron tools. However, the San knew all about the Nguni. For several centuries before any farmer made a mark in their earth, the San were aware of their existence through extended networks of trade, ceremony and kinship - iron and copper beads, shell ornaments, and soapstone bowls dated to around 2,000 years ago speak of wide-ranging movements and contacts. The Khoisan also strangely adopted pottery centuries before the Bantu style appears in the record:

> It has long been observed that pottery appears in the Southern African archaeological record prior to the arrival of the Bantu. A recent review concludes; 'Thin-walled, fibre tempered pottery appears [in Southern Africa] two to four centuries before the arrival of Iron Age agro-pastoralists who were uniformly associated with thick-walled ceramics' (Sadr & Sampson 2006) ... Given that the pottery is broadly contemporaneous with arrival of pastoralism, it would not be extravagant to assume that it was part of the same wave of introductions, although Sadr & Sampson (2006) argue for independent invention.

- Was there an interchange between Cushitic pastoralists and Khoisan speakers in the prehistory of Southern Africa and how can this be detected? Blench 2008

As the Nguni made contact with the San we see an explosion of so-called 'shaded polychrome' rock art style, along with artistic perspective and new animals depicted in the images. The Drakensberg art researcher Aron Mazel argues that shaded polychromes should be dated to the time just before and after contact with the Bantu, as part of a 'defensive traditionalist' response to the changing human situation.

Then a very strange thing happens. The San seem to abandon the Drakensberg for nearly 600 years, before returning back as the climate shifted and many farmers moved away. We'll cover the responses later on, but its possible that many Nguni farmers abandoned agriculture and joined the San in their 'return' to a foraging lifestyle. What the San were doing in the lowlands for 600 years is difficult to know, but all the Nguni languages which branched away during this time contained consonant clicks, so there must have been sustained contact of some form or another, perhaps the San becoming 'clients' of the farmers, providing them with wild meat or honey in return for cheap carbohydrates and alcohol?

The assimilation of the San into the world of the Bantu was probably piecemeal and contained many points of resistance and secrecy. The Drakensberg anthropologist Frans Prins described it thus:

> These new immigrants most probably also introduced a new ideology based on ancestor veneration, witchcraft accusations, and an elaborate pollution concept. Unlike the socially less complex San, most aspects of their religious outlook would have been ritualised. For almost a millennium, if not longer, Later Stone Age hunter-gatherers would have been exposed to this new religious ideology and would have incorporated aspects thereof, albeit selectively, into their own worldview. In addition, they would have been exposed to a people whose socio-political organisation was based on simple chieftainships rather than the band. All these factors would have contributed to the way in which some Later Stone Age hunter-gatherers reorganised their world-views in order to cope with changing political realities.

The Nguni term for the San was 'aBatwa', which is interesting since many contemporary central African Pygmy peoples are known by names like 'Twa' and 'BaTwa', suggesting a deeper Bantu expression for 'wild other' or non-agricultural societies. However, this 600 year period of sustained contact and intermixing also affected the Nguni as well - in particular the aspects of San culture which the Bantu would have found both useful and frightening, such as their extensive knowledge of medicinal and poisonous plants, waterholes, animal migrations, cave systems and the San religious practices of 'trance dances' and rainmaking. As time went on this merging pushed certain Nguni groups - like the Entlangwini - from being considered farmers, to being labelled 'Botwa' or 'aBatwa'. For some, the Bantu were becoming San.

With the consolidation of Bantu chiefdoms and later kingdoms, the colonisation of Madagascar by Austronesian sailors and the exploration of the east African coastline by the Romans, Greeks, Persians, Indians and interlinking traders, the southeast corner of Africa began to be knitted into a wider Indian Ocean political and economic system. The Portuguese started venturing around the Cape during the 15th century, coming into contact with the Khoikhoi, often with violent results, most famously at the Battle of Salt River (1510 AD), where a force of about 150 armed Europeans were driven back by warriors from the !Urill'aekua Khoikhoi clan. Kingdoms such as Mapungubwe (11th to 13th century), Bokoni (16th to 19th century) and the Tswana Kweneng' (15th to 19th century) rose across southern Africa, representing various Bantu peoples, but the Drakensberg remained largely independent. Even as the Nguni and Sotho peoples began penetrating the mountain ranges after 1300 AD, the temperature effectively prohibits the farming of sorghum and pearl millet. It was only after the Portuguese introduced maize to the region that Bantu-led colonisation of the Drakensberg could begin in earnest.

The centuries after contact with the Portuguese thrust southern Africa into a new position of global importance. For millennia the Khoisan had been isolated from the rest of humanity, all of a sudden their shorelines were crucial real estate in the ebb and flow of goods and people between the

Atlantic and Indian Oceans. First the Portuguese, then the Dutch, and then the British came with the same aim - protect the shipping lanes - but expansion from port to fort, fort to farm, farm to settlement seemed inevitable. Not only did this result in the importation of new peoples and settlers, such as the Dutch Boer settlers and the Cape Malay slaves, but it set off a chain reaction of violence as different polities scrambled to control and benefit from the new trade routes.

The major event for our story goes by a number of names - the mfecane or difaqane - meaning the 'crushing' or 'forced migration'. The causes of the violence are hotly debated and decades of books have been written on the subject. The pressures of water-hungry maize, drought, ivory hunting, slavery and the rise of an expansionist Zulu Kingdom under Shaka Zulu (1787-1828) have all been blamed, but ultimately the consequences were over a million people were killed in a bloody series of wars which saw massive internal migration and disruption on the eastern half of the country. The consequences for those Nguni and San living in and around the Drakensberg were profound.

Horses, Raiders & Shapeshifters

Bantu-San relations had deepened centuries prior to the mfecane. Linguistic analysis of the earliest Nguni groups around the Drakensberg postulates that Proto-Nguni diverged, with a Proto-Drakensberg and subsequent Proto-Woodlands and Proto-Uplands communities following on between 1000-1200 AD. Where conditions allowed farmers began terracing, but in other places cattle were the main food source. This is important because foragers often seem more inclined to become pastoralists than farmers, at least to begin with. Proto-Uplands speakers switched out the older term *-tyani for 'grass' with the Khoisan derived *-ngca, but also innovated on speech terms for 'wild places' or non-domestic settings (see Jimenez 2022), indicating both agricultural anxieties but also contact with the San. The Little Ice Age (circa 1300 AD) saw Bantu farmers migrate around the eastern seaboard, and by the time of the mfecane both Zulu and Xhosa Bantu speakers reflected their historical entanglements with the Khoisan through the use and development of click consonants. The Botwa label indicates that the division between 'Bantu' and 'San' was not just one of blood, but of different modes of existence. Just as English speakers use phrases like 'going native', so the agriculturalists would have seen their neighbours becoming hunter-gatherers as a departure from their 'way of life', and thus the initial distinction between San and Bantu became over time more one of domestic vs wild or civilised vs barbarian that we find all over the world.

The history of southern Africa from the mid 17th century to the end of the 19th is immensely complex, including nine Xhosa Frontier Wars, the mfecane and rise of the Zulu Kingdom, the Great Trek, the Cattle-Killing Movement and the formation of numerous new groups and polities such as the Sotho, Mfengu, Swazi, Boer Republics and Matebele. Within this turmoil the San had to adapt to survive. One of these adaptations was mastery of the horse. By the 1820's lowland groups such as the Mpondo had acquired horses from Europeans and by 1835 they were being used by Xhosa, Mfengu refugees, San and Khoikhoi all across the Drakensberg interior. The modern Basuto pony is a legacy of these trades, thefts, gifts and cross-breedings. The second adaptation to the Drakensberg becoming a mess of mfecane victims and expanding European territories was to switch from hunting animals to raiding animals.

It's impossible to say how many original San hunter-gatherers there were in the early 19th century. Both European and Zulu testimonials suggest that differences exist, but also that the San and Nguni Bantu were similar in many ways:

The sole source of physical description is encountered in the records of Pastor P. Filter who interacted with two separate groups of Drakensberg 'Bushmen' who migrated to the eastern Transvaal (quoted in Prins 2004). He remarks on the difference between the 'black Bushmen' and the 'yellow Bushmen', with the 'black Bushmen' being from the foothills of the Natal Drakensberg and the 'yellow Bushmen' coming from Lesotho (Filter 1925: 187). Oral memories of the Drakensberg San also refer to a difference between yellow 'Bushmen' and Black 'Bushmen' (Prins per. comm., December 2004)...

There is some Zulu oral evidence that suggests difference, but is reported in a way that appears more fantastic than real: ' ... Zulus have stories about Abathwa, dreadful to all men because they are like snakes in the grass. They are small people, who live in the rocks up-country and discharge on the unsuspecting traveller their deadly, poisoned arrows' (Krige 1936:359). These stories of conflict may be from the mfecane period and the disruptions in central Zululand that had repercussions for the entire region as peoples shifted alliances and moved geographically (Wright 1983).

As the San disappeared the myths grew into fantastical tales. Zulu-speaking people related that they had grown up learning that Abatwa were not 'Bushmen', but magical mischievous creatures much like a Tokolosh (evil goblin-like creature). Informants in the Drakensberg told me that these fantastic tales were one of the causes of violence against people of Abatwa descent, which would have formed another reason for secreting themselves away as Zulu or otherwise (Fieldnotes 2004). Krige's reference to oral evidence appears to hark back to a time of conflict between the Nguni and Abatwa (1936: 359). Acts of violence by the Nguni began as conflict, and power struggles forced them deep into San territory. Tales of horrible and dangerous Bushmen raining down arrows on 'unsuspecting travellers' and cannibals in the mountains echo these early conflicts Uames Stuart Archive 1905; Krige 1936).

-Silencing the past: historical and archaeological colonisation of the Southern San in KwaZuluNatal (2015)

It seems likely that some phenotypically 'San' groups still existed, and that mixed San-Bantu peoples lived in different forms in and around the Drakensberg. Some of these, under the immense pressure of new refugee groups moving in, banded together and became cattle-raiders. Much like in the American Plains, horses allowed for fast movement over difficult terrain and opened up opportunities to steal more horses and cattle. One of the most infamous groups whose name still survives is the 'AmaTola'.

The AmaTola were almost certainly a hybrid mix of San, Khoikhoi, Xhosa, Mfengu and disparate runaways and outlaws. However, the dominant 'San-ness' of their fleeting culture is hard to ignore. As mentioned, the spiritual power of the San was always revered and feared by the Nguni tribes, and the formation of raiding bands in the Drakensberg seems to have been animated by these supernatural powers. Five elements in particular constitute the AmaTola worldview: the horse, the gun, the medicinal root, the baboon and the rock-painting.

The horse and gun speak for themselves, symbols of frontier power everywhere in the world. The medicinal root belongs to a category of 'war-medicine' shared amongst the Bantu, the San and the KhoiKhoi - they are chewed or rubbed on the skin, or worn around the neck, and the effects are said to include 'bringing mists to conceal an army to making one's adversary forget, so causing one's opponent to be struck down, incapacitated or tied, to affect the flight of projectiles, turning spears aside and changing bullets to water, to allow bearers to pass their adversaries unseen'. The baboon was a magical animal to the San, one who cheats death and passes unscathed. To the Bantu baboons were either demonic familiars or annoying crop-stealing menaces. Amalgamating these two archetypes worked well for the raiders. Rock-art during this period became the only real archaeological data source from within the AmaTola, and although it shares deep continuity with San artistic techniques there are differences in style and composition. The images of raiders transforming into baboons or riding horses wearing wide-brimmed hats alongside baboons are fascinating. Researchers have posited that AmaTola 'war-doctors' are a creolised mix of San 'shamanic' practices and Xhosa traditions - the very name 'AmaTola' is likely a Xhosa word, the singular term for a war-doctor being 'itola' and plural 'amatola'.

The 'Secret San'

To wrap this story up it is worth discussing what happened to the San of the Drakensberg. As we've seen, for the last 1700 years at least they have been in increasingly close contact with the different Bantu, European, Malay and other groups which moved in and around the mountain. Both the San and Khoikhoi were targeted by Bantu slave hunters and sold to Boer frontier communities or were killed as raiders and bandits by commandos and warriors. Trapped between the expanding Zulu and Nguni tribes and the Europeans, the San became herders, farmers, indentured servants, slaves, outlaws, raiders and some retreated as far out of sight as possible. The legacy of mixing with the Nguni gave many the opportunity to 'hide' in plain sight as Ngunis, Xhosa, Zulus and other tribes - their darker skin and more Bantu features shielding them from persecution. But this worked the other way around as well, those Nguni which had become Botwa were seen as Bushmen, reflecting the complex mix of lifestyle and race which defined the different ways of living on the Drakensberg and elsewhere.

By the 1920's there were just hints of free San still living in the mountains. Bundles of arrows left on rocks, poison arrows killing people wandering amongst the caves, old men and women who still spoke the !Ga !ne language or knew where certain important paintings were located. After 1995 there was a revival of San self-identification, and the use of dual ethnicity labels. Hundreds of people have been identified by anthropologists as 'secret San', having been hidden by all sorts of tribes:

> Perhaps the most celebrated 'protector' of the mountain San was chief Moorosi of the Baphuti people. The Drakensberg San aided Moorosi when his mountain fortress was stormed by colonial forces in 1879 (Jolly 1996a: 30–61). However, Moorosi was by no means the only 'protector' of the Drakensberg San: various African groups, such as the BaTau, Mpondomise, Mpondo, Thembu, Bhaca, Duma, and Nthlangwini allied themselves at various periods to the San, and intermarriage frequently occurred (Wright 1971).

> In this regard individuals of acknowledged San descent are still consulted by their Bantu-speaking neighbours

for rainmaking and healing purposes. Unfortunately, their familiarity with the supernatural is also a double-edged sword in this social context. People of San origin, or who are conceptually associated with the San, are often blamed for witchcraft-related incidents. It often happens when villagers are struck by lightning, that the blame is placed on the supernatural abilities of the San.

One way in which San communities ensured 'protection' from African chiefs was to take on the clan or totem name of the chiefly lineage in their area of habitation. Today, many San descendants in the Drakensberg carry the clan names of Duma, Sithole, and Majola – all names associated with the chiefly lineage in the areas where they eventually settled. In Lesotho, a common name encountered amongst San descendants is Kwena, the royal totem of the Basotho people. Typically, San descent is established patrilineally, which is essentially a borrowed African system of kinship.

It is for this reason that they are also called the 'Secret San' (Derwent & Weinberg 2005) – a term that has been embraced by many of them at the present time. 'Secret San' tours are now officially conducted by San descendants of the Thendela community in the Kamberg Valley.

-Secret San of the Drakensberg and their rock art legacy (2009)

Apart from being an interesting story in its own right, one reason to study and learn about this history is to think through the dynamics of how farmers and foragers interact with one another in general. The different strategies of conflict, cohabitation, intermarriage, raiding, slavery, creolisation and hiding were not unique to the Drakensberg, and I think they are useful models to try and understand the Neolithic-Mesolithic transition in Europe, the expansion of agriculture in China and many other places. That farmers sometimes become foragers, foragers become pastoralists and pastoralists fight farmers, for example, is a structural response to the different needs and requirements of each mode of living. Hopefully this was an interesting story and I'd love to hear from anyone who lives or has travelled to the Drakensberg region if they have any other stories to share.

TWO TALES FROM LAOS: IRON AGE BATTLEFIELDS & DEMONS IN THE NIGHT

The Plain of Jars, Hmong guerillas & Sudden Unexplained Death Syndrome

he story I want to tell is something of a rambling tale, one that connects the Taiping Rebellion with Freddy Kruger, an anti-communist jungle war with an ancient archaeological mystery. There's no great moral at the end, just a loose gander around Laotian history. If there is a main character it is the Hmong people, if there is a main event it's the American military campaign of the 60's-70's. The region around northern Vietnam, Laos and southwest China is still somewhat mysterious today, part of that rugged, 'lawless' region dubbed 'Zomia' by historian Willem von

Schendel in 2002. Geographically and politically marginal, home to a mosaic of ethnic and tribal cultures, the uplands of the Indochina are still full of archaeological unknowns and turbulent, colourful histories. This meandering essay is the result of my own attempts to grapple with the formidable range of languages and peoples, especially in Laos, and also covers one of my favourite subjects - that interplay between society and biology we call a 'culture syndrome'. I explored one of these in an earlier essay looking at the 'berserker' phenomenon around the world, and here we'll look at another, the so-called 'nocturnal death' syndrome of the Hmong diaspora. We start our story in 1865.

Flags & Rebels, Wars & Rebellions

The Taiping Rebellion (1850-1864) was one of the largest and most devastating wars in human history. A colossal civil conflict fought between the Qing Dynasty and the Taiping Heavenly Kingdom, possibly resulting in over 20 million deaths. One outcome from the war was a multitude of small warbands based in the south known as 'Flag Gangs', often made up of ethnic Zhuang, who fled across the border into the Tonkin region in 1865. One of these, the Black Flag Army, became a major military force in the area, attacking local populations, plundering temples and harassing traders - including the Muslim 'Haws' and European vessels sailing on the Red River. The confusions between these incoming bandits and the legitimate Haw traders led to them all being collectively known as Haws. One reason for their lengthy campaigns was the backing of the Vietnamese of the Black Flags against the White Flag army, who had created a state of anarchy in Tonkin and defeated Vietnamese military attempts to bring them to heel. Hiring the Black Flags against the White succeeded for a time, but the door opened for the next wave of attacks from China, and in 1868 the Yellow Flag army crossed the border and brought the kingdom close to collapse.

With the French now eyeing opportunities to force open the river deltas and coastline to trade and influence, the Siamese under King Chulalongkorn also started sending troops north to quell the Flag Gang insurgency. The second of these expeditions was accompanied by a British surveyor James McCarthy. McCarthy had been sent from the Raj to the Siamese court to be the Superintendent of Surveys, and his legacy in the history of Thailand is formidable. His documentation of the 1884-1885 expedition was thorough and rigorous, ranging across the military and political disputes, nuances of geography and history, and he was the first to make the formal distinction between the peaceful Haw traders and the insurgents:

> Who and what were these Haw that brought so much misery on large tracts of country, and established such a name for cruelty as to terrorize a whole population? They were, in a word, Chinese brigands. At one time, Chinese traders, known in Luang Prabang as Haw, came down from the north in great numbers to traffic with the inhabitants, and when the peaceful traders gave place to brigands of the same nationality, the name of Haw was naturally transferred to these. Since the appearance of these marauders, communications and trade had ceased, and the whole district had been thrown into confusion. (McCarthy 1900: 44)

McCarthy personally trained seven Siamese officers in the art of surveying, for he was acutely aware that, for Europeans, the entire northern frontier was a blank, and must contain many curiosities. The area that McCarthy focused on was the Luang Prabang mountain range and the Xieng Khouang Plateau - a paradise of limestone, rivers, caves, cliffs, waterfalls and crags, today located in north Laos. To properly map the Mekong River, one must explore the Nam Ngum tributary, which starts in these rugged hills. McCarthy and his team made their way onto the plateau, and there found the most curious expanse of artefacts:

> As we approached our supposed rocks, we were astonished to find that they were gigantic stone jars; some were erect, some were on their sides, others broken. They were of the ordinary shape of water-jars. One that I measured along the broadest girth was 25 feet [7.6 m], the diameter of the mouth being 4½ feet [1.4 m], and it was six feet high [1.83 m]. Some of the people with me, who formerly lived in this beautiful country, say they were made by angels to drink liquors from (McCarthy 1888:126)

This was the first European documentation of the truly enigmatic phenomena known as The Plain of Jars. McCarthy was however, not the only European surveyor and explorer in the area. The French had also seen the chaos in Tonkin as an opportunity to extend their reach into the various river systems, and had selected the royal town of Luang Prabang as the best base for their operations. Luang Prabang had become an independent monarchy in 1707, but had become something of a vassal state to the different regional powers, including Siam. The 1860's had seen a flurry of French mapping activity, focused on the Mekong. The French officer Francis Garnier saw Luang Prabang's weakness as the perfect point of intervention, looking to place the kingdom under suzerainty to protect it from Siam. The Haw invasions from 1865 onwards closed off easy access, but in the 1880's the new Consul-General in Bangkok - Dr Jules Harmand -

appointed French naval surgeon Dr Paul Neis to travel back to Luang Prabang to offer French support. Neis, like McCarthy, documented his adventures, and included a striking anecdote of meeting a Xieng Khouang villager who had been disfigured by a marauding Haw bandit. The man had lost most of his lower face to a revolver, but the royal silversmith had fashioned a rudimentary silver jaw, which allowed him to continue smoking cigarettes.

The French succeeded in establishing a consulate in Luang Prabang, much to the annoyance of the Siamese. They wasted no time in appointing August Pavie and Pierre Cupet to start mapping and surveying northern Laos, focusing on overland and waterway routes that could link this isolated region with the coastline and wider French trade. The two also found the countryside devastated by the Haw wars, but also came across a field of stone jars. Ultimately these tensions over the territory sparked a short-lived war between Siam and France, which resulted in Siam ceding Laos to France. French Indochina had expanded, and the Plain of Jars was now on the map.

The Plain Of Jars

What exactly is the Plain of Jars I hear you ask? To date there are over 100 sites, found in Xieng Khouang and Luang Prabang, which collectively hold over 2,100 large stone jars or containers. Alongside these are around 200 stone disks. The jars are made from granite, sandstone, limestone and other rocks, between 1 and 3 metres tall, usually larger at the base and sometimes with a stone lid. Most jars are undecorated, but some have depictions of frogs, monkeys and tigers. The stone disks are burial markers, and the contents of the jars have included burnt bone, teeth, jewellery, pottery and metal objects. Of course what makes these so enigmatic is their mysterious origins and their function - what were they used for?

Local legend links them to a race of giants, who brewed alcohol in the jars. Viewed as something of a curiosity, the farmers of the region largely ignored them, and the Haws vandalised them. Serious scholarly work began with the colonial French government, who started documenting the archaeological and architectural legacies of Vietnam, Cambodia, Laos and Thailand. In 1903 the first colonial administrator of the city of Vientiane, Pierre Morin, created the first map of the jars, but the real breakthrough came with French archaeologist Madeleine Colani, who arrived in Vietnam in 1899. Her extensive fieldwork and excavation in and around the jars resulted in the authoritative 1930 work The Megaliths of Upper Laos. She concluded that the jars were the product of the Laotian Iron Age and that they were linked to a nearby cave crematorium, whereby certain bodies were cremated and placed into the jars. Work on the jars did not continue until the 1990's. What happened in-between is central to any future investigations of the site, but first we need to take a detour and talk about the Hmong.

Who Are The Hmong?

Chinese history often chronicles their interactions with 'barbarian' peoples. In their own parlance they split these into two categories - 'raw' and 'cooked' (sheng and shu). Late Imperial China struggled to pacify and control in particular five internal frontiers: Hainan, Yunnan, Sichuan, Taiwan and Hunan. One of the collective terms for these barbarians in Yunnan was the 'Miao', which applied broadly to non-Han peoples. Sinicized Miao, or 'cooked' Miao, were differentiated from the 'raw', who often lived in mountainous and marginal areas. One of these Hmong-Mien speaking peoples are known to us today as the Hmong, a label which, according to scholar Yang Dao, means 'free men'.

The Taiping Rebellion saw a massive exodus of people across the barely definable Chinese border into Tonkin, many of which formed and joined the different Flag groups as we saw. The Miao-Hmong may have been migrating as early as 1750, but certainly by the 1860's we have some documentary evidence for their settlement on the Xieng Khouang plateau.

> *The first concrete western record of a Hmong presence in the Indochinese Peninsula dates from 1860, when several thousand Hei Miao (or Black Miao, perhaps Hmu) 'soldiers' were seen entering North Vietnam from Yunnan. Some Annamites had memories of and told Bonifacy (1904) about violent clashes with early settlers in the upper Clear River valley. In Laos, inhabitants of Xiang Kouang province witnessed Chinese Muslims - belonging to the Black, Yellow, White and Red Flag armies - fighting their way through the mountain ranges in flight from Imperial Chinese troops in the north. These rebels were accompanied by (although not necessarily on friendly terms with) members of a number of different mountain tribes, including scores of Hmong. Of the latter, many chose to settle in this fertile area*

> - A Contribution to the Study of Hmong (Miao) Migrations and History. Culas & Micraud 1997

In keeping with their independent ethos, the Hmong found the plateau to be a perfect location to keep themselves free and unconcerned with the wider world, preferring slash-and-burn agriculture and raising animals to rice farming in the valleys. What they could not have anticipated though, was that Xieng

Khouang would soon become one of south east Asia's most valuable strategic locations, and when the titanic forces of national independence and then communism began to rumble through Indochina, the Hmong would find themselves picking sides and casting their lot with fate.

Pathet Lao, Secret Armies And Bombs

Trying to condense the complex history of rebellions, uprisings, wars and politics in Laos and Vietnam between 1865 and 1965 would be an exercise in futility, but nevertheless - Vietnam was a French protectorate until the Japanese invasion of WW2, which ultimately led to the August Revolution by Hồ Chí Minh's Việt Minh coalition, and the formation of the Democratic Republic of Vietnam (North Vietnam) in 1945. Laos similarly saw a communist organisation, the Pathet Lao, form during the 1940's. The Pathet Lao joined the Việt Minh in attacking the French during the first Indochina War, and while the French handed power to the Kingdom of Laos in 1953, the conflict escalated into a civil war between royalists and communists. North Vietnam invaded Laos to establish the Ho Chi Minh Trail, funnelling troops and supplies to the southern Vietnam theatre.

The 1953 invasion of Laos by North Vietnamese forces was aimed at capturing both Luang Prabang and the Plain of Jars, a pair of vital assets in putting pressure on the Laotian royalists. Over the next 20 years the Plain would see dozens of major and minor battles between the US-Laotian military and the various communist groups operating deep in the mountains. But the agonies of the Plain did not begin in earnest until the bombing campaigns. The United States had taken its usual position of not wanting to see either communists or European colonial powers rule Indochina, and had intervened to maintain Laos' neutrality. With the aggression from North Vietnam and the Soviets lurking in the background, the US opted to use airpower to help the royalist forces, specifically targeting the Ho Chi Minh Trail and the Plain of Jars. The exact figures for the amount of munitions dropped onto the Plain varies, but they are staggering. Robert Lawless writes:

> The bombs the U.S.A. dropped on the Plain of Jars in Laos- a country somewhat smaller than the state of Wyoming-between 1968 and 1972 exceeded the tonnage of all the bombs dropped by the U.S.A. in World War II.

Whilst Ian MacKinnon writes:

> The scale of the contamination is mind-boggling. Laos was hit by an average of one B-52 bomb-load every eight minutes, 24 hours a day, between 1964 and 1973. US bombers dropped more ordnance on Laos in this period than was dropped during the whole of the second world war. Of the 260m "bombies" that rained down, particularly on Xieng Khouang province, 80m failed to explode, leaving a deadly legacy.

In descriptions of the 'Secret War' in Laos, it is regularly described as 'the most bombed country on earth', and a significant portion of those bombs landed on the Plain. We'll come back to the legacy of unexploded ordnance at the end, but we can see from the scope of the campaign that the Plain was valued as a hugely important arena in the conflict.

So what of the Hmong and others who lived on the Plain? Prior to the war many Hmong had been pro-French, since the colonial power had treated them relatively equally and many Hmong had outwardly converted to Christianity. However, they were not a homogenous group and when the communist liberation movement picked up steam many Hmong decided to join them. The majority of the Hmong were pro royalist or neutralist, and thus pro USA, and when the US was scouting around to find ways to push the North Vietnamese out of Laos, they found a willing body of men.

The French had not left Laos without any defences. Even as the ink was drying on the 1953 handover treaty, French officers and advisors were busily training Hmong commandos out on the Plain of Jars, stockpiling weapons and preparing them for an invasion from the north. When it came the Hmong had several thousand trained men, but it was not enough, and life under communist rule was intolerable. What happened next is the stuff of novels.

On a fateful night in 1960, in the village of Tha Vieng, three colonels sat together in a darkened room, listening to a Hmong shaman chanting. He tied knotted cords around their wrists together, binding their souls, a deal had been made. The three colonels were Thai Colonel Khouphan, the Hmong Lt. Colonel Vang Pao, and an American intelligence officer and CIA agent they called Colonel Billy. Vang Pao was a wily and brave man, a veteran of guerilla warfare against the Japanese, the Việt Minh and was the only Hmong to reach the rank of General in the Lao Royal Army. Now he was back amongst his people, fighting the communists, and here was a CIA agent promising to deliver them weapons, food, medicine and equipment. The game was on.

Dubbed 'Operation Momentum', the CIA went on to train and equip around 30,000 Hmong soldiers, under the command of Vang Pao and organised by Colonel Billy (James William Lair). The Hmong became a formidable second army alongside the regular Laotian forces, harassing the communists, rescuing downed pilots and coordinating military manoeuvres with the royalists. But it was ultimately futile. With the Americans pulling out of Vietnam, the Hmong and the Royal Army stood alone against the communists, and when the government capitulated and recalled Vang Pao, instructing him not to resist, the Hmong stood alone. They had given it their all - in desperation the Hmong were recruiting teenage boys, then children and women as fighters, maybe 10% of their entire population had been killed, and now the Pathet Lao were promising to exterminate them. The Hmong broke cover. A few thousand were airlifted to the USA, tens of thousands marched the brutal journey into Thailand and the rest disappeared into the hills, where they remain to this day, hunted by the communists.

The Road To Elm Street

Life for the diaspora Hmong was materially comfortable, but socially hard. Their frantic escape left them at the mercy of US authorities, and they were resettled all across the country in 53 cities, fracturing their close, clannish and communitarian ethos. Over time the Hmong would relocate nearer to one another, especially in Minnesota, Wisconsin and the San Joaquin Valley in California. On the 15th July 1977, they were struck by their next tragedy. Southeast Asian refugees, overwhelmingly Hmong, suddenly started dying in their sleep. By the time a Portland medical examiner reported this to the CDC in 1980, over 100 people, predominantly young male Hmong, had died without warning in their beds. Between 1981 and 1983 another 38 deaths were reported. All the victims were in fine physical health, they had gone to sleep normally and appeared to suffer from some kind of nocturnal episode, sometimes relatives heard groans, moans or irregular breathing, but the doctors had nothing to go on. Men who were hundreds of miles apart, healthy, and connected only by their shared ethnicity and culture. The name they gave it says it all: 'Sudden Unexplained Nocturnal Death Syndrome', or SUNDS.

A clue came after extensive interviews with Hmong refugees and family members of the deceased - all the victims had suffered one or more nightmares in which they had foreseen their own death. These reports were largely ignored, but in 1991 the medical anthropologist Shelley R Adler proposed an unsettling hypothesis: the Hmong had frightened themselves to death. Traditional Hmong religion is both animistic and shamanic, and they believe that improper recognition and worship of their ancestral spirits will leave them vulnerable to attack by malevolent entities. As Adler wrote:

> In the Hmong language, the Nightmare spirit is referred to as dab tsog (pronounced "da cho"). Dab is the Hmong word for spirit, and is often used in the sense of an evil spirit, as opposed to neeb ("neng"), which is a friendly or familiar spirit. Tsog is the specific name of the Nightmare spirit, and also appears in the phrase used to denote a Nightmare attack, tsog tsuam ("cho chua"). Tsuam, the Hmong word meaning "to crush, to press, or to smother" (Heimbach 1979:358) is used in conjunction with tsog to mean "An evil spirit is pressing down on me!" or to refer generally to a Nightmare attack (Johnson 1985).

Without access to a shaman to help them, which most new refugee families were, many Hmong started experiencing nightmarish attacks, similar to what we call 'sleep paralysis'. Researchers now know that this phenomenon is a universal experience, linked to REM sleep cycle. Most cultures have some version of this deep in their history:

252

The nightmare syndrome appears to be universal in its occurrence. There are innumerable instances of the nightmare throughout history and in a multitude of cultures. References exist to the Assyrian alu (Thompson 1971), ancient Greek ephialtes (= leap upon), and Roman incubus (= lie upon). Instances of the nightmare are present in many other areas, as evidenced, for example, by terms denoting the experience from the following languages and cultures: Eskimo augumangia; Filipino urum or ngarat (Simons and Hughes 1985:387); French cauchemar (from La. calcare = to trample upon, squeeze); German Alb (Ranke 1977), Alpdruck (= elf pressure), Nachtmahr (Ward 1981:343), or Trud (Röhrich 1973:30); Newfoundland "Old Hag" (Hufford 1976, 1982; Ness 1978), Polish zmora; Russian kikimora; Spanish pesadilla (Foster 1973:109). The Nightmare is very well represented in the literature of ancient Greece and Rome. Descriptions from the writings of ancient Greek physicians refer unmistakably to the nightmare: ... symptoms mentioned are the feelings of the sleeper that somebody is sitting on his chest or suddenly jumps upon it or that somebody climbs up and crushes him heavily with his weight. The sufferer feels incapacity to move, torpidity and inability to speak. Attempts to speak often result only in single, inarticulate sounds (Roscher 1979:19).

A chest-crushing evil, demonic presence, an Old Hag, a feeling of inescapable dread and terror, the sensation of being smothered, sat on, pinned down, hooves trampling across the body, a shadowy figure in the corner of the eye. Adler provides many examples from interviews, such as this one with a 33 year old Hmong refugee named Neng Her:

First, I was surprised, but right away, I got real scared. I was lying in bed. I was so tired, because I was working very hard then. I wanted to go to school, but I had no money. I kept waking up, because I was thinking so much about my problems. I heard a noise, but when I turned - tried - I could not move. My bedroom looked the same, but I could see - in the comer, a dark shape was coming to me. It came to the bed, over my feet, my legs. It was very heavy, like a heavy weight over my whole body, my legs, my chest. My chest was frozen - like I was drowning, I had no air. I tried to yell so someone sleeping very close to me will hear. I tried to move - using a force that I can - a strength that I can have. I thought, "What can I do about this?" After a long time, it went away - it just left. I got up and turned all the lights on. I was afraid to sleep again

Adler's hypothesis was simple. The Nightmare is a universal experience, but within the belief system of the Hmong it took on a particular religious significance (no doubt combined with post-war PTSD), and without the intervention of a shaman the sufferers imbued it a lethality capable of frightening themselves into a heart attack. By the late 1970's the deaths were becoming high-profile news, prompting coverage in the L.A Times and other news outlets. One of the many readers who became fascinated with these deaths was the film director Wes Craven, who was inspired to create the horror franchise Nightmare On Elm Street, wherein the evil spirit Freddy Krueger kills people in their dreams. By the 1990's the death rate had slowed down considerably and researchers now believe that a genetic condition called 'Brugada Syndrome' was largely responsible for the deaths. Found mostly in southeast Asian men from Thailand, Vietnam and Laos, the syndrome causes abnormal heart arrhythmias and sudden cardiac arrest.

However, questions still linger over why so many Hmong men died so soon after the war and why the death rate was so inconsistent.

Life Amongst The Jars

We end our story where we began, back on the Plain of Jars. The legacy of the war, in particular the air bombing campaigns, has been particularly acute in Laos, a forgotten theatre. Millions of tons of unexploded ordnance, primarily cluster bombs, still blights Laos and the Xieng Khouang Plateau, whose residents have remade their lives surrounded by the threat of death and mutilation. There were 30,000 known wartime civilian deaths in Laos, and a further 20,000 casualties due to unexploded bombs after 1973 - between 1990-2008 around 300 people a year were being killed or maimed by the munitions. Disabilities in animistic and rural Buddhist cultures are sometimes seen as the victim's fault, leaving several generations with numerous unmarried and shunned people, sporting missing limbs, eyes and disfigurements. Laos receives aid and support from many countries, faith groups, charities and organisations, primarily to help clear and manage the unexploded bombs. The Plain of Jars itself, a tourist attraction in the ruins, is open to the public, but visitors must keep to the marked paths and risk serious injury or death if they wander off. The villages around Xieng Khouang have learnt to live with the bombs, and turn the casings and scrap into fences, furniture, houses, boats, water troughs and melting them down for tools and cutlery.

For the first time since the 1930's research can be conducted properly on the Jars, even with the limitations of the bombs. New papers are emerging and new Jar sites are being located. One independent researcher in particular, Lia Genovese, has discovered dozens of new sites and discovered a wealth of new information about the Plain. Hopefully we will be able to properly contextualise these truly strange megaliths and uncover the mysteries of the iron age culture which created them. Some landscapes in the world seem to attract the most unimaginable sorrows, and the rugged terrain of northern Laos now has the dubious honour of being the most bombed region on earth. The Hmong who live up here are still persecuted by the Laotian government. Some fighters have never put down their arms, continuing a struggle that began in the 1950's. The Laotian military keeps up a low grade war of disappearances, torture, artillery shelling, helicopter attack and even chemical weapons in their effort to track down those who would resist. Much as it was a century earlier, conflict and death stalks the Plain, one of archaeology's greatest enigmas.

HATING THE SAXON: THE ACADEMIC BATTLE AGAINST THE ENGLISH ORIGIN STORY

Anglo-Saxonism, the post-war struggle against Germanic Studies and the new genetic revelations

O n the 21st of September this year a paper was published in Nature purporting to have solved an ancient conundrum in English history, the origins and arrival of the Anglo-Saxons - the Adventus Saxonum. For most of the public this has never been a real debate - the English were formed through the mixture of pre-Roman Britons and the incoming Anglo-Saxon invaders and settlers. This narrative has been at the heart of Our Island Story for centuries, giving us our national language and character, the formation of the nation being forged through the tug-of-war between Norman and Saxon. But since WW2 there has been a scholarly rejection of this story, one taking on many forms and guises through archaeological and historical trends. This has ranged from arguments that the Anglo-Saxons were actually a very small elite band of warriors, to the wholesale dismissal that anyone arrived at all. Alongside this has come a critique that belief in a unique Anglo-Saxon mentality or race is fundamentally immoral and untrue, a colonial distortion of reality which underpinned the British Empire's claim to superiority. This argument has found a mildly receptive audience in Anglosphere scholarship and its proponents have sought to ban even the term Anglo-Saxon from the academic lexicon. So, what is going on here? Why would the confirmation that England was founded by Germanic settlers be so contentious to so many researchers?

The Origins Of Anglo-Saxonism

Up until the English Reformation the main national myth was largely focused on Brutus, the Arthurian era and the figure of King Arthur himself. With the break from Rome and the development of a separate English church, there was a hurried interest amongst scholars and antiquarians to uncover the roots of a unique English character, one which could shore up claims to a deeper and more legitimate form of Christianity. Archbishop Matthew Parker in particular was responsible for translating and updating works like the Saxon Homily on the Sacrament, by Ælfric of Eynsham, helping defend English Protestantism against its detractors. Both an interest in the English language and in promoting Anglo-Saxon liberties against the Norman yoke found a welcome audience amongst Tudor parliamentarians and Oxford scholars, laying the foundations for the conflict between Crown and Commons. Certainly, by the 17th century there was a growing consensus that the Anglo-Saxons were a people of exceptional liberty, who created free institutions and the common law, and who were later subjugated by the Normans. The Great Struggle through the use of Magna Carta, common law juries, Parliament and the Saxon spirit triumphed over autocratic foreign rule.

Alongside the flourishing of English antiquarianism came the fraternal connections to the Germanic peoples in general. Translations of Tacitus had been available since around 1470, but his descriptions of the Germanic people exploded in popularity between 1600 - 1649, which saw 67 editions of the Annals and Histories published across Europe. The eminent antiquarian William Camden (1551 - 1623) in particular emphasised the founding stock of the Saxon peoples, that powerful Germanic tree from which flowered the English branch. Leaning on Tacitus' description of the Germans as a peculiar and pure people, untainted by marriage with others, Camden and his colleagues, such as Richard Rowlands, connected England's Saxon heritage with the Germanic languages and the cluster of northern peoples - the Danes, Germans, Normans and Dutch. This was to have profound consequences for how the nascent British Empire came to view itself, with a magnificent national story of freedom-loving Germanic settlers, capable of self-discipline and self-rule, free from outside interference, England could confidently project its destiny out into the world. This is what others have dubbed 'Anglo-Saxonism', the belief in the unique and masterful qualities of the English race, which could be traced back to the primaeval forests of Germania. Self-government, free institutions, conventions of liberty, common law and the English language defined Anglo-Saxonism prior to WW2.

Excavating The Past

This brief overview of Anglo-Saxonism touches on major

themes that came together over many centuries into a coherent vision, but the messy reality for scholars and treasure-hunters through those long years was anything but crystal clear. In both the fields of physical excavations and historico-legal studies, the men who pioneered 'Anglo-Saxon studies' found the past confusing and uncertain, sometimes even unpleasant and frightening. The Tudor revolution in English history probably marks the moment when the English became truly cognizant of their ancient past, through the recovery of both the early English language and their laws and literature. The historical narrative that Britain had been invaded by Germanic settlers and warriors was nothing new to the Tudor ear, works ranging from Bede to Henry of Huntingdon were readily available, but it took the work of two men in particular - Laurence Nowell and William Lambarde - to convert the Anglo-Saxon legacy into something living, continuous and inspirational.

Laurence Nowell and William Lambarde, both born in the 1530's, came of intellectual age during a major inflection point in English history. Drawn to the figure of William Cecil, arguably the most important and powerful man in Elizabethan England, both found themselves providing tactical, geographical, historical and legal information which was to help set England apart during her precarious break with the Continent and its Catholic powers. Cecil employed Nowell as a tutor for his ward, the Earl of Oxford, and he funded and housed many of the preeminent scholars of the day, including Nowell, John Hart and Arthur Golding, who translated Ovid's Metamorphoses. Nowell and Lambarde went on to study, research and ultimately publish an astonishing array of books. These included: the first accurate map of England, *A general description of England and Ireland with the costes adioyning*, which Cecil always carried with him; the first English county history, The Perambulation of Kent; the first translated compilation of Anglo-Saxon laws, the Archaionomia, and the first Anglo-Saxon dictionary, the Vocabularium Saxonicum. It is hard to overstate the influence these texts had on English history, they were read by later thinkers such as Francis Bacon and Edward Coke (who envisaged Parliament as the successor to the Saxon witanagemot), they passed on copies of Beowulf and provided the material needed to bind England together as one nation under the aegis of the Saxon past.

Archaeologically the Elizabethan period had yet to catch up with the revolution in Anglo-Saxon thought and work. The majority of primitive excavations and fieldwork focused on Roman and Celtic Britain, the historical documentation of the Saxon arrivals being clear enough to deter curious antiquarians. With the Civil War and Restoration came obvious Saxonist triumphs, but it wasn't until the mid 1700's that Anglo-Saxon archaeology really began in earnest. Camden had written about Saxon era coins, which were clearly in scholarly circulation back in the 1600's, and the Alfred Jewel had been discovered in 1693 in Somerset, but the time had come to open the barrows. Of the new generation of antiquarians, none was perhaps so industrious as the Reverend Bryan Faussett, who excavated over 750 Anglo-Saxon burial mounds and graves between 1757 and 1773, recording every detail and object in minute details. By the time of his death in 1776 he had amassed the world's largest collection of Anglo-Saxon artefacts, from swords to brooches, belt buckles to bejewelled pendants. Faussett's work, and those of his and his contemporaries, fed into the major archaeological text of the period - the Nenia Britannica: or, a sepulchral history of Great Britain; from the earliest period to its general conversion to Christianity, by James Douglas in 1793.

This work, a masterful compilation of all the excavations to date, formed the foundation for later Victorian efforts and visually depicted the Saxon soldier as both a mythical romantic figure, but also a living spirit who permeated the souls of those excavators digging into the barrows. This growing quasi-racial image of the Saxon then found its apogee in the 1799 publication The History of the Anglo-Saxons, written by Sharon Turner, a self-taught student of English and Icelandic literature. Turner studied the artefact collections and Tudor/Elizabethan manuscripts extensively, putting forth a full-throated defence of the cleansing power of the Germanic barbarians and the Anglo-Saxons in particular, "in the shape of a good constitution, temperate kingship, the witenagemot, and general principles of freedom". Turner believed in a single human family, but stressed the importance of liberty, parliamentary institutions and hatred of the Norman yoke to the English character.

The Victorian Imagination

Without delving into the wider history of Germanic and Indo-European studies which flowered in the 1800's, it is crucial to at least underscore the importance of Anglo-Saxonism to the Victorians to understand the post-war backlash against the entire field. With Turner's and Douglas' books came not only a wider public appreciation for their Saxon forebears, but a cultural cementing of Anglo-Saxonism as an explanation for the success of the British Empire. Writers like Sir Walter Scott brimmed with pride for the manly, chivalrous and truthful Saxon, one blessed by God to conquer and rule the world. Carlyle, Arnold, Kingsley and Disraeli leant on phrenologists and ethnologists like George Combe:

> *Combe praised the Caucasians above all other races, the Teutonic branch over other Caucasians, and the Anglo-Saxons over all Teutons*

The belief in Anglo-Saxon liberties and freedoms had become enmeshed with the wider Germanic conviction that Teutonic virtues and virility were exceptional and would become globally dominant. As English-speaking institutions came to rule significant portions of the world, it was hard for anyone brought up with the story of Anglo-Saxon superiority not to feel giddy with a sense of destiny. John M Kemble's work, such as his 1849 Saxons in England, solidified a core belief that the Aryan Germanic spirit was one of regeneration. As the Germanic tribes re-invigorated a dying and corrupt Rome, and the Anglo-Saxons infused a backwards marsh with a freedom-loving martial ethic, so would the expansion of the Anglosphere into the wider world revitalise and energise the sordid and primitive corners of the Earth. As the anatomist Robert Knox wrote:

The Saxon, or true German, that is, the Scandinavian race. The only race which truly comprehends the meaning of the word liberty... their laws, manners, institutions, they brought with them from the woods of Germany, and they have transferred them to the woods of America

The Post-War Backlash

The century between the 1840's and 1940's could fill another article on the subject of Anglo-Saxon archaeology, but in tracing our story here we can accept that the heady brew of Empire, Germanic and Anglo race science, European war and doctrines like Manifest Destiny helped produce a post-war generation which fully rejected all intellectual movements related to cultural and ethnic supremacy. With the defeat of Nazism came a move away from Culture-

History, national origin stories and the belief in an intrinsic volk or people bound to collective terms like Celtic, Viking or Anglo-Saxon. The mood looked forward to the advent of scientific techniques and a more objective eye towards the past, untinged by misty-eyed nostalgia. Historical periods were subdivided, guided by radiocarbon dating. Isotope and geochemical analyses broke new ground, as older methods of comparative osteology and linguistics fell away. Scientific hypotheses were offered and scrutinised, and grand historical narratives such as Indo-European prehistory fell into disrepute.

Primarily the focus has been to deconstruct these meta-narratives, going right back to Rome. Since the story of the Anglo-Saxon arrival is predicated on a number of fundamental axioms, the goal has been to strip them of any explanatory power. Starting with the distinction between Roman and Germanic, oceans of ink have been spilled pulling apart what these two civilisational terms mean. Since the concept of 'being Roman' underwent a radical shift towards the end of the Western Empire, and since 'being Germanic' largely depended on nationalist constructions of a 'Germanic ethos', both have been attacked as historical fictions. Taking Gildas and Bede's accounts of the Saxon invasions as true came under immense fire, and the Victorian archaeological method of linking distinct material cultures with the Saxons, Angles and Jutes was dismissed as lacking rigour and saturated with romanticism. To quote archaeologist James M Harland:

> *Substantial scholarship has been devoted to critiquing the concept of 'Germanic' cultural identity… numerous studies have grappled with various aspects of the early medieval record held to embody authentic remnants, preserved from before the Völkerwanderung, of the protohistoric 'Germanic' past, and in almost all cases these are found to be lacking.*

Thus, to the deconstructivist eye, there is no basis for claiming that Anglo-Saxon is a meaningful concept. It is simply a projection backwards into time, grouping together disparate and unrelated peoples into an unreasonable whole. This debate has been unusually emotional for academics, and probably nowhere better illustrated than the battle over the idea of ethnicity in archaeology, which has focused on the Germanic peoples.

In 1961, the mediaeval historian Reinhard Wenskus published his masterpiece Stammesbildung und Verfassung, loosely translating to something like 'tribal formation and constitution'. This landmark text formed the core of a school of thought, known as the Vienna School of History, which aimed to abolish the idea that Germanic barbarian identity was founded on biological, racial or kinship lines. Instead, their proposed 'ethnogenesis' concept posited that the Germanic peoples were a diverse alliance of groups, led by a core elite which preserved and maintained the Traditionskerne, or 'core-traditions'. Only in this way, the school argued, could there be truly be a stable Germanic identity which stretched from North Africa to Iceland, from the Balkans to Norway. In opposition to this line of argument came the recent Toronto School, which takes a strident position against any framework which supports any idea of ethnicity. Scholars like Walter Goffart, Andrew Gillett and Michael Kilukowski have gone so far as to dismiss Germanic literature such as Old Norse poetry as having anything of value to archaeology, and to attack the Vienna School as crypto-nationalists. In their eyes, archaeology should never attempt to trace ethnicity or even the migrations of peoples. As Wolf Liebeschuetz says in his 2015 book, East and West in Late Antiquity:

We cannot trust what Roman historians, especially

*Caesar and Tacitus, say about Germanic customs
because their descriptions are hopelessly distorted. The
Romans applied to the Germans their own classical
preconceptions of what barbarian peoples must be like.
Archaeology can trace cultural diffusion, but it cannot
be used to distinguish between peoples, and should not
be used to trace migration. Arguments from language
and etymology are irrelevant.*

In a similar vein, Sebastian Brather in the important
2002 volume On Barbarian Identity: Critical Approaches to
Ethnicity in the Early Middle Ages rails against all approaches
in archaeology which rely on ethnicity.

*My view is in a sense a 'pessimistic' one. I cannot
see any way that archaeology could identify 'ethnic
identities' of the past. The search for ethnic groups
follows the national(istic) imagination of the last two
hundred years, and does not meet the expressiveness of
archaeological sources... 'Ethnic identity' is beyond the
reach of archaeology, whether it was important in early
history or not (this is a question for historiography).
The archaeological search for 'ethnic identities' was
not of scientific interest, but more or less a matter of
national discourse and nationalistic emphasis. It was
used for the construction of modem national identities.*

This is a remarkable sentiment, and not one shared by the vast
majority of archaeologists around the world, many of whom
spend their lives researching national and ethnic origins. But it
underscores the disdain the later generation of archaeologists
have for any line of argument which could lead to the
legitimisation of distinct biological/ethnic peoples in history.

'There Were No Anglo-Saxons'

Hopefully by now we can see how sharply post-war scholarship diverged from its earlier iterations. The battle-lines have cut deeper and deeper into the intellectual suppositions of ethnicity, race, culture and migrations, to the point where archaeologists actually forbid interpretations which suggest any form of cultural distinction between peoples. While these fights have been played out in the larger sphere of Germanic studies more broadly, they have obviously found their way into Anglo-Saxon research.

To pick on two recent books in the popular literature on British history, Francis Pryor's Britain AD (2005) and Susan Oosthuizen's The Emergence of the English (2019), we see a new consensus position being cemented across the field. Broadly it runs something like this - the Gildasian 'Dark Age' and post-Roman social breakdown is wrong, archaeology shows a clear pattern of continuity in farming and social life, the arrival of the Anglo-Saxons is based on circular reasoning and conservative interpretations of the data, there is no evidence for mass warfare, strife, elite imposition or ethnic segregation. A better explanation would be a slowly changing continuity of Latin Britain with a reorientation towards Germany and Scandinavia for trade which results in the diffusion and spread of the English language and Germanic artefacts and styles. To quote Pryor:

> *It is probably fair to say that serious scholars who believe in largescale Anglo-Saxon mass migrations are now in the minority. Most people, myself included, accept that there was a certain amount of movement in and out of Britain, just as there was in the Iron Age and the Roman period. We might well discover one*

*day that certain Anglo-Saxon cemeteries in, say, East
Yorkshire, contain the bodies of immigrant populations.
I do not believe, however, that such discoveries will
invalidate the consensus that the changes attributed
to the arrival of Anglo-Saxons were usually caused by
people changing their minds, rather than their places of
residence*

Pryor attacks older studies, such as J.N.L Myres influential
1969 work Anglo-Saxon Pottery and the Settlement of
England, which painstakingly shows how Saxon pottery and
cremation urns arrive in successive waves from the Continent.
Decrying his love for Bede and Gildas, Pryor waves Myres away
with the simple 'pots are not people' refrain. This is in line
with many decades of arguments against the correlation of
'Germanic' artefacts or burial traditions with 'German' people
themselves. To quote archaeologist Julian Richards in 1992:

*Mortuary ritual reinforces cultural differences and
helps classify Anglo-Saxon
society. It provides a means of describing social
identity... we must accept that many of those given
a Germanic burial rite were not immigrants from
North Germany and Scandinavia. The form of burial
is a symbol being used to assert the domination of
Germanic culture, not the annihilation of the previous
inhabitants*

Early genetic studies on the Anglo-Saxon legacy, now known
to be incorrect, have helped buttress this line of argument.
Both Stephen Oppenheimer and Bryan Sykes, analysing papers
in the early 2000's, arrived on the consensus that the Anglo-

Saxons left little genetic legacy, and that British population genetics have been largely unchanged since the end of the Ice Age. Anyone familiar with post-2015 genetic studies will find this almost amusing, but for scholars like Pryor and Oosthuizen, both traditional pot-and-soil archaeologists, these confirmations shored up the position that the migrations and invasions were a myth.

To bring us fully to date, with the strident anti-racist ideology percolating into Britain from America, we have seen some very public attacks on the term Anglo-Saxon itself. Under immense pressure from younger researchers, in November 2019 the International Society of Anglo-Saxonists voted to change its name to the International Society for the Study of Early Medieval England, citing the long history of American imperialism and racism bound up in the title. The campaign has probably over-reached in attempting to force scholars, universities and museums to relabel everything Anglo-Saxon and there has been push-back from academics in the field, but it is sobering to think that even the phrase is at risk of extinction within the halls and laboratories of research.

The Turning Tide

With the advent of comparative full-genome studies we seem to have entered a new phase of debate in Anglo-Saxon studies. Those on the offensive for the last few decades are very much on the defensive, and statements that 'no-one believes in Anglo-Saxon mass migration' already look very dated. This recent paper seems to have blown away the accumulated layers of obfuscation and argument to reveal a clear truth - the migration did happen. Granted the details are now open for further investigation and hopefully we will see constructive rather than hostile responses. Certainly nobody fully accepts Bede and Gildas as the absolute truth, if they ever did, but with scholarly acceptance of oral tradition amongst indigenous people as preserving not just centuries but millennia of accurate information, and with genetics cutting a swathe through the old guard, we should be nothing but charitable to those early chroniclers. I've attempted to lay out something of a potted history of Anglo-Saxon historiography and the politics and science of its continued study. Whatever one makes of national origin stories, we should see here a wonderful tale of scholarship and passion - Our Island Story - no longer relegated to romantic myth, but one returning with youth and vigour.

WHY ARE YOU
SO WEIRD?

*Individualism and kinship: The
Bronze Age, Anglo-Saxons
& mediaeval England*

W hy are you so WEIRD? By this I mean of course Western, Educated, Industrial, Rich and Democratic. If you haven't heard this acronym before, let me introduce you. WEIRD psychology is the brainchild of several academics - Joseph Henrich, Steven J. Heine and Ara Norenzayan - from their 2010 article 'The weirdest people in the world', where they argue that psychologists have been making assumptions about standard human nature from possibly the strangest subset of people of earth. They describe it thus:

WEIRD subjects are particularly unusual compared with the rest of the species – frequent outliers. The domains reviewed include visual perception, fairness, cooperation, spatial reasoning, categorization and inferential induction, moral reasoning, reasoning styles, self-concepts and related motivations, and the heritability of IQ. The findings suggest that members of WEIRD societies, including young children, are among the least representative populations one could find for generalizing about humans.

Henrich went on to write a bestselling 2020 book 'The WEIRDest People in the World: How the West Became Psychologically Peculiar and Particularly Prosperous' where he extends the original idea into a big history narrative, explaining the origins of Western individualism through the dynamics of Catholic social policy, and later Protestant sensibilities. The changes in kinship relationships, rise of the nuclear family, mass literacy, and voluntary, rather than obligatory institutions, led to a peculiar psychological disposition that in no way reflects the majority of human beings.

Although far more nuanced than its proponents, Henrich's book dovetails nicely with a rising 'postliberal' mood across the West. Books like David Goodhart's 'The Road to Somewhere' with its divide between the rootless 'anywheres' and the rooted 'somewheres'; J.D Vance's 'Hillbilly Elegy'; Patrick Deneen's 'Why Liberalism Failed', and writers such as Giles Fraser and Sohrab Ahmari often position the Enlightenment and the subsequent rise of individualism and capitalism as the source of many modern evils. Holding hands with the contemporary academic Left, who have long railed against 'neoliberalism', the result is a strange blend of 'trad' virtues and a firing squad of many ideologies against the Great Enemy - Western-style liberal individualism. For both political wings there is a crude but effective story about a more collectivist past giving way to a more individualistic present.

This is nothing new however. The idea that the past was a more primitive, communal place, which changed with the disruption of modernity, beginning with the Scientific Revolution and the Enlightenment, goes back centuries. Historian and activist R..H Tawney excoriated capitalism and individualism over a 100 years ago; Saint-Simon and the Owenites likely invented the pejorative 'individualism' a century before that. A broad academic consensus exists which posits that the Industrial Revolution and the market economy developed out of a violent expropriation and enclosure of common rural peasant land. It isn't easy however to actually define what we mean by an 'individualistic' vs 'collectivist' mode of life, especially when dealing with archaeological or historical evidence, but here are some suggestions:

A spectra of kinship relationships and obligations.
Whether legal systems, be they oral or written, regard the individual or group/family/clan as the basic unit of society.
A focus on self-differentiation through career, bodily modification/adornment, expectations or other ideological manifestations.
Whether the individual, or certain types of person, have moral worth in themselves.
Social methods of rule enforcement - private guilt vs group shame for example.
Personal mobility during an individual's life.
Family structure - multi-generational, nuclear, extended and so on.
Whether land is directly inherited through the group or family.

Others exist of course, and it becomes very difficult to produce a coherent system of thought when you take all the different factors into account. But taking a deeper look beyond the narrative of Western Enlightenment individualism, Europe and especially England have a different story to tell.

Bronze Age Warriorhood & Aristocratic

Individualism

The Neolithic farming communities of Europe are typically described as sharing a communalist approach to life and death. Group burials in large tombs without distinctions, a lack of exotic grave goods for individual people and a material culture which emphasises the group rather than the person.

> In LBK [Neolithic] communities, group deaths seem to have effectively caused the identity and individuality of the victims to be erased. This stands in stark contrast to more traditional burial treatments, in which selected information pertaining to the role and standing of the deceased was routinely preserved through an individualised funeral rite

> -Patterns of Collective Violence in the Early Neolithic of Central Europe. Meyer et al 2018

We find similar expressions all over the world, for instance in the way many Andamanese islanders would dig up bones of loved ones and wear them:

> Like all their other relics these possessions are lent or exchanged, passing from one person to another, until sometimes a skull may be found in possession of a man who does not know to whom it belonged

> -Radcliffe-Brown, 1992

One of the great shifts in human history was the rise of the bronze age individual, or more specifically, the male warrior. This can be seen both in the material culture of the period (chariots, personal drinking vessels, individual graves, personal grooming objects, bodily adornments), and in the development of a broader Indo-European cultural sphere which emphasised weaker kinship bonds, monogamy, small nuclear families and social militarism. The results from Bell Beaker cemeteries support the view that early Indo-European expansion resulted in a shift towards monogamy, exogamy and the mobility of young men through fostering:

> *The buried individuals represent four to six generations of two family groups, one nuclear family at the Alburg cemetery, and one seemingly more extended at Irlbach. While likely monogamous, they practiced exogamy, as six out of eight non-locals are women.... This provides evidence for the society being patrilocal, perhaps as a way of protecting property among the male line, while in-marriage from many different places secured social and political networks and prevented inbreeding. We also find evidence that the communities practiced selection for which of their children (aged 0–14 years) received a proper burial, as buried juveniles were in all but one case boys, suggesting the priority of young males in the cemeteries. This is plausibly linked to the exchange of foster children as part of an expansionist kinship system which is well attested from later Indo-European-speaking cultural groups.*

Contrast this with ethnographic descriptions of Kurdish kinship systems, which are both endogamous and clan-oriented:

> *Young men, nevertheless, had few possibilities of challenging the senior men who were in control of property and women. One had access to these 'valuables' as one went through the life cycle of growing up, going to the military, marrying, having children,*

and finally separating one's own household either from the parental or the fraternal household

This Bronze Age individualism had its limits of course, and we are likely looking at a system in which elite warriors and their families maintained a form of egalitarianism, whereby reciprocity, host-stranger conventions, gift-giving, oaths of loyalty and meritocratic battle prowess forged strong bonds between unrelated groups of men.

First, all Indo-European cultures from the "earliest" times in the 5th millennium have seen the presence of warriors who sought to demonstrate their standing and wealth, by dressing in "ostentatious" ways; for example, with long or multiple belts and necklaces of copper beads, copper rings, copper spiral bracelets, gold fittings in their spears and javelins – with variations of styles depending on place and time but all demonstrative of an "individualizing ideology" (Anthony: 160, 237, 251, 259–63). Second, the Indo-European warriors "were interred as personalities showing off the equipment of life and their personal position in a final coup de theatre, rather than joining a more anonymous community of ancestors" (Sherratt 2001a: 192). Kurgan burials commemorated the deaths of special males; the stone circles and mounds, and the emphasis on "prestige weapons and insignia," were intended to isolate and self aggrandize the achievements of warriors (Anthony: 245). Third, they developed a distinctive tradition of feasting and drinking, in which "individual hospitality rather than great communal ceremonies" dominated the occasions.

-The Uniqueness of Western Civilization.

Ricardo Duchesne. 2011

English Individualism - Loose Kinship, Germanic Origins

Due to the rejection of 19th century scholarship on Indo-European history and archaeology, there has been an awkward tension between even modern researchers on the European Bronze and Iron Ages and the later historical understanding of Medieval Europe. Whilst debates go back and forth on how much modern liberal bias influences our perception of the Bronze Age individual warrior, the gulf between the final 'Germanic' period and popular understandings of the Mediaeval world could not be greater. In this sudden jump we are placed into a world where the bulk of the population are 'peasants', that is to say an unfree people who work the land for the benefit of their lord or landowner. Unsurprisingly peasantry, serfdom and the whole concept of traditional agrarian societies have been a battleground for all kinds of ideologies, Marxism in particular. Crucial to any reading of Marxism is the existence of a pre-market, undifferentiated rural economy, where families are tied to the land, labour performed in service of the family and patriarchal households hand down inheritances.

England has long been the best source material for studies of mediaeval peasantry, sometimes called "most thoroughly investigated of all peasantries in history". In an extraordinary book by Alan MacFarlane entitled The Origins of English Individualism, he argues that this image of the English peasantry is entirely wrong, and that by the 13th century England had nothing resembling a traditional serf or peasant class:

> ... in thirteenth century England, single women,

married women and widows all had very considerable property rights as individual persons. In many peasant societies, the household goes through a phase when there are two or more married couples in the same dwelling and eating from the same table. There is no evidence that this was prevalent in the thirteenth century, and there is a certain amount of evidence that households were predominantly nuclear

There is strong evidence of considerable individual mobility, as well as long-term differentiation between the landed and the landless. Doubt is even being cast on two other supposed features of the medieval peasantry, namely that they married young and that there was more or less universal marriage. The consequence of all these features is that there is a growing impression that the thirteenth century countryside was not broken up into self-contained and self-sufficient local "communities" with strong boundaries and highly differentiated from other communities. The society is beginning to appear much more like the sixteenth century, where people and money flowed through the countryside, where the individual was not born, married and buried amongst his kin

If we look at the writings of travellers and social commentators, we find that they did regard the English system as peculiar, particularly stressing the absence of communities, of family ties, of a fixed division between the "peasantry" and the rest. The contrasts are drawn very sharply in the work of De Tocqueville, particularly in his Ancien Regime. But he was only able to work back in the historical documents to the late fifteenth century. From that time, it was clear to him, England was inhabited by people with a social structure fundamentally different from that in France

If MacFarlane is right, and he does have his detractors, then English notions of kinship and individuality diverged from many other European nations, where a true 'peasantry' emerged, complete with the communalistic features of traditional, agrarian life.

In fact this argument goes deeper than mediaeval England, and traces its roots back into the Iron and Bronze ages. Towards the end of the 19th century and during the early 20th, there was an explosion of legal scholarship and thought surrounding the English Common Law and its antecedents. German and American scholars temporarily embarrassed the English with their advanced historical research into the foundations of common law:

> *lawyers who knew nothing but law, and only the common law at that. But for history the disaster was enormous. In proportion as Englishmen have made themselves good lawyers they have become bad historians. The whole fabric of the common law rests on a quantity of assumptions which as history are destitute of any sound basis of fact, and these assumptions have decisively influenced the ideas even of those English historians who, technically speaking, knew no law*

Maine's Village Communities - Henry Adams, 1872

The two most important legal history books by English scholars of the age, and maybe still today, were Ancient Law (1861) by Henry Maine, and The History of English Law Before the Time of Edward I (1895), primarily written by Frederic Maitland. The second book was something of a reply to the first, since Maine's argument followed perhaps a common line of thought for readers. Namely that English law originated with the collective, patriarchal family lineage in a pre-State condition, where the group ruled over the individual and the transformation has:

> been distinguished by the gradual dissolution of family dependency and the growth of individual obligation in its place. The Individual is steadily substituted for the Family, as the unit of which civil laws take account

Maine pointed to Roman and Hindu law as examples of the pure Aryan or Indo-European legal system, where the absolute power of the male was celebrated and codified. In contrast Maitland, Adams and his American school of thought, rejected this claim and instead looked to Germanic law as the wellspring of Anglo-Saxon jurisprudence:

> Adams argued, by contrast, that Roman law and family structure were not typical of archaic law and the archaic family. He emphasised the extent to which archaic German law and family structure differed substantially from their Roman counterparts. The absolute power of the Roman paterfamilias did not exist in Germany, where a son had unlimited rights to acquire and own property, a daughter was not excluded from her family when she married, a wife could easily obtain a divorce to protect herself against her husband's authority, and kinship was determined through the mother's as well as the father's side of the family.

-From Maine to Maitland via America. David Rabban. 2009

This last assertion about the emphasis on the dual lineage from both mother and father is very important. Anthropologically this is called 'Eskimo Kinship' - where the nuclear family has special terms, then other relations are lumped together as 'cousin', 'aunt' and so on. Bilateral descent is crucial, neither fatherly nor motherly ancestry is prioritised. This would seem to be the case for northern Europeans and especially the English since time immemorial. MacFarlane thinks that this system was in place since the 7th century AD; Adams argues for a much older rootstock:

> Immediately after announcing his central theme, Adams dismissed the relevance of Maine's theories of development from the patriarchal family to the state, though he did not cite Maine himself. He observed that scholars remained ignorant of societies antedating the Indo-European family, but did have sufficient information to reach meaningful conclusions about early Germanic society. The evidence of early German laws indicated a society of small families without a patriarchal chief, whose able-bodied male members united in a council as equal individuals rather than as families. The council elected civil and military officers, protected property, and arbitrated disputes, proving the supremacy of the state. The council did not, however, control the private affairs of families, decided according to family custom.

Although deeply unfashionable now, there is probably a great deal of low-hanging fruit available to the eccentric thinker who could link together recent archaeology, genetics and these older, forgotten legal histories of English law. Similarly with MacFarlane's work, modern genetics may be able to help prove or disprove this thesis, as well as new archival work. There is a lot for the taking here, someone just needs to pick it up.

The Forgotten Indo-European Legacy

Henrich's thesis about the origins of WEIRDness seem to me to be half-true. His argument that the Church is largely responsible for transforming Western Europe from a clannish, communalist culture to an individualist one rests strongly on what his conception of this culture was like:

> *Here are some broad patterns in the tribal populations of pre-Christian Europe:*

> *People lived enmeshed in kin-based organizations within tribal groups or networks. Extended family households were part of larger kin-groups (clans, houses, lineages, etc.), some of which were called sippen (Germanic) or septs (Celtic).*

> *Inheritance and postmarital residence had patrilineal biases; people often lived in extended patrilineal households, and wives moved to live with their husbands' kinfolk.*

> *Many kinship units collectively owned or controlled territory. Even where individual ownership existed, kinfolk often retained inheritance rights such that lands couldn't be sold or otherwise transferred without the consent of relatives.*

Larger kin-based organizations provided individuals with both their legal and their social identities. Disputes within kin-groups were adjudicated internally, according to custom. Corporate responsibility meant that intentionality sometimes played little role in assigning punishments or levying fines for disputes between kin-groups.

Kin-based organizations provided members with protection, insurance, and security. These organizations cared for sick, injured, and poor members, as well as the elderly.

Arranged marriages with relatives were customary, as were marriage payments like dowry or bride price (where the groom or his family pays for the bride).

Polygynous marriages were common for high-status men. In many communities, men could pair with only one "primary" wife, typically someone of roughly equal social status, but could then add secondary wives, usually of lower social status

It's interesting how much of this was refuted by earlier legal scholars, and increasingly contradicted by modern archaeology. In the 1905 landmark volume Essays in Anglo-Saxon Law, Ernest Young disagreed with the conception of Anglo-Saxon law as grounded in private property held by a patriarchal chief, to whom the family yielded. He held that the family was a collection of individuals, all of whom had rights:

> *It is not the subjugation of all descendents to the will of an ascendant, but the voluntary association of the near kindred; and the control exercised by the family council in such a group as little resembles the despotic power of a patriarchal chief ... as the free democratic constitution of primitive Germany resembled the highly aristocratic constitution of early Rome*

The shadow of Roman family law still holds sway in the imagination of academics, who have inherited a strand of thought which saw the paterfamilias as the 'purest' expression of pre-Christian domestic life. Many feminist critiques of modern patriarchy trace what they see as the 'traditional' Western family from Rome, ignoring the very different family and state structures of the Germanic north.

This is really something of a primer or an introduction into whole areas of thought surrounding kinship, individualism, private property, the free market and the legacies of pre-Christian life which make up the character of modern populations and nations. As it stands I think the fundamental break was the end of the Neolithic and the development of an aristocratic cultural and biological substrate during the Bronze Age, one which ushered in a form of individualism which set Europe on a different path.

THE MĀORI GENOCIDE OF THE MORIORI

The Māori Musket Wars, the invasion of the Chatham Islands and its aftermath

An interesting dynamic often occurred when Europeans encountered other peoples and civilisations. The entrance of firearms into politically divided and complex regions would set off a powder keg of explosive violence, as different groups would scramble to acquire the weapons and use them to gain territorial advantages over their neighbours. This happened in North America during the famous 'Mourning Wars' and in South Africa during the mfecane, which I've looked at before. It also happened in New Zealand, where access to the musket unleashed the most incredible violence and aggression between different Māori peoples, culminating in one of the worst genocides in history, as the Māori sailed to the Chatham Islands and annihilated their pacifist cousins, the Moriori. The subsequent enslavement of the Moriori by the Māori, and their attempts to eradicate them as a people, have rarely been examined outside of New Zealand. The contrasts between the two peoples could not be greater and the story deserves to be widely known.

The Māori And The Moriori

The arrival of the Māori heralded one of the last great moments of human global expansion, although no-one knew it at the time. New Zealand, unlike its continent-sized neighbour Australia, had been devoid of people until the early 1300's AD. The Māori have many legends of the small-folk who inhabited the island before them - the patupaiarehe - in a manner similar to all Polynesian peoples, but otherwise there is no evidence for any earlier settlements in New Zealand. Despite creative efforts to show how the Aryans or Celts or Phoenicians arrived first, we must stick with what can be proved empirically.

The Māori are a part of the wider Polynesian family, with roots going back to Austronesian Taiwan. Colonising New Zealand was like gravity in some sense, these pioneers of ocean exploration were always going to find such a large land mass. Mother Nature's reward was an island paradise, complete with an ecosystem which had never encountered such an apex predator. 80 million years of isolation had bred creatures unknown to the rest of the world, and the Māori set about harvesting them, in particular the large flightless moa bird, which quickly went extinct. The colonist's rats also did their work, and the island has never fully recovered.

It might be somewhat unfashionable to say today, but there can be no doubt that the Māori were a proud, warlike people, full of vigour, energy and a will to expand themselves. If not at sea, then on land. Conflict, fortified settlements called pa and cannibalism are well known in the record. One undeniable piece of proof for this was the development of a strictly pacifist culture on a small set of islands off the New Zealand mainland.

The Chatham Islands, along with the Auckland Islands, are the last stop for sailors before hitting Antarctica. Indeed Polynesian oral history is replete with stories of sailing into freezing water, with islands made of ice sticking out of the sea. Several studies and articles have been written in the past few years, and maybe one day some archaeological evidence will be found to confirm the legends. The Chathams were likely colonised between 1300 and 1500 AD, but our knowledge of that period is extremely limited. We do know that the people who settled there and flourished in that harsh environment named themselves the Moriori.

Much of Moriori history is shrouded in mystery and uncertainty. Moriori traditional knowledge describes a dual colonization, first by the ancestor Rongomaiwhenua from East Polynesia and subsequent migrations from mainland New Zealand. The standard scholarly view is that Moriori are an East Polynesian people descended from or closely related to the same East Polynesians who settled in New Zealand and became Māori. The date of their arrival is unclear. Michael King, whose history of Moriori is currently the authoritative treatment, estimates that 'on the balance of probabilities', Moriori arrived on the Chathams 'around the thirteenth or fourteenth century'. It is possible the settlement of the Chathams was as late as the mid sixteenth century.

-'The miserable remnant of this ill-used people':

colonial genocide and the Moriori of New Zealand's
Chatham Islands. André Brett. 2015.

One point of agreement is that around the year 1500 AD, a
particularly prominent chief called Nunuku-whenua arrived
or emerged in the Chathams and established a new moral code
for the people. He was disgusted by the violence and warfare
on the mainland, and established 'Nunuku's Law' - this forbade
murder, warfare and cannibalism - which should give us a clue
about conditions elsewhere. Some versions of the story say
that warfare had broken out between the two main Chatham
Islands: Rēkohu (Chatham Island) and Rangiaotea (Pitt Island),
and that Nunuku stopped the fighting. Either way, the code
held, and the Moriori became a strictly pacifist culture.

*The Morioris do not appear to have had the same
amount of energy or vivacity as the Maoris, nor were
they an agressive or war like people, although somewhat
quarrelsome among themselves, caused chiefly by curses
(kanga) of one section or tribe against another, which
generally originated in the infidelity of the wives. To
obtain revenge for this, they organised expeditions
against their adversaries, in which they went through
and recited incantations for the success of their party,
just as if in actual warfare. All fighting, however, had
been forbidden,-and had ceased since the days of their
ancestor Nunuku shortly after their arrival in the island
about 27 generations ago, since which time they have
been restricted to the use of the tupurari (quarter-staff)
only. It was ordered by Nunuku that man-slaying and
man-eating should cease for ever? "Koro patu, ko ro
kei tangatāme tapu todke" and that in all quarrels the
first abrasion of the skin, or blow on the head or other
part causing any blood to flow, was to be considered
sufficient, and the fight — so-called — was to cease.
The person sustaining injury in such cases called out,*

"Ka pakarū tanganei ūpokō?" "My head is broken;" but, although the quarrel ceased for the time, it did not prevent the injured party endeavouring at a later period to get satisfaction for his "broken head." Nevertheless, apart from such disturbing incidents, their general life was a very peaceable one.

-The Moriori People of the Chatham Islands: Their Traditions and History. Alexander Shand. 1894

With this new social framework in place, the Moriori were able to settle into a life of foraging and gathering, freed from the violence and destruction of constant war. The horticultural system which had spread with the Polynesians across the Pacific finally failed this far south, and the Moriori switched to becoming marine hunters, living primarily off their seals, fish and seabirds. At most there were 2,000 individuals on the small archipelago, and for several centuries life was fairly good. Many tree carvings exist from this time which testify to their animistic religion. Tattoos seem to have disappeared, along with excessive bodily ornamentation and markers of rank. Staying alive at the ends of the earth demanded a social conversion to something more egalitarian and peaceful. But it was not to last.

The Musket Wars On Aotearoa

European contact with the Māori came late. Cook's first voyage between 1768-1771 discovered Tahiti, where a priest called Tupaia joined Cook's crew for the sake of adventure and discovery. His life and skills were remarkable, and when Cook ended up on the shores of New Zealand staring at the Māori his presence was to be more than decorative. Having brought him from Tahiti, a journey of around 2,700 miles, Cook bore witness to Tupaia speaking with the Māori, despite never having visited the islands. The realisation that the Pacific was inhabited by people, separated by thousands of miles, but connected by a common tongue was a revelation. The process of working out the relationships between these people has taken a long time, beautifully narrated in two books by the writer Christina Thompson - Sea People: The Puzzle of Polynesia, and Come on Shore and We Will Kill and Eat You All (the apocryphal phrase said by the Māori to Cook upon first contact).

Muskets were extremely valuable from the get-go for the Māori. Their traditional weapons made of greenstone, bone, ivory, wood and so on (the Wahaika, Tewhatewha, Patu etc) were largely for close quarters combat, where a warrior was renowned for his bravery and could increase his personal and collective power (his mana) through dominating his enemies. The musket changed everything, and from the instant Cook's men opened fire, the Māori knew they needed to acquire as many as possible. Slowly through sealers and whalers, through corrupt missionaries and flax traders, different groups (iwi) stockpiled muskets, powder and lead. The flashpoint came in 1807. A year earlier a small trading vessel, the Venus, had been seized by a group of onboard convicts and sailed from Tasmania to the north of New Zealand. Here the crew went on a remarkable kidnapping spree, making landfall to drag away many highborn Māori women to be used as sex slaves. Two of the women were related to Hongi-Hika and Te Morenga, names which are now synonymous with the Musket Wars. The crew of the Venus dropped off the women with different iwi down the coast, groups which were already hostile to one another, and reports came back to both sides that their women had been killed and eaten. The two main iwi, the Ngāti Whātua and Ngāpuhi, then came to blows at the Battle of Moremonui, which marked the opening of the Musket Wars. Although the muskets were not very useful during that battle due to their long reloading time, the Māori could see that he who had the most muskets could win the war.

A full account of the Wars needs a book length treatment, such as Ron Crosby's The Forgotten Wars: Why The Musket Wars Matter Today. In his own words:

> During the Musket Wars era, there were more than a thousand conflicts, ranging from major taua, sieges and battles to more minor ambushes, skirmishes and other engagements.

> The casualty figures resulting from the Musket Wars greatly exceeded those of the later New Zealand Wars.

> The Musket Wars affected every iwi throughout the length of the country, either directly or indirectly.

> The numbers of people affected by the Musket Wars, whether through death, injuries, permanent migrations or temporary displacements, were massive — the lives of 50,000 people were affected over the 30-year span of the wars, against a background population of between 100,000 and 150,000.

> Major permanent migrations occurred, displacing or subjugating the original occupying iwi, and in one case effectively eliminating Ngāti Ira in the Whanganui a Tara area.

As a result of migrations and displacements, large areas that were particularly vulnerable to raiding taua were depopulated and left vacant, sparsely populated or only intermittently occupied for the gathering of food or other resources.

New Zealand would never look the same. Whole communities were destroyed, their men killed and women taken as slaves. Massive parts of the country were left empty, and European settlers moved in. The balance of power shifted and many heroes performed great deeds for their iwi. The musket had unleashed the energy of the Māori, whose style of warfare was unprepared for the devastation of firearms. The equilibrium had been broken.

Sailing To The Chathams

While the Musket Wars raged on New Zealand, the Moriori were blissfully unaware of any danger. But their lives had changed with the coming of European ships and sealers. In 1791 lieutenant William Broughton, commander of the Chatham, sighted the islands and made contact with the Moriori. Twenty years later whalers and sealers began arriving in numbers and spread diseases the Moriori had never encountered - measles and influenza - their numbers dropped from an estimated 2,000 to around 1,650 people. Still, the ravages of war had not touched them, yet.

As the wars picked up their bloody pace many Māori left to find peace and security on the European merchant and fishing vessels. It was from these journeys that the Māori learnt of the existence of the Moriori and the Chatham Islands. Some chose to stay when they arrived, relaxing in the calm of their pacifism. Interestingly the Māori did not see the Moriori as cousins or kin, in fact they looked upon the Moriori with quite a different eye. In 1805 the Māori chief Te Pahi visited Australia where the millennia old barrier between Polynesians and Aboriginal Australians was finally broken. He viewed them with disgust, scorning their more egalitarian and primitive culture. The European term 'blackfella' for Aboriginals came to enter the Māori language as 'paraiwhara', which came with valences of savagery, inferiority and natural slavery. It was through this lens that the Māori saw the Moriori - a weaker, lesser people, more akin to the Aboriginal than the Māori.

By the 1830's the Musket Wars were in full swing. Two iwi around the central North Island - the Ngāti Mutunga and the Ngāti Tama - were suffering the effects of constant insecurity and raiding, particularly at the hands of the Ngāti Raukawa. They decided to flee. In November 1835, Pomare of the Ngāti Mutunga negotiated with one Captain Harwood of the Lord Rodney to take them all to the Chatham Islands, away from danger. Around 900 people crowded onto the vessel and disembarked not long afterwards. They fell on the Moriori who sheltered them and provided food, hoping they would go away. The Māori had been careful not to aggravate their British hosts while sailing, but once ashore, they quickly revealed their true intentions.

The custom of takahi, or 'walking the islands' began at once. This was a defiant, violent claim of territory. The aggression came swiftly and brutally:

> *The killing of Moriori was not random; it was quite clearly targeted at their elimination. The few Pākehā on the Chathams were not targeted. Moriori leaders testified before the Native Land Court that Māori*

hunted down those who fled; they 'killed us like sheep ...wherever we were found'. Moriori who lived on claimed land became vassals of their conqueror, and some were killed to verify the claim; any Moriori bold enough to resist also died. Koche, a Moriori survivor of the invasion, recounted that Ngāti Mutunga swept Pitt Island, killing or enslaving its entire population. Killing varied based upon the temperament of individual Māori chiefs and the confidence they had in their own mana. However, this was not random, isolated violence and Moriori endured horrendous, targeted atrocities. One chief roasted fifty Moriori in an oven; another attacked all Moriori within his land and laid their bodies on the beach, some still alive and left to die of their injuries.

-'The miserable remnant of this ill-used people':
colonial genocide and the Moriori of New Zealand's
Chatham Islands (2015), André Brett

The Moriori, traumatised and terrified, gathered at Te Awapātiki for a council. The young men urged the elders to lay aside their pacifist convictions, that they had the numbers on their side and could defend themselves if allowed to fight. The elders refused and even in this, their darkest hour, clung to Nunuku's Law as the right course of action. The consequences were predictable. The Māori proceeded to rampage through the islands, shooting, clubbing, eating and enslaving their hapless victims. Some were staked out on the beach to die slowly, others were marched to their sacred sites and forced to urinate and defecate on their shrines. The remainder were enslaved. They were forbidden to marry one another, to produce a new generation of Moriori. They were forbidden to speak their language, which is now extinct. Some Māori left the Chathams with their slaves and colonised the Auckland Islands, where the miserable Moriori toiled growing flax for their masters. By 1862 there were 101 Moriori left. The Māori disdained to marry Moriori women, although they sired them many 'mixed-race' children, who were loathed by the Māori and disenfranchised. The last 'pure' Moriori, Tommy Solomon, died in 1933 - although many mixed descendants still live on the islands today. The intention of the Māori was to wipe them out, to brutalise and humiliate them, ripping away any succor that even their religion might have provided:

At least Moriori who were killed fell into merciful oblivion. Those who survived the first killings were separated, moved around, and forced into slavery of the most onerous kind... They faced a life in which those they had loved were not only absent, but whose remains could still be seen intermittently, defiled by Maori and dogs alike. Perhaps worst of all, they faced a world in which everything in which they had believed spiritually and culturally was shown to be leached of fertility and value: their gods did not protect them from these horrors; their gods were dead.

Aftermath

In 1863 the resident British magistrate on the Chathams ordered the remaining Moriori to be set free. In 1870 a Native Land Court was set up to investigate claims of ownership and territory on the islands. The ruling went in favour of the Māori, who were awarded over 97% of the land, despite most having returned to their homeland. The Treaty of Waitangi, signed in 1840, had laid down a framework of British suzerainty over the main islands of New Zealand, but the Chathams and other remote islands proved difficult to control. The first magistrate on the islands, Archibald Shand, was sympathetic to the plight of the Moriori. Shand's son, Alexander, would go on to be their greatest ethnographer and helped preserve what details and records we still have of pre-contact Moriori culture. The Moriori themselves were not totally passive, and they petitioned to the Governor in New Zealand to be allowed their lands back:

> We were a people who dwelt in peace, who did not believe in killing and eating their own kind. Our word for that kind of person is kaupeke: a flesh-eating demon. The manner of this people was like that of a flock of lost sheep ... when the shepherd went away, the wild dog came to eat them ... The sheep were many, but what was that to the wild dog ... It simply went on eating until its teeth were blunted and the sheep's numbers dwindled ... Friend, we must have the rights to our own lands, because we are the rightful owners of our ancestors' home — of that land planted here by God at the time our forefathers arrived at this place

By 1852 the Auckland islands experiment had collapsed, both the Māori and their Moriori slaves returned utterly sick of the barren freezing cliffs and rocks. The eventual judgement about Moriori ownership may seem surprising, giving only 2% of the land back to the original inhabitants. But legal decisions about ownership and settlement in the aftermath of the Musket Wars were extraordinarily complex, and a general rule was adopted to honour possession since 1840, which gave the conquering Māori the greatest rights. To the victor the spoils indeed.

The debates, politics and legality of the Māori invasion of the Chathams has been ongoing ever since. The Moriori have been used as weapons in many arguments, some Māori have denied they ever existed, angrily insisting they are a fiction used to deny them their territories. Some politicians have pointed to the Moriori as an example of Māori brutality, arguing it far exceeded anything perpetrated by Europeans. The Moriori themselves have downplayed this, refusing to let their experience be used to attack the Māori, which is a fairly astonishing move given what happened. Instead the Moriori have claimed against the Crown and New Zealand government through the Waitangi Tribunal (a permanent commission tasked with redressing grievances relating to the Treaty of Waitangi). In 2020 this was concluded with a settlement of redress, including transfer of land and $18 million in compensation from the government. Remarkably this claim was centred on the failure to protect the Moriori and teaching subsequent generations that they were extinct. Nothing was demanded of the Māori. Scholars of genocide have held their nose and tentatively chipped in from the side-lines, quietly admitting that the Māori destruction of the Moriori counts as one of the worst genocides ever committed in history

Unsurprisingly perhaps, contemporary study of the invasion has attempted to partially shift the blame onto Europeans, for allowing a flow of arms into New Zealand, and for providing the Māori with the 'ideological tools' of racism in order to eradicate the Moriori:

> *The key point demonstrated by the Moriori experience is that perpetrators of genocides in the colonial sphere do not by necessity have to be colonial authorities or settlers. Colonialism can and did influence genocide between indigenous peoples as well as against them. On the Chatham Islands, colonialism shaped the broader context of warfare and population movement, introduced ideas and language of racial hierarchy to justify extermination and facilitated the encounter between Māori and Moriori. Colonial encounters*

motivated behaviour that diverged radically from Māori custom.

-'The miserable remnant of this ill-used people': colonial genocide and the Moriori of New Zealand's Chatham Islands. André Brett. 2015.

In the end, the Māori invasion should be seen for what it was, the expansion of a warrior people who held warfare and the ability to conquer in high esteem. Their response to the introduction of the musket was not inevitable, but perhaps predictable by anyone familiar with their pre-contact culture. The pacifism and survival of the Moriori speaks to a people which framed themselves as radically different from their neighbours, and they paid the ultimate price. If we can manage to examine and understand these types of events dispassionately, then we can gain a fuller picture of both the Māori and the Moriori and their temperaments and societies. It is a tale of both war and peace, militarism and pacifism, slavery and the freedom to take a boat and explore the world. It is human, all too human.

ATHEISM IN THE ANCIENT WORLD

*The Comanche, Pirahã
and Greek Mindset*

O ne of the most pre-caricatured images today is that of the online atheist. He is a figure of mockery and ridicule - bearded, fat, unkempt, donning a fedora hat - in a word, low-status. Prior to this atheism has long been associated with left-wing thought, or as a consequence of left-wing thought. Atheism otherwise has connotations of cultural Judaism, the hippy movement, the rational freethinking scientist or some kind of unorthodox fringe character. Atheism in historical periods is not given much thought, with the exception of the 'New-Atheist' project to create a pedigree from Antiquity onwards. The presumption from many strands of thought is that religion belongs to a primal age of human development; this meta-story that humans are 'storytellers' who need to create gods and deities to 'make sense' of the world. On this point I am not so sure. Many simple hunter-gatherer peoples do not seem to possess complex systems of religious thought, some even disdain to believe in a Creator at all. The distinction between strict materialism and atheism should be maintained of course, one can believe in supernatural phenomena without recourse to a god. We shall examine three such peoples - the solipsistic Pirahã, the militaristic Comanche and some ancient Greeks. Three very different mindsets, but united in a rejection of the theological life.

No Gods, No Numbers: Life With The Pirahã

The Pirahã people belong to a particular class of anthropological curiosities, those who defy categorisation and break all the rules of human universals. They are a small group of Amazonian foragers, between 500-1000 people strong, who live around the Maici river in the northern Brazilian state of Amazonas. Prior to the 1970's the Pirahã were famous amongst linguists for their strange language, which was believed to be an isolate - unrelated to any living languages. But it was not until the missionary work of Daniel Everett that the world came to learn about the sheer strangeness of these remote people.

To fully grasp the Pirahã mindset I recommend readers hunt down a copy of Everett's book Don't Sleep There Are Snakes: Life and Language in the Amazonian Jungle. In it he explores their culture as an outsider, as a scholar, as a father and as a missionary. What he comes to understand is that the Pirahã have developed a radically empirical mentality, one which fervently rejects any abstractions of any kind. He calls this the 'immediacy of experience principle':

> *The immediacy of experience principle accounts as well for Pirahã's simple kinship system. The kinship terms do not extend beyond the lifetime of any given speaker*

in their scope and are thus in principle witnessable—a grandparent can be seen in the normal Pirahã lifespan of forty-five years, but not a great-grandparent.

Anthropologists often assume that all cultures have stories about where they and the rest of the world come from, known as creation myths. I thus believed that the Pirahãs would have stories about who created the trees, the Pirahãs, the water, other living creatures, and so on. So I would ask speakers questions like "Who made the Maici River? Where did the Pirahãs come from? Who made trees? Where did the birds come from?" and so on. But I never had any luck. No one had ever collected or heard of a creation myth, a traditional story, a fictional tale, or in fact any narrative that went beyond the immediate experience of the speaker or someone who had seen the event and reported it to the speaker.

Eventually numerous published experiments were conducted by me and a series of psychologists that demonstrated conclusively that the Pirahãs have no numbers at all and no counting in any form... Not one Pirahã learned to count to ten in eight months. None learned to add 3 + 1 or even 1 + 1 (if regularly writing or saying the numeral 2 in answer to the latter is evidence of learning).Only occasionally would some get the right answer.

Some of the strangeness of Pirahã culture includes: their lack of numbers and ability to count; the lack of terms for colours other than those in their immediate surroundings; their reluctance to preserve food, preserve metal tools from rust or learn how to make canoes; their Darwinian approach to healthcare, pregnancy and child-rearing and their extremely strange habit of 'becoming' new people and forgetting that their previous personalities ever existed. On top of these the Pirahã became particularly famous for their apparent lack of linguistic 'recursion'. Grammatical recursion is a feature which allows for a potentially infinite number of sentences with a finite number of words. The phrase "I went to town and saw Sam's red car" contains two elements. The sentence "Sam's red car" is embedded inside the main sentence, and is much easier to communicate than separating the elements out. The famous academic Noam Chomsky, and others, have argued that recursion is a universal feature of human language, one which provides the tool to create an infinite number of sentences. Pirahã appears to contradict this rule, and arguments have raged for decades trying to understand whether this absence of recursion is true or not.

Turning towards religion, the Pirahã again seem to disobey the general rules of anthropology and do not have a Creator deity. They do believe in spirits and supernatural phenomena, but oddly they only believe in these because they directly experience them. This leads to some truly odd moments in Everett's book, where he struggles to make sense of the Pirahã mindset:

> "Don't you see him over there?" he asked impatiently. "Xigagaí, one of the beings that lives above the clouds, is standing on the beach yelling at us, telling us he will kill us if we go to the jungle."

> "Where?" I asked. "I don't see him."

"Right there!" Kóhoi snapped, looking intently toward the middle of the apparently empty beach.

"In the jungle behind the beach?"

"No! There on the beach. Look!" he replied with exasperation.

In the jungle with the Pirahãs I regularly failed to see wildlife they saw. My inexperienced eyes just weren't able to see as theirs did.

But this was different. Even I could tell that there was nothing on that white, sandy beach no more than one hundred yards away. And yet as certain as I was about this, the Pirahãs were equally certain that there was something there. Maybe there had been something there that I just missed seeing, but they insisted that what they were seeing, Xigagaí, was still there.

In trying to evangelise to the Pirahã, Everett encountered the brick wall of empiricism again and again. When they discovered that Everett had never met Jesus, and nobody he knew had ever met Jesus, they immediately dismissed the Biblical stories. No matter how hard he tried, their recalcitrance to accept anything beyond immediate experience was absolute. Not a single Pirahã has ever been recorded as converting to Christianity, from the time of the Spanish Jesuits to today. Something about their unique mentality will not admit the Gospels. In fact, their bizarre habit of getting dressed up as spirits and believing themselves to be possessed came to a head with Everett:

> The morning after one evening's "show" an older Pirahã man, Kaaxaóoi, came to work with me on the language. As we were working, he startled me by suddenly saying, "The women are afraid of Jesus. We do not want him."

> "Why not?" I asked, wondering what had triggered this declaration.

> "Because last night he came to our village and tried to have sex with our women. He chased them around the village, trying to stick his large penis into them."

> Kaaxaóoi proceeded to show me with his two hands held far apart how long Jesus's penis was—a good three feet.

> I didn't know what to say to this. I had no idea whether a Pirahã male had pretended to be Jesus and pretended to have a long penis, faking it in some way, or what else could be behind this report. Clearly Kaaxaóoi wasn't making this up. He was reporting it as a fact that he was concerned about. Later, when I questioned two other men from his village, they confirmed his story.

Thus the Pirahã belong to that subset of tribal peoples who

do not have a deity, have no creation myth and have no need of a god. So sure are they in their worldview that they often dismiss any and all foreign knowledge, words, technologies and beliefs, out of a simple and naïve xenophobia. Everett's faith was so shaken by his time with them, that at the end of the book he admits that the Pirahã are happy without God, and he becomes an atheist himself.

The Comanche - Warriors And Sceptics

The Comanche notions of religion are as crude, imperfect, and limited, as of geography or astronomy. They believed in, or have some indefinite traditional idea of, the Great Spirit; but I have never discovered any distinct mode or semblance of worship among them. ... I perceived no order of priest- hood, or anything analogous to it, among them; if they recognize any ecclesiastical authority whatever, it resides in their chiefs; but I think their religious sentiments are entirely too loose, vague, and inoperative, to have produced any such institution. The elevation of the shield is the only act I ever noticed among them, that afforded the slightest indication of religious concernment; and I doubt if they have any opinions relative to future rewards and punishments that exercise any moral influence upon them. They have nothing like a system of mythology, and neither do they entertain any religious myths of a traditionary or settled character ... .Their minds are too little intent upon the subject of a future state, ever to have formed a connected system of opinions in relation to it. If the doctrine of metempsychosis has ever been presented to them, it has not received a national or general credence; indeed, I doubt if they have any common plan of religious belief, or of a supernatural agency operating on the affairs of this life, beyond the mystic vagaries of witchcraft; and of these they do not distinctly believe in anything beyond the potentiality of human means. It may be assumed of them, as to all practical results of religious sentiment, that "the fool hath said in his heart, there is no God"

-Comanches and Other Tribes of Texas and the Policy to be Pursued Respecting Them (1851) David Burnet.

This intriguing passage comes down to us from one of the earliest Anglo-American observers of the Comanche, David Burnet. He, like other witnesses to the expansionist, militaristic power that was the Comanche Nation, struggled to understand their loose and quite vague religious beliefs and practices. The Comanche were obviously one of the Plains peoples, having descended from the Eastern Shoshone, and they presented many Plains traditions such as the suttee practice of killing a dead man's wife to place her in his grave, or taboos on mentioning the names of the dead. They shared some rituals and a personal focus on amulets and spiritual medicine, but observers from the 19th to the 20th century, through the different anthropological schools, consistently described the Comanche as sceptics and largely irreligious:

Commenting on a tearful Kiowa memorial service, a man told me "Comanches don't do that. You can't bring 'em back. We just find a good place to put them, and that's the end of it" (Gelo 1986)

Men who lived so dangerously were and had to be deeply religious, although their beliefs were primitive and, according to their cosmology, entirely practical ....

The people never had time for abstract thought.... The Nermernuh understood each other's secret incantations and personal taboos and respected them without ever attempting to correlate them into a coherent body of belief (Fehrenbach 1979)

The Comanches have often been designated as the skeptics or unbelievers of the plains.... They had no dogma and no professional priestly class to formulate a systematic religion .... It was not in the nature of the Comanche to be introspective. Nor was it in his nature reflectively to state his motives or ways of acting in formulae. The Comanche was oriented to see things as isolated episodes, not as a patterned unfolding of a great schema (Wallace and Hoebel, 1941)

"The Comanche do not know anything; they do not think"; by which they meant that the Comanche possessed no "spiritual knowledge," rather that than they were ignorant of anything pertaining to warfare, the chase, and other temporal matters (Curtis, 1930)

Nearly every important tribe, excepting perhaps those aboriginal skeptics, the Comanche, has or did have a tribal "medicine" equivalent to the taime, around which centers the tribal mythology and ceremonial with which the prosperity and fate of the tribe is bound up (Mooney, 1898)

These selected passages and quotes emphasise a familiar

position over many decades. The Comanche comes across as practical, concerned with war, hunting, life and death, and satisfied to let individuals find their own way spiritually, without dogma or expert guidance. It is tempting to wonder if these qualities were not also part of their overall conquering mentality, an almost imperial aloofness compared to their more ritualistic neighbours. Sometimes these divisions between the Comanche and the other Plains nations border on comical:

> While the Cheyennes and Arapahoes thought of bears as their ancestors, and believed that they were capable of sexual intercourse with human beings, so that to eat a bear was an act of cannibalism, those "aboriginal skeptics" the Comanches found bear very good eating when they could hunt it down (Marriott and Rachlin, 1968, 159)

One of the few rituals mentioned by observers is their habit of 'shield-sunning', which involved placing their hide shields on tripods to face the sun all day and absorb its power. Grease and menstruating women were kept away from it, lest it be defiled. Other traditions such as dances, the presence of healer 'medicine men' or shamans, vision quests and sweat lodges all seem to be present, but with no coherent religious framework. All the trappings of a traditional way of life existed, but were never used like the Kiowa or the Pawnee.

Is this an example of atheism, as we moderns might understand it? Not in the truest materialistic sense, but it is an intriguing example of a warrior society which developed a practical and sceptical mindset towards religious beliefs. What spiritualism did exist seemed oriented towards the hunt, towards war and success. It is possible that anthropologists were simply denied access to some inner sanctum of dogma,

and the Comanche protected their beliefs against outsiders.
We may never know.

Critias, Alcibiades And Ancient Greek Atheism

So, speaking words like these
Most cunning doctrine did he introduce,
The truth concealing under speech untrue.
The place he spoke of as the God's abode
Was that whereby he could affright men most,—
The place from which, he knew, both terrors came
And easements unto men of toilsome life—
To wit the vault above, wherein do dwell
The lightnings, he beheld, and awesome claps
Of thunder, and the starry face of heaven,
Fair-spangled by that cunning craftsman Time,—
Whence, too, the meteor's glowing mass doth speed
And liquid rain descends upon the earth.
Such were the fears wherewith he hedged men round,
And so to God he gave a fitting home,
By this his speech, and in a fitting place,
And thus extinguished lawlessness by laws.
Thus first did some man, as I deem, persuade
Men to suppose the race of Gods exists..

-Sisyphus Fragment

A curious feature about modern atheism is the presence
of moral teachings and givens. Scratch the surface on just
about disbeliever today and they will be committed to
egalitarianism, democracy and human rights. There is really
no justification for this, other than the general social milieu
they find themselves in. Many thinkers from Democritus to
Dostoevsky have battled with the ethics of atheistic thought.

The writer Peter Hitchens has pointed out that atheism historically leads to Felix Dzerzhinsky, whose brutal reign of Leninist terror is symbolised for him by Dzerzhinsky's funeral wreath, fashioned out of bayonets. The Bolshevik and the New Atheist sceptic are not logically separated by any real creed, and any period of 'real' atheism will lead to the rule of Nature, that is, the rule of the strong.

> *... how can a man be happy who is the servant of anything? On the contrary, I plainly assert, that he who would truly live ought to allow his desires to wax to the uttermost, and not to chastise them; but when they have grown to their greatest he should have courage and intelligence to minister to them and to satisfy all his longings. And this I affirm to be natural justice and nobility. To this however the many cannot attain; and they blame the strong man because they are ashamed of their own weakness, which they desire to conceal, and hence they say that intemperance is base. As I have remarked already, they enslave the nobler natures, and being unable to satisfy their pleasures, they praise temperance and justice out of their own cowardice. For if a man had been originally the son of a king, or had a nature capable of acquiring an empire or a tyranny or sovereignty, what could be more truly base or evil than temperance—to a man like him, I say, who might freely be enjoying every good, and has no one to stand in his way, and yet has admitted custom and reason and the opinion of other men to be lords over him?—must not he be in a miserable plight whom the reputation of justice and temperance hinders from giving more to his friends than to his enemies, even though he be a ruler in his city?*

-Callicles to Socrates, The Gorgias

Callicles' point to Socrates, his argument for the right of the strong to rule the weak, is developed more fully in Nietzsche's Genealogy of Morals, where he lays out the psychological movement from good and bad, to good and evil. The rage of the weak against the strong, like the lambs against the eagle, leads to the development of morality proper, and the use of morality to bind the powerful. Nietzsche may have been inspired here by reading about the Athenian period of tyranny, known as the Thirty Tyrants in 404 BC. One of the main instigators of the tyranny, a man called Critias, is often described as portraying one of the earliest examples of atheism. He and Euripides are both touted as possible authors of the above Sisyphus Fragment. Critias is one of the best examples of the Calliclean 'master morality' at work, unconcerned with the divine judgement of the gods, and brimming with an aristocratic lust to crush democracy and restore the rule of the mighty. Critias and his friend, the general Alcibiades, were both suspected of desecrating a statue of Hermes. Alcibiades himself was further accused of profanity against the Eleusinian Mysteries, underlining the reality that mockery of the gods was a public evil in Athens.

The outrage against the Tyranny, and the execution of Socrates, clearly left a deep scar within the Athenian and wider Greek psyche. The shocking brutality of Critias and his cronies, their corruption and violence, demanded a response against whatever ideology propelled them. Plato and subsequent philosophers turned to morality to defend themselves and their vocation, changing the course of philosophy and enquiry forever:

> Plato here develops some of his most important and worked-out ideas about the nature of deity, and in particular focuses on proofs that gods exist. These take two forms. The first is a cosmological one. The regular

motions of the heavenly bodies demonstrate that a divine hand is at work. Anything that moves must have something that animates it, the Athenian supposes. In the case of living beings, that is the soul. In the case of the heavens, that is god. The second argument is a moral one: if we do not accept that humans have share in the divine, in the form of our souls, then we cannot aspire to moral perfection that is the property of the gods alone.

These are not just philosophical arguments; they are also justifications for the legal repression of atheism. The Athenian pitches his arguments in response to 'certain clever moderns', some 'young men' who hold disreputable views about the gods. There are, he claims, three types of position that such people hold: either they hold that the gods do not exist; or that, if they do, they have no involvement in the affairs of humans, or that they do, but they are easily swayed by sacrifices and prayers. Is he talking about a real community? Does he mean that there was a sizeable movement among the young in Athens who held such beliefs? One respected scholar has argued exactly this: that there was an 'atheist underground' at Athens, on which Plato is here shining a light. He may well be right. But the primary target of this designedly non-specific attack is, surely, the phantoms that have haunted Plato ever since the trial of Socrates. Book 10 of The Laws is ultimately about disavowing all traces of philosophy's origins in (real or perceived) atheism.

-Battling the Gods: Atheism in the Ancient World (2015). Tim Marsh.

Going one step further, Costin Alamariu, in his dissertation work Selective Breeding and the Birth of Philosophy, argues that the atheistic master morality of Callicles and Critias was the Nazism of ancient Greece. The response to the Tyranny, he outlines, was akin to the modern terror of any work being associated or leading towards fascism. This is why Plato and the rest of the philosophical world took a turn towards moral thinking, to disavow any hint that the materialistic coldness of Critias could be connected to such a way of approaching the world and Nature:

> Critias, Socrates' student, was the Hitler of the ancient Greek world. He and his friends established a regime based on atheistic biologism so to speak; on "Sparta radicalized," a eugenic antinomian dictatorship. He was maybe what Hitler's most hysterical detractors claim of him today. Critias killed more Athenians in his short rule than died in the decades of the war with Sparta. He expelled almost everyone from the city, and burned the docks, which were the perceived source of democratic power. He wasted all the priests of Eleusis for being tedious religious moralists. He saw the purpose of the Spartan constitution as the creation of one "supreme biological specimen," and Critias sought to found a state based on such ideas. He and his friends were overthrown quite quickly. Against this catastrophe, carried out in the name of philosophy and nature (of biology) there was a predictable reaction. Socrates' other students, most of them at least, as well as Isocrates and others, went out of their way to distance themselves from Critias and what he was perceived to stand for: "We are not like that guy. We are good boys. Philosophy isn't actually about that. We're doing something different. We're socially responsible good guys." Does this sound familiar? It doesn't matter if someone like Critias represented a distortion of

philosophy as it existed at the time, or a distortion of the idea of nature as biology and eugenics. The reaction against him, and the eagerness of other prominent members of his "tribe" to distance themselves from him caused an equal distortion in the opposite direction.

Thus atheism in ancient Greek thought may have been one of the prime movers of the Western intellectual tradition, though an inadvertent one. The action and reaction of the Tyranny and its aftermath could be one of the most important drivers of philosophy, hiding the roots of natural inquiry behind a veil of morality.

Two Forms Of Atheism?

The three manifestations of atheism and scepticism I have presented here are all different from one another. The Pirahã are a profoundly strange people, and their insistence on a radical immediacy and empiricism make them almost the opposite of the ancient Greeks. For them, an extended intergenerational discussion of Nature and her phenomena seems utterly irrelevant. The Pirahã refuses all intrusion from the outside, whereas the Greek mind was fertilised by contact with the foreign. The Comanche charted a different path again, distinguishing themselves from their more ritualistic neighbours by adopting a conqueror's mindset, and valuing what is pragmatic, expedient and useful. Personal charms, medicine and beliefs are fine, but codifying a system of thought and practice was the custom of a less vital people. This perhaps comes closer to the master morality of Callicles and Critias, who see the merit of religion as a system for lesser men, but see it as a set of constraints and shackles for men like themselves. These types of atheism are of course nothing like the contemporary form, which is suffused with ethical and moral concerns. It would be better described as humanistic, or even a type of secular Christianity, rather than atheism, which has never held a great popular appeal in its purest forms. Perhaps it should remain the preserve of warrior aristocrats and social refuseniks.

PART FIVE-
REFLECTIONS

A STILLBORN FUTURE: WHERE IS THE ART?

*Aesthetics, music and the
death of the artist*

Where does a novel art style come from? What factors or ingredients are needed to leaven culture into something new? An aesthetic can sometimes be born, or grow, in a fertilised soil which yields the most exciting and important fruit - a way of seeing the world. Can you imagine the thrill of being in the early Romantic movement, seeking a transformation of nature, the individual, the emotions? That shifting motion across a void which has no obvious landing spot until it is created, is the essence of being creative, giving birth to, or generating - being captured by or letting something flow through you. I'm pondering this because it feels like this motion is currently impossible, it feels blocked.

When one looks around at the aesthetic landscape - culture -

there is an obvious dearth of anything fresh or inspiring. The only motion is a shallow democratisation. In classical music there is a sense of impending doom, only kept at bay through the compositions of film scores and video games. Many of these are good pieces, in and of themselves, but they lack the fire and internal coherency of their forebears. Alexander Scriabin, a man possessed of almost divine genius, someone who dove into the dark recesses of mysticism and synesthesia and returned with a vision to remake the world through art, how could such a man survive today? Would he compose music for a Disney remake? Searching online for trends or schools in modern classical music, there is just a flabby splash of a dying corpse - how to arrange chairs in the concert hall; getting more X minority or class of person to play music; mixing old, pale and stale tunes with electronic beats to attract the youth.

Poetry and literature doesn't seem much healthier. Jack London once wrote: "Have you lived merely to live? Are you afraid to die? I'd rather sing one wild song and burst my heart with it, than live a thousand years watching my digestion and being afraid of the wet. When you are dust, my father will be ashes". Today literature, and even less so poetry, fails to concentrate that kind of energy, either in the writer or the reader. Questions of authenticity, irony, sincerity, standpoint, life experience and one's relation to power (marginal or not), dominate endless discussions, exactly the sentiment of watching one's digestion. Meanwhile, where is the fire? How could a Lord Byron arise from this now? He would be on medication, his work never glanced at by a publishing house.

In all things the flame of genius and youth has vanished. George Mallory, a young man described as an Arthurian hero, with a face like a mystery of Botticelli, threw himself onto the rocks of Everest to conquer the roof of the world. Thomas Young was appointed a professor of natural science at the age

318

of 28. He was the 'last man to know everything', including in his accomplishments the deciphering of the Rosetta Stone and inventing modern physics. Mozart's brilliance was of such a pitch that his contemporaries described him as Orpheus reborn, a renewal of the Apollonian Greek spirit. These people, energised by something beyond mere life, would be stifled if they were young men today. Where are our Mozarts and Beethovens? What new creed or belief would anyone die for now? What intellectual or artistic movement could you devote yourself to, forsaking all else?

In part the sticky parochialism of origins binds people to their supposed roots, and in part there is an exhaustion which hangs in a pallid cloud over the world-spirit. The mood is depression, apathy, not even an anarchic schizophrenia of thought, but the most low-energy lane-gazing imaginable. The suspicion of straying outside your ethnic heritage is now ever present. If you came to work dressed in cutting-edge Japanese fashion, not only would it be unusual and different, but the eyes would narrow, "oh, do you have Japanese heritage?". Under such a smothering gaze, how would a young artist experiment in Life, in creativity, in the necessary blending which precedes generation? Everywhere the type of individuation of a truly unique being is cut short. Imagine making art that lacked moral content, some wider point about 'society' or politics, art that just forcefully and energetically punched you in the gut and made you feel. I am suspicious that anyone can feel like that anymore - hear a piece of music that keeps you awake for days on end with pure excitement, or a sensation that grips you so tight it changes your life there and then.

Maybe I am wrong, but looking around at the aesthetic output of the world - architecture, fashion, cuisine, music, painting, sculpture, literature - I can't see any mainstream energy that could awaken the old gods and bring them back to us. All is dabbling, all is tinkering, all is striving in place. Maybe these are the weeds that need to be cleared before the soil will sprout something new?

LIFE ASCENDING & DESCENDING: ON THE TWO FORMS OF PRIMITIVISM

The popular television show *Alone* presents some of the most impressive human specimens by way of their abilities and skills. The game show involves dropping off individuals into areas of harsh wilderness, with a minimum of equipment, no supplies, and the expectation that one of them will last the longest. They have to build a shelter, find and boil water, hunt and fish, and protect themselves from animals such as grizzly and polar bears. Despite their extraordinary skills in bushcraft, carpentry, bow hunting, improvised fishing, building boats, nets, fish traps, and so forth, many of them suffer from a peculiar set of psychological dispositions and traits. Men crave the company of their wives and girlfriends, to the point where they might try meditating to connect with them; many struggle with having to kill animals in order to survive in what amounts to a frivolous competition; others explain how their love of nature and the outdoors stems from childhood bullying; most see their vocations as hunters, trappers, primitive skill teachers, as a means of escape from civilisation, which is viewed as soft and ultimately fake. This is what I call 'egalitarian primitivism', a set of overlapping beliefs which craves Man's return to the primitive as a form of levelling, a spiritual horizontalism. We can contrast this to a second type of primitivism, one we could call 'hierarchical primitivism', which is animated by a metaphysics of 'strife' - the impulse of which is to engage in a struggle, a struggle which glorifies Life. The first is descending, the second, ascending. The first is present in many corners of many philosophical and political movements today, the second is barely visible at all.

How can Man overcome his current debased condition? He can look to the future with optimism and hope, or he can seek to plant one foot firmly back in the past. But the past is dead, is it not? The fleeting moments of kings and dynasties all end, like so many mayflies, but the real, deep, True past is Nature herself. You can return to her bosom and dismantle every shackle of civilisation, but why, and for what purpose? The roots of egalitarian primitivism obviously run deep, the psyche wants to dismantle existence and join the great multitude, the swamp of all primal being. A man who seeks freedom from his drab office life, or maybe he never had such a job, but was repelled by the mere thought of it, such a man seeks solitude in the woods, as he always did from boyhood. He thinks of the trees as friends, he observes the squirrels in their domestic coming-and-goings, he learns the songs of the birds. This is his secret garden, Nature is a portal through which the world of conformity and regularity can be escaped. He was a sensitive boy, now a sensitive man, some sensations dulled by being forced to interact with modernity. But he learns to hunt, to harvest Nature's bounty and live among her boughs. Some men like this turn such experiences into painfully private mental spaces, to inhabit at will, as a refuge and cool watering hole for the spirit. Other men might actually find employment or a vocation here. More insidiously some men will twist and wring it all to squeeze out a drop of morality, and oh will they run with that. Every environmentalist NGO is staffed with these men and women, who have warped Nature into a morality play about human greed, excess, waste, selfishness, cruelty. The parables they tell themselves are about wise indigenous stewards, obliterated by boorish and crude colonisers, they talk of biodiversity and of capitalism, and a thousand more abstractions. "Man Must return to Nature, to live within his Limits!". What are Man's limits, and how can these people claim to know them? Limits are those mechanisms which funnel energy towards differentiation. To the egalitarian, energy should be diffuse, quiet, smooth, flat, amorphous. You may *not* harvest those trees, you may *not* fish this week, you may *not* take more than you *need*. This ethic is common - the veneration of Bare Life, life for the sake of life, with modest and unflattering victories: a little mushroom here, a feather for your hat there, a community dance night which fills you with that warm, fuzzy feeling of being 'connected'. This is not dissolution in its ecstatic, Dionysion state; no this is dissolution like a sandcastle being reduced to nothing by the lapping tides.

There are many branches to this spirit however, and not all primitivists become fruitarian hippies. I would diagnose this same spirit within the Tolkienite conservative right as well. The ethos of the Hobbit does have a certain nobility to it, but it depends on external protection, and cultivating a deliberate ignorance about the wider world. The fantasy has the nostalgic allure of comfort, cosiness, gentle orderliness, an organic whole, all of which have their charms. The border between the Shire and something far more degraded lies within the heart of each resident and their love of privacy, individualism, personal liberty and a closed garden gate demarcating that which is my property and no others. Remove this and the entire constitution will sink into the rule of petty-minded moralists and zealots. I would argue the same dynamic is at play with homesteaders, Christian home-schoolers and boomer-run villages that reek of marijuana. The nightwatchman of private property and individual liberty maintains his eternal vigilance.

Further away again are the short-lived communes, intentional living communities and other such experiments in communalism, for which the European and especially the northern European is not built to excel in. No other nation needs to create test laboratories for collective living, they already do it by instinct. This is why these egalitarians always gravitate towards the Third World and the Indigenous, they believe themselves to be victims in a historical game of differentiation, where their ability to nestle into the folds of the longhouse have been excised. They feel deracinated, lost, unmoored - and this exact sentiment binds all those who accept the premise that the human animal has been severed, *and this is a bad thing.*

> *I am also inclined to agree with Freud and Nietzsche—*
> *whose rather gaudier explanations of the evolution of*
> *morality don't seem to tempt de Waal very much—that*
> *human beings seem psychologically damaged, in ways*
> *that suggest some deep break with nature*

This quote from Christine Korsgaard, a moral philosopher by profession, seems accurate to me. The neat 'just-so' stories of the evolutionary thinker must be seen as a Procrustean trap, which seeks to straighten out the entirely crooked timber of the human animal. People are a confused, horrid jumble of drives, impulses, nasty little loops of vengeance and meanness. Most people have always lived 'closer to the earth', in the sense that the egalitarians wish for, but they see only the benefits of this and forget the utter suffocation of life in the village. 'Live within your means' could be a proclamation from a respected tribal grandmother, or a modern climate activist - they become one and the same at some point. The egalitarian does recognise this deep break with nature, and wrestles endlessly as to where the blame should be laid. The birth of capitalism, the industrial revolution, the peasant enclosures, Christianity, the domestication of various animals and plants, agriculture itself, maybe the use of fire as a tool?

> *And it was not until our species that any creature developed the psychological perceptions, and then*

> *the behavioral manifestations, that allowed it to stand distanced from that world-indeed, in many ways opposed to it -so that it was able to expand its control and dominion in a totally unprecedented way, justified in the name of survival.*

> *Our secular, rational, industrial society, with its amazing scientific insight and technological skills, has established the first radically anthropocentric society and has thereby broken the primary law of the universe, the law of the integrity of the universe, the law that every component member of the universe should be integral with every other member of the universe.*

The two quotes here, the first from Kirkpatrick Sale and the second from Wendell Berry, are typical of the genre. Hand-wringing, concerned with levelling the consciousness of Man back to that of an animal, anxious that the 'break' with Nature has violated a kind of treaty, that we shall suffer the consequences of being fully apart from the world. Sale goes further than most in arguing that humans should attempt to re-adopt the mindset and behaviours of *Homo erectus,* truly a return to nature if there ever was one. Of course, there are parts of this every sentient human recognises are correct -

cruelty to animals, both industrially and at the small scale, is a profound injustice; the annihilation of wild animals and wild spaces is a tragedy, there are too many slums and too many people extending their garbage-lives outwards like locusts. Noone said these complaints were entirely without merit. But we must turn to that second type of primitivism now, that seeks not to annihilate Man's capacity for action, but to refine it and wield it in his service.

We have stretched our iron nerves in the sun,

we have arched our metallic spines,

and opened our mouths to a joyful gust,

inhaling gigantic bursts of life

Song of the Airplane Hangers. Luciano Folgore. 1912

One can have *too much* civilisation, by which I mean one can feel suffocated by the weight of history and time, and feel trapped in a sticky and dying morass of 'culture'. The way out of this is to breathe the fresh air of something clean and pure, through speed, pace, vitality, life. Much of settled history from the Bronze Age until the invention of firearms came with an escape clause, for anyone bold and strong enough in body and mind, they could cross the frontier of domestication and join the barbarians on the steppe. Now there are few physical realms like this, but through art, music, literature, the development of friendships, instincts, the training of the body, the celebration of life - it is possible to tap into that strain of primitivism. Nihilism even has its allure, if only as a cold, cleansing breath to purify the mind. I said before that this is not a house of peace however, this is a house of metaphysical strife, a *Dar al-Harb* where the possibility of Life depends on Death. Darwinism is just one version of this thought, certain pre-Socratics were another. Red in tooth and claw is not a *moral* lesson from nature, it is a description of basic reality. Civilisation has overcome this problem, of the strong against the weak, and provided for the default human unit all he needs to live, in the greatest comfort.

A young man of such a disposition, who wants only to see Beauty in the world, may find life in this civilisation intolerable. Everything he encounters seeks to defang and declaw him, remind him of his place, insist on rote-learning the moral lessons of the day. "If everything is irredeemable" he thinks, "then it all needs to go". In this he shares with the egalitarian the impulse to destroy, but comes instead to see the fight, the conflict, the challenge, as the greatest point of spiritual ascension. Not just in the ability to overcome through a test of wills, but in the instant of any struggle when the chattering, broken mind of habitual Life is silenced, and the body can take over. Ask any athlete and they will answer that the greatest moments of their lives were during the final moments, where a leap, an extra unknown surge of speed, a well placed jab, won them the day. Musicians in the flow, lost in the swirl of notes must also know this feeling. How much more intense, how much greater would this feeling have been for the first charioteers? The first mariners? The first to climb a summit? To have conquered a city? "*Strife is justice*" as Heraclitus said, insisting on the primacy of tension between opposites to generate Life. Entropy isn't just Death, it's the absence of motion and the possibility of conflict. Death itself can be a vital force which elevates and exalts Life.

I have laid these out as maybe you see bits of both within yourself. Maybe you don't want to succumb to the low energy and lethargy which accompanies the dissolution of form and difference. We must all learn to recognise the impulses and where they lead, and guard against their consequences. I see too many men now who are strong enough in body, but utterly broken in their spirit, a mere reflection of their potential, twisted into the service of mere Life. Seek out what is ascending, and rise.

Printed in Great Britain
by Amazon

38671851R00185